THE CHILDREN
MONEY CAN BUY

THE CHILDREN MONEY CAN BUY

Stories from the Frontlines of Foster Care and Adoption

Anne Moody

ROWMAN & LITTLEFIELD
Lanham • Boulder • New York • London

Published by Rowman & Littlefield
A wholly owned subsidiary of The Rowman & Littlefield Publishing Group, Inc.
4501 Forbes Boulevard, Suite 200, Lanham, Maryland 20706
www.rowman.com

Unit A, Whitacre Mews, 26-34 Stannary Street, London SE11 4AB

British Library Cataloguing in Publication Information Available

Library of Congress Cataloging-in-Publication Data
Names: Moody, Anne, author.
Title: The children money can buy : stories from the frontlines of foster care and adoption / Anne Moody.
Description: Lanham : Rowman & Littlefield, [2018] | Includes index.
Identifiers: LCCN 2017034191 (print) | LCCN 2017037267 (ebook) | ISBN 9781538108031 (Electronic) | ISBN 9781538108024 (cloth : alk. paper)
Subjects: LCSH: Foster home care—United States. | Adoption—United States.
Classification: LCC HV875.55 (ebook) | LCC HV875.55 .M65 2018 (print) | DDC 362.73/30973—dc23
LC record available at https://lccn.loc.gov/2017034191

Printed in the United States of America

Contents

Introduction

ONE MORNING EARLY IN MY MARRIAGE, my husband, who is a writer, told me about a dream he'd had the previous night. In this dream, I (who was not a writer) had nevertheless written a collection of beautiful and poignant stories.

Many years later, I realized that over time I actually had become a collector of unwritten stories like the ones the dream described. They were brought to me by children in foster homes and orphanages and by the parents who, in a kinder world, would have been able to raise them. They were also brought by adults who had suffered the loss of children through infertility or relinquishment. The beauty in these stories lay in the hope and resilience of the people who lived them, and—for many of them—in their eventually finding love, happiness, and one another.

The stories first came to me through my work with children in foster care whose parents had lost custody of them due to abuse, neglect, or some other form of tragedy. More stories came through my work with a large private adoption agency and children from Korea, India, Colombia, China, and various other countries, as well as children coming out of the U.S. foster care system. After becoming the director of an agency specializing in in-country infant adoption, I collected stories about the struggles adoptive parents endured in their efforts to bring children into their lives and about the selfless love and sacrifice of birth parents who chose adoption for their children. Some of the most inspiring and instructive of these stories are now gathered in *The Children Money Can Buy*. The first section of the book focuses on the years I spent as a child welfare worker. The second focuses on my work with a large adoption agency that handled international adoptions and was an early promoter of openness in domestic adoptions. The third concerns my own experiences as an adoptive parent of a child of a different race. The fourth focuses on the agency I direct and my work with pregnant women considering adoption for their babies. The final section examines some currently relevant issues in infant adoption, international adoption, and foster care.

The nature of my work has given me entrée into the lives of many people, sometimes seeing them at their worst and sometimes at their most loving and joyful. Like others with long careers in child welfare and adoption, I have worked with hundreds of people over the years; these are just a few of the stories that I feel best illustrate the changing states of American foster care and adoption practice.

The Children Money Can Buy is the result of my desire to share the stories I have collected and my hope that the people and experiences they describe will offer insight to the reader. It is a collection of observations about real people and real situations that I believe help illustrate larger life lessons about the way our society values—and fails to value—parents and children.

I have borrowed the stories in this book from the people who lived them, in some cases without their knowledge and in others with their assistance and encouragement. In all cases, I have changed the names of individuals and I have altered specifically indentifying information unless it was already part of the public record. All of the other information in this book is factual and as accurate as memory allows. This book would not exist without the stories brought to me by the parents and children to whom they belong.

I
FOSTER CARE

1

Why Do I Want This Job?

"**D**O YOU PROMISE that you will always work to reunite the family?"
I wasn't sure.

My husband and had I expected to return to Seattle as soon as we completed our graduate degrees at the University of Michigan, but when he was offered the job of his dreams at Ardis Publishers, a Russian-literature publishing company, we decided to stay in Michigan. Once we'd made that decision, I looked around for a job and found an opening for a child welfare worker at the Department of Social Services. Although I had just gotten a master's degree in social work, my focus had been on administration and policy rather than casework; as with many fateful decisions in life, the decision to apply for this job was made by chance and did not reflect any careful thought about my career goals.

Now here I was, in a dreary, windowless conference room, finishing up my interview with the social services director, Charles, a mild-mannered ex-minister, and feeling pretty optimistic until he got to what appeared to be the final question:

Do you promise that you will always work to reunite the family?

I searched Charles's face for a clue to the correct answer but came up with nothing, so I decided that it must be a trick question. For one thing, there was the problem of that "always." As any good student knows, answers that contain that word are rarely correct. And then there was the more significant question of exactly what the purpose of this job was. Could it really be to always work to reunite the family? I didn't think it could be that simple. What about the times when reuniting the family clearly wasn't in the child's best interests? What about when it was dangerous for the child?

I decided to cap off what seemed to have been a successful interview by showing this man that I was someone who could think for herself and who understood the ethical complexities of child welfare work. "Well, I would work to do what is in the child's best interests. Reuniting the family might not always be the right thing to do."

Instead of acknowledging my answer with any sort of approval, Charles repeated the question. "Yes, but do you promise that you will always work to reunite the family?"

I was puzzled by his insistence, but naïvely continued to emphasize that I could imagine circumstances in which I could not ethically work to reunite the family. I guess I thought that I could impress Charles with the subtlety of my reasoning or perhaps with my conviction that the child's interests should come first. But this was not the case. After sparring with me for a bit, he began to express a hint of exasperation, never a good sign, and particularly disconcerting when it comes from someone with the comportment of Mr. Rogers, the world's most tolerant man. Charles and I eventually reached a compromise. I agreed that, in an ideal world—which we certainly were not dealing with here—I could see that it would always be best if there were no circumstances in which parents abused their children, or became mentally ill, or succumbed to substance abuse, or were sent to jail for many years. In that world, I would always work to reunite the family. I could also see that in the real world, there were times when parents made mistakes, when life circumstances overwhelmed them, when mental illness and substance abuse were untreated, and when parents were given no assistance, encouragement, or even any sort of fair shot at overcoming the problems they faced. These parents and their children certainly deserved their caseworker's best efforts. I definitely wanted to work to make life better for these families. But I wasn't sure that "better" always meant reuniting the family.

That was not the answer Charles wanted, but he offered me the job anyway. Apparently they didn't have many qualified applicants because, with my brand-new degree and no relevant experience, I brought little to the table other than an ability to learn.

I had a pretty vague idea of what to expect when I took the job. Soon enough, I found that becoming a child welfare worker put me on a frighteningly steep learning curve littered with lessons made painful by the nature of the problems our clients faced. The other caseworkers in my office, four women and three men between the ages of twenty-five and thirty-five, had either a little prior experience or, like me, an appropriate degree in lieu of experience. Half of us were married, and none of us had children. The University of Michigan School of Social Work was highly respected and served as a productive source of employees for the department, particularly for graduates who wanted to settle in Michigan for a while.

The job of a child welfare worker in our foster care unit began after a child was removed from his or her home and placed in a foster home. The initial turmoil surrounding the allegations of abuse or neglect, and the legal work involved in obtaining a court order authorizing foster care, had been handled earlier by a caseworker in the child protective services division. Once the child was settled in foster care, usually within a matter of weeks, the protective services case would be closed and the foster care worker would take over the job of working with the family. It didn't take long for me to get a grasp of the general parameters of the job, which were daunting; but far more daunting was the level of responsibility handed over to someone like me, who had absolutely no experience working with children or dysfunctional families other than a brief stint answering phones on a crisis line. Since the previous caseworker had already moved on to her new job, I received virtually no training or preparation other than the opportunity to read over the files on the fifty-eight families that made up my caseload. I was shocked by how quickly I was given what appeared to be immense power over the lives of my clients.

When the initial court work justifying the need for foster care was completed by the protective services worker, another court date, usually three months after the first court appearance, would be set to review the case. The foster care worker's task was to determine what needed to happen for the child to return home safely. This involved the creation of a "service plan," which included a set of tasks for the caseworker and a set of tasks for the parent. Ideally, the parent's part of the service plan would consist of straightforward statements about what actions the parent could take in order to have the caseworker recommend that the child be returned home. Caseworkers were supposed to come up with specific, understandable, and attainable tasks for the parent. For example, rather than saying that a parent needed to stop beating up the child, the plan would say that the parent needed to take part in parenting classes. Instead of saying that the parent needed to become mentally healthy or stop using drugs, the plan would say that the parent needed to attend counseling or rehab. This system had obvious flaws in that it was perfectly possible for a parent to meet the standards set out in the service plan without actually changing the behavior in question. Parenting classes, counseling, and rehab could be ordered and attended faithfully, yet to no avail if the problem behavior didn't change (as it usually didn't). But creating the service plan was at least a good place to start.

The tasks specified in the service plan were presented to the parent as soon as possible after the child was placed in foster care. The parent would then have a few months to work on correcting the problems and to demonstrate to the court that he or she was committed to changing. If, for example, the child had been removed from the home because of physical abuse when the parent was drunk, the parent would be ordered to attend rehab and parenting classes and the caseworker would assist him or her in connecting with the appropriate resources or programs. The service plan also included a visitation schedule, with supervised visits usually taking place either at the parent's home or in the child welfare office.

This all sounds straightforward, but it never was. We all know that there is nothing straightforward about alcoholism or anger-management problems, and none of us expected our clients to suddenly change their behavior. But the fact that many of them couldn't or wouldn't take even the first few steps toward improvement was truly dismaying. And equally dismaying was the fact that so many parents, for whatever reason, didn't visit with their children while they were in foster care, despite the often-elaborate arrangements put in place to make this possible. It was depressingly common for the parent to be absent when the caseworker or foster parent showed up with the children for a visit or, if home, to be incapacitated by drink or drugs.

Most often, my clients would initially approach the service plan with at least a flicker of optimism. Our goal, after all, was to help them regain custody of their children, and most people were able to understand that they would need to change their behavior. Even among abusive parents, there is general agreement that children shouldn't be abused. (We're not talking about a vigorous spanking here. We're talking, at best, about a loss of control resulting in injury and, at worst, sadistic ritual torture.) The reasons for removal of their children were strong enough that the parents usually didn't try to justify their abuse—with the notable exception of those whose "religious" convictions prompted and/or supported child abuse. These people were the hardest clients to work with because they believed that abusive "discipline" was exactly what their child needed; they were unlikely to be amenable to treatment or service plans.

One of the most surprising discoveries I made as a beginning child welfare worker concerned my own reaction to abusive parents. The first such parents I encountered were a young couple who had sexually abused their three- and five-year-old daughters, and I remember feeling so enraged after reading through their file that I didn't know how I would manage to talk with them. But at our first meeting, I found that my reaction to these poor, scruffy people was just a profound sadness. It seemed so clear to me that they had been abused children themselves not so long ago, and that anger on my part now would be a futile and simplistic response. This does not mean that I wanted them to have their kids back. Not at all. I wanted to keep those little girls far away from their parents and to protect them from further abuse. Even so, it was evident that an adversarial relationship with these parents wouldn't be helpful to any of us, least of all the children.

Another surprising discovery was how few expressions of anger were directed at me and my fellow child welfare workers. Many of the parents on our caseloads were mentally ill or had a history of criminal behavior, a serious problem with substance abuse, or some combination of these problems. Quite a few also had a history of domestic violence, and they all had a history of child abuse or neglect of one form or another. Typically, the parents were people who had difficulty with aggression and impulse control. Yet despite the anger they must have felt toward us—the embodiment of the system that had taken away their children—there were relatively few instances of overt conflict. There were plenty of borderline situations in which it would seem as though the client was about to lose control but would manage to regain his or her composure. Perhaps these were mostly bluffs, and when the caseworker didn't take up the challenge (unlike many of the other people with whom our clients interacted), everything would calm down again.

There were scary moments, however. One of my first home visits was to see three young children who had recently been returned to their mother's care. They lived in a ramshackle row house, on the upper level. The street level had a narrow porch across the front of the building, and I could see about eight men sitting along it and on the stairs up to the second level as I approached. I wondered for a moment if it would be wise to go up those stairs, then decided just to act confident and hope for the best. Halfway up, I heard one of the men say, "Let's get her." The woman upstairs opened her door quickly, so I never found out whether they were serious. I did think later, though, that if something had happened to me it would have been more than reasonable for people to wonder about my stupidity in blithely walking into that situation.

When I came back down the stairs, the men were gone, and I was with an eight-year-old girl, Missy, a wispy, white-blond child who appeared to have found her way out of a photograph of a hollow-eyed family in Depression-era Appalachia. She seemed smart and feisty, though, and very much in charge of her two younger brothers—and even of her mother, who had a hapless, beaten-down demeanor. I was taking Missy to the doctor because her eczema was so severe that she had clawed bloody wounds into her hands and arms. The poor child had no medicine to relieve the itching, and it was obvious that the skin was now infected. Getting her medical care wasn't going to solve the problem of the filthy apartment where she and her little brothers slept on stained mattresses without bedding. It didn't address the problem of the mom who had let the eczema get so out of hand even though the child had state-provided medical coverage that would have paid for treatment. I wanted to take care of that child in so many ways, but I had to content myself with the idea that I could at least get her some medical attention.

I took Missy to the nearest walk-in clinic. Since I was only twenty-five, I thought it seemed obvious that I wasn't the mother of this child. I also thought that my business attire and general level of grooming made it clear that I wasn't the sort of person who would allow a child in her care to be so grubby and thoroughly neglected. So I was startled when a young doctor assumed I was the parent and started questioning me about Missy's condition, with obvious dislike of me and distaste for the task. For a moment, I realized what it must be like for Missy's mother to be on the receiving end of a doctor's frustration and scorn—another surprising discovery.

It turned out that Missy had impetigo as well as eczema and needed various medications regularly administered along with showers, clean clothes, and clean sheets. Of course the likelihood that she would actually get any of these things was nil.

This was my first lesson in accepting the reality and futility of child welfare work. I don't remember exactly why Missy's mother had lost custody of her three children for a while. I think she was just incapable of maintaining a reasonably safe and healthy home, probably because she had never lived in that sort of home as a child herself. But despite the risk to her children, Missy's mother's inadequacy in this area didn't constitute grounds for permanently removing them from her care. She couldn't be compelled to upgrade her standards and she wasn't amenable to encouragement, particularly since she didn't even recognize that there was a problem in the way she cared for her children—or for herself. She wasn't at all interested in my explanations about how to tend to her daughter's wounds, but she did seem to think it was nice that I had taken Missy on a four-hour outing.

Not long after that visit, the mother regained full custody, and her children were removed from my caseload. It was frustrating to have been able to do so little to improve those lives. But it wasn't a hard call for the judge to decide it was time to close their case; despite what we might want for children like Missy, their parents have the legal right to raise them in squalor and deprive them of non-urgent medical care. I needed to understand that while it's hard for kids to grow up in these conditions, it's not as hard on them as being separated from their parents.

Fortunately for me, there were no immediate crises when I started my job, and I wasn't suddenly faced with making life-altering decisions. I had a little time to get my bearings before any really hard decisions came my way. But not everyone in my position was so lucky.

Consider what happened to Miles, a friend of mine from graduate school. Hired as a caseworker immediately after getting his bachelor's degree, he was smart, conscientious, and ethical, and would go on to be highly successful and well-respected in his long career. He was an earnest, idealistic twenty-three-year-old when he was sent out to complete a home study for a young woman new to the area who was hoping to regain custody of her three-year-old daughter. The child was in foster care in another state, and Miles was able to get only minimal information from the social workers there who were handling her case. There was no mention of child abuse or neglect in their reports, and it appeared that the child had been removed from the mother's care primarily because of a lack of family support—misfortune, in other words, rather than cruelty. Miles went to the woman's home, saw that she met the basic home study requirements, and found no grounds for denying the return of her child. When the little girl did return to her mother's care a short time later, Miles was assigned responsibility for supervising them. Things seemed fine for a while, but then the child was admitted to a hospital with scald burns that the mother reported as accidental. After a short period of treatment, the little girl was released and returned to her mother's care. Within a few days, she was readmitted with what was diagnosed as a subdural hematoma; she died of this injury.

Miles was responsible for investigating the death for his agency, while the local police department investigated it as a possible homicide. The mother insisted that her daughter had been injured while in the care of a friend/babysitter. Miles recalled that on his first visit to the home after the child had died, he arrived just as two police detectives were leaving. He later realized that they must have lingered by the front door, because they apparently heard him tell the woman that she might want to consider getting a lawyer. When the case became a high-profile matter in the press, the detectives told the reporter that this statement indicated to them that Miles seemed to be more concerned about the mother than the child. The tragedy was top-story news for a number of weeks, and Miles figured prominently in the reports and subsequent investigation. The newspaper coverage was so negative toward Miles that it prompted one woman to write a letter to the editor comparing him to Hitler. The hospital spokesman made things worse by telling the reporter that they had sent Miles a letter expressing concern about the child's safety. In fact, Miles had received no communication from the hospital until more than a week after the child's death and days after the spokesman's statement had been reported in the paper, when a letter with neither stamp nor postmark mysteriously appeared on Mile's chair at work one morning. At about the same time, Miles spoke with an intern who had seen the child during the first hospitalization. He told Miles that he had observed symptoms consistent with a subdural hematoma at that time but that the doctor in charge had dismissed his concerns. It seemed that the hospital was worried about its possible culpability in not paying proper attention to the intern. The creation of the letter, after the fact, was probably not so much an effort to discredit Miles as to distract from the fact that the hospital might have missed the child's most significant injury and consequently missed the opportunity to save her life.

To complicate matters for Miles, he was not allowed to speak with reporters for several weeks, so the stories kept running without his input. After he was finally interviewed, the reporter concluded that he had an admirable command of the facts, and she said she was sorry that she hadn't spoken with him earlier. Of course, this was after weeks of vilification; there were no subsequent stories exonerating Miles or clarifying the difficulty of his position. Fortunately, he had great support from his family and friends. And he certainly had the understanding of his colleagues, some of whom expressed amazement that he didn't quit his job. They all must have realized that it was just blind luck that separated them from Miles, and that this sort of tragedy could hit any of them at any time.

I vividly remember when Miles first told me this story. I was rendered speechless—a rare condition for me—as I took in the enormity of the tragedy to the little girl and the injustice to him. I couldn't imagine a way to offer comfort or make sense of any of it. But I could easily understand the media reaction. When bad things happen, we want clear explanations and someone to blame. How quick and convenient to conclude that Miles was negligent and that children wouldn't die in these circumstances if caseworkers weren't so inattentive.

The mother was ultimately found guilty of manslaughter, and Miles recalls the judge saying something to the effect of "someone has to be held responsible" for this child's death.

I had remembered Miles during my interview with Charles, the social services director. I couldn't stop thinking about how he had been working to reunite the family. And I wondered why I wanted this job.

2

Service Plans

THE COMBINATION OF HUMAN misery and mind-numbing bureaucracy can quickly render people who work in places like operating rooms, police stations, and child welfare offices depressed and ineffectual if they don't find a way to cope. To a certain extent, you have to harden yourself to the reality around you in order to simply get through the day without being overwhelmed by sadness and frustration. Gallows humor prevails in these settings—as it did in our office. We worked in a large, open room with short partitions between the desks. Consequently, we all knew a lot about each other's cases, and our secretary, Joyce, who typed up all our case narratives, knew everything about everyone. We all came and went to and from the office frequently, but Jim, our supervisor, was usually there along with at least two or three other caseworkers at a time, and there were frequent informal discussions about our cases.

There were always people to turn to when one of us needed advice or emotional support or just needed to vent about the latest frustration in working with a client. I remember one conversation with two other caseworkers, all of us female and in our mid-twenties, about a call one of us had received from a foster mother who was fed up with repeatedly finding all the family's towels stuffed under the bed in her thirteen-year-old foster son's room. She wanted my colleague to come out and tell the kid that masturbating was fine and his own business, but that the disappearance of all the household's towels created a problem for everyone else. So the poor caseworker, Connie, was trying to gather information about the etiquette of teenage male masturbation from people who—like her—had never been a son or had a son and certainly hadn't

learned anything about this subject in graduate school. We heartily sympa-
thized, though, and tried to suggest alternatives (washcloths? socks? doing his
own laundry? more uninterrupted time in the bathroom?) that were by turns
serious and frivolous. After about thirty minutes of uninformed speculation,
we heard Jim laughing in his office and realized we should have turned to
him for advice. In the end, he was the one who had a talk with the boy, which
solved the problem of the missing towels and preserved Connie's ability to
work with him without crippling embarrassment for both of them.

Interactions of this sort took place in our office practically every day, so it
didn't take long to establish close bonds and a feeling of camaraderie between
us all. It also wasn't long before we started socializing. My husband, being a
writer, was especially fond of gatherings of social workers, all of whom had
stories (non-identifying, of course) that could command any room.

There were innumerable discouraging aspects to our job, yet things often
would start off on a quasi-optimistic note, with clients seeming to have a glim-
mer of understanding about what they needed to do to regain custody of their
children. This was when the "service plan," with its detailed instructions for
improvement, would come into play. At the outset, parents might do something, such as attend an AA meeting or two or show up for visitation with the
children a few times, just as called for in the service plan. But then, for many,
all forward progress would stop and we wouldn't hear from them or be able
to reach them for weeks or months. When we did finally manage to connect,
we would hear a string of excuses, and new promises would be made, only to
be broken again—usually immediately. Typically, about two weeks before the
next review hearing was scheduled, the parents' attorney would swing into
action and get his or her client back on track enough to show up for a visit
or attend an anger-management class. Sometimes the attorney would only be
able to make contact with the client at the courthouse moments before the
hearing and would then extract a promise to make the necessary changes in
the future. This feat was accomplished just in time for the attorney to be able
to tell the judge with a straight face that the parent had seen the error of his or
her ways and was once again committed to regaining custody. I saw this routine repeated every three to six months for years, while the parents changed
nothing and the children grew older and more disillusioned.

So, where's the gallows humor in all this? It was often provided by Mike,
a good-humored, good-looking caseworker who got along famously with almost all his clients—particularly the women. He was funny and approachable
and seemed softhearted and even a little self-deprecating. One of his best stories was about the day he and a female caseworker were sent out to a sketchy
neighborhood in Detroit to investigate an abuse allegation. They were greeted
at the door by a man with a shotgun, and Mike and his companion responded

by repeatedly jumping behind one another until they both fell off the porch. They then took off running without a backward glance.

No one held Mike's lack of chivalry against him—particularly since he generally told this story at his own expense.

Mike had been on the job for a while when I joined the department, and he had developed substantial self-protective cynicism. This was particularly evident when he came back from visits with his most trying client—an obnoxious, belligerent, abusive single father of six bedraggled children. This man found Mike to be not at all charming, and he regularly threatened to treat him the way he treated his children. These poor kids ranged in age from grade school to high school; they had all been in and out of foster care repeatedly, and it was abundantly clear that their father was never going to change his ways. The family home was what we called a "pee house"; the stench of urine hit you the minute you walked in the door. (I had the misfortune of having several clients with "pee houses," whom I had to visit regularly. In one, I had been trying to act nonchalant and not breath too deeply while sitting on the edge of a decrepit, overstuffed armchair when a four-year-old boy walked up to it and peed into the arm.) Mike had been working with this particular man for several years, and despite numerous service plans, there was no discernible improvement of any kind. The children always did well when they were in foster care, but things would fall apart as soon as they were returned to their father. The oldest daughter, who was about sixteen, wanted out but felt responsible for all the younger siblings since their mom was long gone. She knew she couldn't leave them alone with Dad. And Dad knew exactly how far he could take his abuse without giving Mike grounds to terminate his parental rights. (The bar for removal of children from an abusive home was criminally high.) So Mike was confronted with a stalemate in which there was virtually nothing he could do in his dealings with this cunning man to ease the suffering of the children. His only recourse was to concoct ever-more-fanciful "secret service plans" as a way of taking refuge in his imagination from the anger and hopelessness he faced whenever he thought of this family.

I remember my husband telling me that my coworkers and I were like the cops in a Joseph Wambaugh novel, constantly getting together outside of work to drink and commiserate because no one else understood what they went through on the job. It was at one of these frequent nights out with my colleagues that Mike, a gifted storyteller, was venting to my husband, who could never hear enough of these stories. Mike had blazing blue eyes that grew brighter and brighter beer by beer. He'd knocked back quite a few by the time he got around to talking about the man who made him so frustrated. "My secret service plan, next time the kids are in foster care, is to go over and blow up this guy's house."

As it happens, I had a case where a father actually did disappear (un-harmed) at an opportune moment. There were two tremendously appealing children, Cori and Sam, on my caseload. Nine-year-old Cori was a lanky little chatterbox with a sometimes disarmingly straightforward, though always well-intentioned, manner. She was bright and sensitive and worried a lot about her mother, Madeline, who was a drug addict and couldn't provide a safe home for her kids. Madeline's failings had led to Cori being sexually abused by at least one male acquaintance, and she and five-year-old Sam had been put into foster care about a year before I met them. Since there were no similar allegations of abuse involving Sam, he had been returned to his mother's care about six months before their case was turned over to me. This added immeasurably to Cori's distress, and she alternated between agonizing over what might be happening to Sam and wondering why he got to be with mom and she didn't.

I certainly didn't have any reassuring answers. Fortunately, Cori's foster family consisted of a genuinely nice young couple with two kids, a boy and a girl, who both really liked Cori, and she responded well to the family's hon-est and uncomplicated desire to take care of her. She was clearly suffering emotionally, but on a scale of one to ten, Cori's foster home was a nine (they lacked the horse that would have made it a true ten in Cori's eyes), and I think she genuinely appreciated the lack of drama in her new life.

After meeting and being charmed by Cori, I got down to the work of fig-uring out what to do for her. It seemed obvious that her mother's most im-mediate problem was drugs. Sometimes when I spoke with her on the phone, Madeline was alert and engaging and could make reasonable plans regard-ing Cori; but far more often, she couldn't manage to drawl out more than a couple of disjointed sentences before nodding off for a while.

Clearly, my service plan needed to address this issue. But I couldn't get anyone to even acknowledge that Madeline was using drugs, let alone con-vince her to get treatment. She denied having any sort of problem, and both her doctor and her therapist refused to provide me with any information. After my first visit with a groggy Madeline in the basement room of the seedy Detroit hotel where she and Sam were living, it became head-thumpingly clear that he was not safe with her. And even in her drugged state, Madeline apparently realized that she had not made a good impression; while I was busy obtaining a court order to have Sam join Cori at the foster home, she vanished with him.

Six months later, a policewoman in Las Vegas called to tell me that Mad-eline was dead. The officer told me that Madeline had been in a crowd of people waiting to cross a busy street, had stepped out into traffic, and was killed instantly. The policewoman had gotten my name from Madeline's mother and was calling to tell me that they had Sam in custody and wanted to know what they should do with him.

These days, most people know much more about drug users and the fact that dying a violent, early death is a distinct possibility for them, but we weren't as knowledgeable or as jaded back then, and the news of Madeline's death stunned me. I was sad for her and for the kids, and depressed about the life she had been leading. But amid all this horror, I was also aware of how relatively easy it had suddenly become for me to create a long-term plan for Cori and Sam.

The most pressing concerns were to get Sam back to Michigan and to tell Cori about her mother's death. I cringe when I think about how totally inadequate I was to the task of telling Cori, but I managed to stumble through it, and then she and her foster mother and I sat there talking and crying for a long time. Cori was a smart, strong little girl who, unlike many abused and neglected kids, hadn't shut down emotionally. I knew she had been slowly losing faith in her mother over the past year and a half, but like a lot of kids in foster care, Cori had held on to a certain bravado regarding her mom, and now that been abruptly stripped away.

There was one bit of good news, though: Cori now believed that Sam was safe and would be coming to live with her.

When I got back to my office, I had another call from the policewoman, this time informing me that Sam was now in the custody of his father, who had somehow gotten word of Madeline's death. The father, Dan, said that he had flown to Las Vegas immediately upon hearing the news about Madeline. Dan told the policewoman that he hadn't taken Sam earlier because he hadn't known about the problems Madeline was having.

Of course I knew that many efforts had been made to find Dan, all of which had been unsuccessful. The speed with which he suddenly appeared was perplexing, to say the least. I could never tell if Madeline and other family members were trying to protect Dan from my office by not revealing his whereabouts or if they had just given up on him. But I knew that he had been absent from his children's lives for a long time, long enough that Sam probably barely remembered who he was.

Fortunately, Dan's plan included bringing Sam to Madeline's funeral. After that, the policewoman told me, Dan had mentioned that he might take Sam to live with him. He hadn't said anything about plans for Cori.

My single-minded focus at that point became getting Sam and Cori together. I knew that Cori was counting the minutes until she saw Sam, and I felt that she would be the best person in the world to give him comfort. They were both so fragile; they needed each other so badly, and any delay in getting them together seemed unconscionable. I decided to appeal to a judge who— thank goodness—agreed with me and gave me a court order to take custody of Sam. So with paper in hand, I met Dan and Sam that night at the Detroit airport as they got off their plane. In appearance and manner, Dan evoked a taller and handsomer "Man in Black" Johnny Cash—definitely intimidating. He was clearly displeased to see me, but with the help of airport security, he eventually seemed to grasp the idea that the kids really wanted and needed each other. Poor Sam was stunned and exhausted, but he perked up at the idea of being with Cori, and Dan finally conceded that I could take him to her.

Seeing the two children together an hour later was an overwhelming combination of heartbreaking and heartwarming. Cori immediately turned into exhausted little Sam's proud and protective big sister, and he clung to her. The kids both kept breaking into grins of delight as they shyly sized each other up after their long separation. But I feared their happiness would be short-lived. I knew that Dan would get custody of Sam if he pursued it, and he had said that that was what he intended to do. None of Dan's failings as a father—knowing of Madeline's problems, knowing that his kids were in and out of foster care, refusing to provide any sort of financial or emotional support for them, failing even to make contact—would be enough to deny him custody. I knew that the courts and I would soon lose control of this situation, and how likely it was that Sam would be taken away and Cori would feel devastated and abandoned once again.

The funeral and wake were held the next day, and I stayed away in the hopes of not further agitating Dan. My information about what happened that day came from Cori's foster parents and from Lou Ann, the caseworker who had worked with Cori and Sam before I did. Lou Ann had established a good relationship with Madeline's mother and stepfather, and had a level of insight and street smarts about the situation that I lacked. Madeline's parents lived in an upscale community in the same town as Cori's foster family but had minimal contact with Cori. They told me they were happy that she wasn't with Madeline and they acknowledged that Madeline "had problems," although they wouldn't get specific about her drug use. Much of their anger was focused on Dan, whose lifestyle they felt had been a bad influence on Madeline and had led directly to all of her difficulties. I got to know these grandparents a bit when I did a sort of mini–home study so that they could be approved for a weekend visit with Cori. I remember being surprised by the discrepancy between their reported income and their relatively lavish lifestyle and complimenting them (with stunning naïveté, in retrospect) on their money-management skills. It turns out there was a whole lot of unreported income—supposedly from consistent good luck at the racetrack.

I spent that day dreading the call informing me that there had been a confrontation at the wake. I couldn't imagine that Dan would give up easily.

I was caught completely by surprise by the calls I finally received from Cori's foster mother and Lou Ann. They told me about the scene at the cemetery, where Dan had appeared to be inconsolable in his grief. Then came the subsequent scene at the wake, held in a private room at a local restaurant: Dan was sitting at a table socializing along with everyone else when suddenly a group of older men walked in and surrounded his chair. There was a brief, inaudible discussion, after which Dan rose and was escorted out the back door. A short time later, the group returned with Dan, took him past his table without anyone saying a word, and went out through the front door. At which point, Madeline's stepfather turned to Lou Ann and said, "He won't be giving you any more trouble."

Dan called me the next day to say that he had reconsidered and now felt that both children would be better off with the foster family. I tried to start a conversation about plans for the future and he cut me off with, "I'd talk more but I have to run—my flight's about to take off." It was the last time I ever heard from him.

I had stumbled upon a "secret service plan" that was every bit as effective (and almost as troubling) as the one Mike fantasized about. Although there was much speculation in the office after that about how useful the grandfather and his friends could be to us, no one asked for his contact information.

3

Who Are These Parents and Children?

M Y CLIENTS (THE PARENTS) GENERALLY FELL into one of three categories, the first two of which made up only about one-third of my caseload but took up most of my time. Those two categories were (1) people who were seriously mentally ill and/or thoroughly drug or alcohol addicted, refused any sort of treatment, and consequently were disconnected from reality much of the time; and (2) people who were severely antisocial (sadistically abusive, sexually abusive, violently criminal). A small but insidious hybrid of these two groups consisted of "religious" fanatics who appeared to function normally most of the time but genuinely believed that God called them to regularly beat the devil out of their children.

There were varying degrees of dysfunction in these groups, but you could hold out hope for only a few of them, which made our mandate to work to reunite the family particularly unrealistic.

The third and largest group consisted of people who were abusive and/or extremely neglectful but who showed potential for improvement. Some had problems with substance abuse and anger management but at least understood that hurting children was wrong. Others were women who weren't ready to end a relationship with men who had abused their children. Still others were parents who had grown up in such deprived environments themselves that they had never learned even the most basic child-rearing skills necessary to protect children from injury and illness. These people weren't necessarily easy to work with, but there was a much larger degree of hope for them.

The most typical storyline would begin with a child spending time in foster care after an incident of abuse. Rarely was this the first incident of abuse; it was just the first time the child's plight had come to the attention of child protective services. While the child got settled into the foster home, the parent and caseworker would begin working on improving things enough to warrant a try at bringing him or her back home. The goal was to make this happen quickly, but I had lots of kids on my caseload who had lingered in foster care for years. Their parents' problems proved serious enough to keep the children in foster care but not serious enough for the courts to terminate the parents' rights and free the children for adoption. The ensuing stalemate had these kids essentially growing up in foster care.

This would have been somewhat less damaging if the children had been able to stay in the same foster home. But often, there were numerous moves and changes, with the children cycling not only between home and foster care but between foster homes as well. Even after a child had been in foster care for years and it became clear that he or she would never be returning home to live, there was still no assurance of living in the same foster home throughout childhood. It was depressingly common to get calls from long-term foster parents asking that the kids be moved when they hit puberty and became more difficult to live with. While it was hard to blame the foster parents for needing respite when the children's problems were extreme, the consequences of a move were devastating to these already damaged children. Another upheaval in their lives thoroughly undermined the normal adolescent effort to gain independence by testing parental limits. Instead of achieving the desired independence and maturity that adolescence was supposed to bring about, another move would plunge these children back into insecurity and chaos, further reducing their chances of ever being able to form normal attachments. The world just continued to prove to them that it wasn't safe to let yourself care about or depend upon other people.

For some reason, most of my clients didn't elicit the expected anger from me when I dealt with them directly. While I was tremendously angry about whatever they had done that warranted putting their children in foster care, I couldn't help but see that many of them simply had no concept of what it meant to be a decent parent. Their own parents had been abusive, and no one had ever stepped in to put a stop to it or even let them know that this wasn't normal. Now, as parents themselves, these people probably knew intellectually that children shouldn't be abused, but emotionally they struggled to come up with a different response when they were angry or frustrated, as they often were.

Many of my clients elicited outright sympathy. One woman I expected to loathe had lost custody after she began disciplining her three children by biting them on the cheeks. When I first read her case file, I was horrified. I expected her to be a monster, but when I went out to meet her, I found

Deirdre to be a highly intelligent woman and—even more incredibly—a loving parent who (through no fault of her own) was mentally ill. The children were two somber little girls and a seemingly happy toddler boy. After they were removed from their home, the children were placed with their paternal grandparents. They were well cared for and attached to their grandparents, but it was evident that the girls, at least, missed their mother terribly. Deirdre appeared to have been a good and devoted parent most of the time, and there was no question that the children loved her and that she loved them. But it was also probably true that she was not going to get well enough to be a reliable caretaker any time soon. Her service plan called for her to go to counseling and take her medication, but these steps, if they were being taken, didn't appear to be having any beneficial effect. She frequently stopped by my office in an effort to convince me that she didn't need treatment, and she would talk circles around anything I said to try to convince her otherwise. Deirdre was extremely articulate and pretty and could seem quite normal—even convincing—for a while. She could engage me in conversations that held out no hope for resolution. Reasoning with her was like trying to reason with a drunk. She exhausted me and frustrated me practically to the point of tears, but she didn't make me angry; she was far too sad for that.

In general, it was hard to know what sort of relationship to establish with my clients. I tried to seem friendly and helpful most of the time, but every three to six months, the inevitable court hearing would come at which I would have to recommend whether the child should stay in foster care. Most of the time I was recommending against a child returning home, and my clients were unhappy about that, but it didn't take long for them to resume acting friendly toward me. It was as though we had an understanding that, while they really did want their child back, they wouldn't actually be expected to live up to their part of the bargain by changing their behavior quite yet, and therefore I couldn't be expected to recommend the return of their children.

I did have one client who didn't follow this depressing pattern. She was a young mother of three- and four-year-old sons and a thirteen-month-old daughter; and as is all too common, her boyfriend, who was not their father, had abused the children. They were placed in foster care, and Darcy—the mother—remained with the boyfriend. When I was assigned the case, the boys were in one foster home and the little girl, Shelby, in another, and Darcy had been told that she needed to find a safe place to live without the boyfriend if she wanted to get her children back. I got to know her and the kids as I supervised their weekly visitation.

The routine for these visits was always the same. I would first pick Shelby up at her foster home, where she lived with a pleasant couple in their sixties. She was adorable and easygoing and didn't seem to be suffering any obvious ill effects from either the abuse or the separation from her family. (Of course, she really was suffering terribly; it just wasn't obvious to her inexperienced caseworker, who knew so little about children at that point.) Next we would drive to the home where her brothers were living, and Shelby always reacted with excitement when they got into the car with us. During the visits, she clung to Darcy.

This pattern of visitation went on for several months while Darcy extricated herself from the relationship and living situation with her boyfriend and waited for a spot in low-income housing to become available. Finally she called me with the news that an apartment in an approved building had opened up, but she needed a $400 deposit within twenty-four hours in order to hold it for her family.

I decided to just go ahead and ask for the $400, and a tremendous uproar made its way up the chain of command in my office. It seemed obvious to me that keeping the three young children of a mother who had lived up to her end of the service plan bargain in foster care simply because she was jobless and couldn't come up with the money for a deposit made no moral, psychological, or common sense. Her service plan assignment had been to extricate herself from her abusive boyfriend and to find adequate, safe housing for her family, and she had done that. To deny her access to her children at that point was tantamount to finding her guilty of—and deserving punishment for—poverty. And the children were being punished as well.

I also thought it made financial sense in this situation for the state to just give Darcy $400 instead of continuing to spend more than that every month to keep the three children in foster care. But when I pled her case to our assistant director, he told me that there was no precedent for this sort of payment and that therefore it couldn't be done. He did allow me to talk with Charles about it, though, and Charles (who was so committed to reuniting families) finally agreed that we could, just this once, dip into an emergency fund and gamble on this woman. But both men made it clear that I was "overinvolved" in this case, and that they fully expected that Darcy would soon be in financial trouble again and would feel entitled to keep coming back to ask for money.

Indeed, Darcy did continue to struggle financially. One day when I visited, she told me that she had only a few diapers left and joked that she needed to start toilet training Shelby. Safely out of sight of my supervisors, I spent a whopping eight dollars of my own money (1975 money) on a case of diapers.

I closed Darcy's case a few weeks later. I'm sure life continued to be hard for her, but she never contacted me again, the kids didn't come back into foster care—and my tendency to overinvolve myself was off to a flying start.

* * *

The kids on my caseload ranged from newborn to eighteen years old. Most were Caucasian, about one-fifth were African American, Hispanic, or of mixed racial heritage, and a few were Native American. This was a fairly accurate representation of the general population in that part of Michigan at the time. A few of the kids had significant developmental delays or mental health concerns, and most of the kids had been traumatized, first by the abuse or neglect that had brought them into foster care, and then by the separation from their families and their familiar lives. There were kids who (rightfully) raged against a world that had treated them so cruelly, and there were other kids who had given up on that approach and kept a low (and depressed) profile. Staying under the radar may have been an effective way of coexisting with their birth parents, and it was certainly a reasonable approach to the unknowns of living in a foster home.

There was also a group of kids who had figured out that if they worked extra hard at being charming and affectionate, the world was likely to treat them more kindly. These kids were usually upbeat and compliant, and they made life easy for the adults in their lives. They made life easy for their caseworker, too, until she started thinking about what was behind all that people-pleasing behavior, which was most likely the child's assumption that he was somehow in control of/to blame for the way other people treated and mistreated him. It was hard not to envision a miserable future for a child with such damaged self-esteem and such a finely honed ability to manipulate others. These qualities would ultimately not serve him, or the people who were drawn to him, well.

I usually had between fifty-five and sixty-five children at a time on my caseload. There were a few sibling groups, which brought the total number of cases down a little, but still there were too many children for me to be able to establish any sort of meaningful connection with most of them. Although I spent a lot of time on their behalf, I didn't spend a lot of actual time with the babies and little kids on my caseload except when I was transporting them to visits with their parents or other appointments. They were too young to know who I was or to care about my role in their lives anyway. It was the older kids who commanded the greatest amount of my in-person time. Talking with them was rarely a formalized activity but was sneaked in around the edges of other things that needed to be done, such as monthly trips to the dentist. If we didn't have the excuse of an appointment, I would suggest that we run an errand or go get a treat, and would always take back roads to prolong the trip. This one-on-one time was perfect for the sort of low-pressure conversation that the kids needed, and they were able to express themselves in ways they wouldn't have if we had been sitting together in a quiet room.

I remember a detailed fashion critique by a teenaged girl as we drove through the University of Michigan campus one day. She was extremely scornful of the ripped jeans and flannel shirts she saw everywhere and said the students looked like they belonged in the woods. She made it clear that her own standards of dress would never allow her to look so ragged and foolish. Of course we both knew that she had just moved into a new foster home with one garbage bag carrying all her meager possessions. Her clothes may not have been flannel, but they were definitely ragged. (Not once did I see that girl looking foolish, though.)

At first I was surprised by her strong feelings, but it made perfect sense that this girl, who had so little, would try to elevate her own standing in the all-important world of fashion by criticizing someone else's style. Disparaging others is what people, especially fourteen-year-old girls, do when they feel inadequate. I told her that the college kids thought they looked terrific; she feigned disbelief, and we didn't delve into the deeper meaning of her comments that day.

The subject of fashion came up again a few months later, though—in a big way. Every year, the foster care department would receive wrapped Christmas presents for the caseworkers to distribute to the children on our caseloads. Each gift would have a tag, sometimes with the name of the specific item (e.g., baseball) and sometimes saying something like "clothing, girl, size 10." We were supposed to gather together a couple things for each child so that the foster parents wouldn't be overburdened. I sure wish I had that first Christmas as a caseworker to do over again. I followed the rules and sought out the appropriately labeled packages, but it was a disaster. My fashion-loving teenager opened up a size large cotton housedress (in a box labeled "clothing, girl, size 10") and an orange-and-gray striped knit hat and muffler made of yarn so stiff and thick that they could stand up on their own (in a box labeled "hat and scarf, girl"). Not only were the gifts completely unsuited to her taste (or pretty much anyone's taste), but they screamed "I have no idea who you are." A horrible message for a gift to give, but especially sad when the recipient is a child who is already plenty worried about being unknown and unloved. We were able to laugh together about the ugly clothes later, but I know she wasn't laughing on Christmas morning.

The following year we revamped the whole Christmas present system. We got specific information from the foster parents about exactly which items the kids were hoping for, and we did all the wrapping ourselves in order to ensure that there were no mix-ups in delivery. Sometimes it seemed weird when kids who had never been able to have expensive things became quite specifically demanding. For example, a kid without a winter jacket wouldn't just put "warm jacket" on his list but would name the precise jacket (designer, store, size, color, and often, team name), and anything else would be a disappointment—just as it would be for the lucky kids in regular families. Things didn't always work out, and kids didn't always get exactly what they wished for (also just as in regular families), but Christmas in our department was no longer a time when people cleared out their closets or tossed their leftover yarn supply in our direction. The kids in foster care were just as materialistic as most kids are, and they enjoyed their presents for what they were. More importantly, they enjoyed what the presents represented: that there were people paying attention to them as individuals rather than as random "needy children" who were expected to feel unquestioning gratitude for anything they were given.

Children who have been abused and neglected and have come into the foster care system often haven't had an opportunity to develop a normal sense of self-worth. Sometimes the chaos of their early lives made it impossible for the children I knew to establish reliable bonds with their parents or other caregivers, and they continued to struggle to form attachments or even meaningful connections with other people. More often, they did form strong (albeit troubled) bonds with their parents, but were then traumatized by abuse and by the separation brought on when they were removed from the home. Common sense suggests that children in this circumstance would learn to reject the abusive parent and quickly place their trust in someone—such as a good foster parent—who provided proper nurture, but I saw that happen only with children who were very young. Older children usually held on to the attachment to their parent no matter how serious the abuse or how long the separation had been. Sometimes the attachment had little to do with the actual parent or even the child's whitewashed memories of the parent but was instead a fantasized version of how things should have been. With some kids, the worse the abuse, the stronger their need to deny it and to defend their parent. It makes perfect sense as a coping mechanism, especially for a child.

The typical image of an abused or neglected child is of someone who is hurt, frightened, sad, confused, pitiful, and so on. Once the initial trauma surrounding removal from the parent's home has subsided and the child is settled into a stable foster home, we revise our image a bit. Now we hope the description will include words like *grateful, humble, cooperative, undemanding*, and the ever-popular *plucky*. In other words, we want this child to leave all the drama behind as soon as possible and take advantage of the opportunity she has been given to thrive.

I had one girl on my caseload who embodied all the qualities of the deserving and ideal foster child. Alison was sixteen years old, and her mother was mentally ill and an alcoholic. By the time I met Alison, her mother was so volatile that it had become unsafe for Alison to remain at home. The situation was greatly complicated by the fact that Alison was pregnant, and there were apparently no relatives who could or would take care of her. So Alison came into foster care and had decided that since she didn't think she was ready for parenthood, she would plan an adoption for her baby. Alison was only about five feet, two inches tall and, even in the later stages of pregnancy, was extremely delicate in appearance. She had long brown hair, big blue eyes, a gentle manner, and a face that was Madonna-esque.

Things hadn't been good at home for a long time, and Alison was, to a degree, used to taking charge of her own life. She was a straight-A student, well liked at school, and definitely had plans for the future, including college. The pregnancy had derailed all of that, and she had become dependent in ways that made her terribly uncomfortable since she absolutely hated to impose on others. One bright spot in all of this was Alison's boyfriend, Chad, a classmate who was not the father of the baby. They had started dating before she realized she was pregnant, but unlike most young men in this situation, he remained supportive and didn't end the relationship. Chad clearly adored Alison, but he was sixteen years old and did not have the support of his parents, who were understandably unhappy about the sudden drama in their son's life. Chad wasn't going to be able to contribute much in the way of practical assistance to Alison, but his friendship and emotional support were invaluable.

Alison was living in a nice foster home, and the plan was for her to stay there, place the baby for adoption, and resume her life as a high school junior. She and Chad started attending the church that the foster family belonged to, and it wasn't long before I was told that she had selected a family from the church to be the baby's adoptive parents. Everything went along smoothly for a couple of months; then the baby was born, and Alison, who had received nothing in the way of unbiased decision-making counseling regarding her adoption decision, decided that she could not, after all, give up her child. I'm sure the prospective adoptive parents were devastated, but to everyone's credit, it appeared that the entire church community rallied around Alison. She was instantly and fully supplied with baby clothing and equipment as well as offers for babysitting and other forms of assistance. Women gave her much-needed parenting information and advice, and Chad spent time with older men who provided him with lessons about fatherhood and responsibility. The fact that he wasn't actually the baby's father and that he and Alison had only been dating for about six months didn't seem to be of much concern. Both teenagers, and baby Alex, were suddenly bathed in attention and approval. The only people who didn't seem supportive were Alison's and Chad's parents. Alison's mother's condition didn't improve, and Chad's parents kept a careful distance from Alison and the baby. I'm sure early marriage and parenthood were not what they had envisioned for their son.

Early marriage didn't seem to be the answer for Alison, either. As long as she and the baby were on their own, they qualified for a subsidized apartment and enough other forms of assistance to be able to get along reasonably well. Alison was an amazingly relaxed and competent parent. I greatly admired her matter-of-fact attitude as she met the various demands of parenthood, all without complaint. In retrospect, she had to have been putting on a good show, but she never seemed exhausted or overwhelmed the way you expect new parents to be. She also never seemed resentful about the position she was in or angry with her mother or with the baby's father, both of whom had effectively abandoned her. Mostly what Alison seemed to be was responsible and devoted to baby Alex, who was the picture of health and happiness and absolutely thrived in her love and care. My admiration for her grew even more after I became a parent myself and understood how truly remarkable it was that she managed everything so well as a sixteen-year-old who was on her own most of the time. She even managed to keep up with her schoolwork.

I feel a little guilty using Alison as an example of what parenthood was like for a teenager in foster care. Her experience was by no means the norm. Much more typically, when a girl got pregnant, it was cause for enormous concern. Obviously there was concern for the girl and how parenthood would affect her future. There was also concern for the baby, whose mother was likely to have had either abusive or neglectful parenting herself and was unlikely to have had positive role models to emulate. This put both mother and baby in jeopardy. Hopefully the mother would agree to stay in foster care for a while longer so that she could receive practical and emotional support as well as a crash course in parenting. More likely, the girl would decide that she could now live on her own, with the help of the extra government assistance she now qualified for. Usually these young mothers were raising their babies on their own from the beginning and, tragically, were at increased risk of turning into the next generation of parents whose children would come to the attention of the child welfare system.

4

Foster Home Highs and Lows

Jim and Kevin started arguing over toast. I told them how silly it was to argue over bread and asked them what they would do if Christ was sitting down at the table. Kevin seen the light and said he was sorry but our almighty Jim sat there and said he didn't do anything wrong. And I said if he was so perfect and never did anything wrong then why has he been in so many different foster homes? He never batted an eyelash.—Anonymous Foster Mother

IT WAS RARE IN OUR OFFICE TO terminate parental rights. Judges were willing to rule that a child was not safe at home for a given period of time, but generally stopped short of determining that the family situation was so hopeless that the parent/child relationship should be legally severed. This meant the caseworker was often put in the position of choosing either to risk a child's safety by recommending that he return home to a dangerously inadequate parent or to recommend that he continue to live in a foster home that (as far as could be determined) was at least meeting his basic needs. My work in these situations in which children lingered in foster care year after year often involved managing what we called "long-term foster care"—something similar to a guardianship arrangement.

Good foster homes were always in short supply, and there was no guarantee that I could maintain equilibrium in a foster child's life for long, even when he or she was officially in a long-term foster home. This was particularly true during adolescence. Rather than cope with the problems that teenagers present, foster parents too often would ask that children be moved when they became teenagers. In some cases, it was because the child's problems had become too severe for any family to handle, and some sort of residential care (such as a group home or treatment facility) was called for. But more often a family would ask to have a child moved after an episode of more or less normal teenage rebellion. The family had handled similar levels of defiance when the child was younger, but now they were looking down the road and worrying about not being able to control the child's physical and sexual behavior. The foster care system, at least in those days, didn't offer much incentive or reward to foster parents confronted with the exhausting struggles of troubled adolescents.

It wasn't unreasonable for foster parents to want some relief from these problems, but moving the children was likely to cause their behavior to worsen, particularly since there were few foster homes willing to take teenagers with behavior problems. When a long-term foster care situation was disrupted, the options for the child were bleak.

I also came to learn that foster homes sometimes provided substandard care or, tragically, abused the children who were placed in them. And foster parents could be as devious as my official clients.

One unforgettable foster mom came across as a model foster parent—in fact, she had received at least one Foster Parent of the Year award. She was always dressed and groomed like June Cleaver (of *Leave It to Beaver* fame), and she and her husband lived in a sprawling, immaculate home on about five acres outside the city. It seemed as though every time we visited to check on the children in her care, she was pulling something yummy out of the oven just as we arrived. We marveled at her and the serenity of her household, despite the fact that she always had at least two babies in her care. They were quiet babies.

The babies were always napping no matter what time of day we visited. They would be awake and sitting up in their cribs when we went into their rooms with the foster mother to "wake" them. I didn't have a baby from my caseload in her home, but I visited there a few times for another caseworker on maternity leave. I remember being led down a dark hall and into a dark room where a baby girl, who was about fourteen months old, was supposedly sleeping. Instead, she was sitting quietly in her crib and paid little attention to us as we entered the room. There was no crying—but there was also no sign of greeting or expectation. She did not jump to her feet, lift her arms to be picked up, or make a single sound. It was eerie; my first thought was that there must be something wrong with the baby. I mentioned what I had seen to my supervisor, Jim, and it turned out that another caseworker had similar concerns with this foster home. She and Jim started to make unannounced visits to the home, and it didn't take long for them to figure out that there was virtually no time of day when the babies in this woman's care weren't confined to their cribs.

The baby I had seen had been deemed a "failure to thrive," but once she got out of that home and started to receive proper care, she did fine. Naturally, the foster mother denied any wrongdoing; she had no doubt convinced herself that babies just need to sleep all the time. But it seemed evident to us that the babies in this woman's home had either been drugged into passivity or had simply given up on the idea that their crying, or anything else they did, mattered to her, or to anyone at all. Despite the extremely serious nature of her mistreatment, there was no consequence to the woman other than losing her foster care license and the admiration she had so enjoyed.

As far as we knew, instances of physical and sexual abuse were rare in the foster homes we used, but they did occur, and we always took accusations seriously. I had a sixteen-year-old girl call one day to say that she had to move immediately because her foster father was sexually abusing her. This girl had lived with her foster family for the past three years, and it seemed like one of the most secure placements on my caseload. She had been a school friend of her foster parents' daughter and the family had gotten licensed specifically to care for the girl when her own family fell apart. Her mother was dead and her father had been convicted of sexually abusing the girl and an older sister, who was now living on her own. I visited the foster home numerous times during her stay there, and there had never been a hint of difficulty. The parents were open and loving, and the children—the two sixteen-year-old girls and a younger boy—all seemed happy. The father was the last man I would have thought could be an abuser, and in all probability he wasn't. But once the child made that accusation, there was nothing to be done except to remove her from the home and arrange for counseling. I never suggested to the girl that I doubted her story, but each time she told it, the details would change dramatically. The foster family was devastated and confused by the allegations, and also understandably frightened.

The girl moved in with a family that specialized in fostering teenagers. Neither she nor I was happy about that choice, but there were no other homes available. I remember the night I took her to that home and watched the new foster mother make a big show of welcoming her in a contrived ceremony held in front of all the other kids. She gave a tearful, overwrought performance in which she assured the girl that she had now found her "forever family." The woman was incredibly self-centered and annoying, and it didn't take that girl long to find an older guy to run off with. The foster care system clearly failed her—whether or not the abuse allegations were true.

One of the nicest and most impressive foster families I worked with was a couple in their sixties who had taken in the four older siblings of a three-year-old boy who had died of starvation because, as an older sister explained, there was "no food but jam" at their house. The older children included a fifteen-year-old girl, fourteen- and twelve-year-old boys, and a ten-year-old

girl. They had come into care four years earlier with no plan in place to reunite them with their mother. By the time I met the children, their mother
hadn't been heard from in more than three years, and they were in long-term
foster care. The four children had initially been placed together, but within
a year, the fifteen-year-old developed some behavioral problems the foster
parents couldn't handle, and she was moved to another home nearby. Her
siblings said they were pleased to have her gone, and she seemed pleased to be
in a home with no other children. The move apparently suited everyone, and
all four children appeared to be doing amazingly well, given their traumatic
history.

The three younger children were exceptionally tall and thin and grace-
ful and had some developmental delays. They had all been traumatized by
extreme neglect, the death by starvation of their little brother, the ensuing
legal issues, the separation from their mother, and undoubtedly other horrors
we didn't know about. Fortunately, the foster mother had a lovely, gentle,
nurturing manner. She and her equally likable, easygoing husband had been
married since their teens but had never had their own children. Their rural
home was small and humble but extremely pleasant and well cared for, and
although money was obviously tight, it looked as though they lived well.
For their part, the children always behaved wonderfully, at least when I was
around. They were polite, cooperative, and responsive and appeared to have
an appropriate attachment to their foster parents. Whenever I visited, the
whole family, including the father, would gather around to talk, and I was
impressed by how seriously the parents took their responsibilities to these
children. It was a pleasure to be around them all, and I was always sent off
feeling happy and carrying a gift of something delicious. In the winter, they
would send me home with a jar of jam or something freshly baked. In the
summer it was fresh vegetables from their huge and abundant garden and
Concord grapes from the arbor. In many ways, going to their house felt like
stepping back in time to an era when hard work and a bit of productive land
could meet most of a family's needs.

These happy visits continued for about two years. Then, seemingly out of
the blue, I got a call from the foster mother asking me to come and move the
children. I was stunned. When I got to the house, I found that all three children were asking to be moved. They couldn't tell me about anything specific
that had happened, and no one had any particular complaints about anyone
else, but the foster mother reported that the children said they wanted to leave
so they should be allowed to do so. I couldn't extract anything more from her
or from the children about what had led up to this situation, and the foster
father just said he needed to respect his wife's decision. So, with a heavy heart,
I arranged to take the children to visit another foster home. I had never been

to the new home before, but it was the only one available in their school district that could take all three of them.

A few days later, when I came to get the kids, they acted as though we were going on an exciting field trip, and the foster parents looked as though their hearts were breaking.

The new foster home turned out to be a dilapidated old farmhouse in the middle of a dirt yard strewn with broken appliances, tangled barbed wire, old car parts, and other cast-off items. Unwelcoming as it looked from the outside, the inside was even worse. The bedroom the woman showed the children had nothing in it except for rusty bed frames, filthy bare mattresses, and large shreds of ancient, peeling paper hanging from the ceiling. The kitchen walls were thick with grease that had turned the light-colored wallpaper around the stove dark brown, and the air was so filled with flies that I had to constantly wave a hand in front of my face to keep them out of my mouth and eyes. The children were their characteristically polite selves during the visit, but were dead silent as I drove them back home. As soon as we arrived, they quietly went to their rooms, no doubt with a new appreciation for the fresh sheets and fresh food that this home provided. I explained to their foster parents that we would have to look further for a suitable new foster home.

When I called a few days later, the foster mother reported that the children had now decided they wanted to stay where they were. The next time I visited, everyone was happy, life was back to normal, and no one wanted to talk about the aborted move. I was never able to find out what precipitated the children's request to move or why the parents didn't try to talk them out of it. I suspect that the foster mother had just been calling their bluff after an angry episode in which one of the kids said they wanted to leave. I suggested as much to her in private, and she acted surprised, saying "No" with a sweet little smile that seemed to indicate she and I shared our little secret. That strategy isn't one that would work well in most situations, but this time, with these children and the stark contrast between the foster homes, it was most effective.

I have long since lost touch with that family, but I have a vision in my mind of the parents sitting at a big table, surrounded by children and grandchildren and lots of terrific food, and embodying everything that is good about foster parents.

5

The Cycle of Dysfunction

MICHELLE WAS NINETEEN when I officially met her. But along with lots of other people, I had long known of her as the crazy girl who shouted abuse at random passersby and got in fights with people. Her problems were obvious, and trouble had probably always hovered nearby; but until she had a baby with her, there was apparently no reason or authority that could compel her to get the help she clearly needed. As a younger teenager, Michelle had been "looked out for" by the older street population, but her hair-trigger temper and aggressive demeanor made it hard for anyone to get along with her for any length of time. Michelle's mother, who was a drug addict with obvious mental health problems, was also on the streets, but she lacked Michelle's overtly confrontational manner and generally just seemed too stoned to communicate.

Michelle had been raised primarily by her maternal grandmother, a frail but feisty woman in her seventies who looked much younger than seemed possible for someone who had raised two generations of children with such severe problems. She may have had her own psychiatric problems, but the fact that she was often difficult to deal with could just as well have been due to all the turmoil and defeat she had endured for so long. The overwhelming sadness of watching helplessly as your daughter and granddaughter self-destruct had to have taken a tremendous toll. I admired the grandmother for simply continuing to be there for Michelle, and for doing everything she could to advocate for her granddaughter and great-granddaughter.

Michelle's fourteen-month-old daughter, Ayla, had come to the state's attention because of various complaints from people who had observed Michelle's dangerously inadequate parenting. The most specific and startling complaint was that she would frequently take Ayla outdoors wearing only a diaper in the frigid Midwest winter weather. Child Protective Services investigated and determined that Ayla was not safe in her mother's care and that there was no one else in the family who could parent her. Although the grandmother was not found to be an inadequate caretaker herself, CPS felt that she lacked the ability to protect Ayla from Michelle. So the baby was placed in a foster home and had lived there for about a year when I met her. Ayla was a beautiful, happy baby, and her young foster parents, who had no other children, doted on her.

My most immediate responsibility was to arrange for and supervise Michelle's visits with Ayla. I was also supposed to figure out their future, but for that I needed some time to get to know them and their situation.

It didn't take long to figure out that the situation was abysmal. Michelle lived in an empty shell of an apartment that was dark, quiet, and almost devoid of furniture or any other personal effects. It never seemed as though anyone was actually living there, even Michelle. I would often hear the sounds of other people from an upstairs bedroom, but Michelle denied their existence and no one else's presence was ever made known to me or acknowledged.

Our visiting routine was invariable. I would arrive at the foster home and find Ayla being readied for the visit. She would be dressed beautifully and bundled into multiple layers of clothing, perhaps because the foster mom could never get over knowing how cold Ayla must have been when she was taken outdoors wearing only a diaper. The first time I met the foster mother, who was lovely, I found myself wondering about her decision to bundle Ayla in a snowsuit on a mild day. I didn't say anything because she obviously knew far more than I did about appropriate clothing for babies. But even with no heat on in the car, Ayla was drenched in sweat by the time we reached Michelle's apartment, only fifteen minutes away. After that, I learned to stop a few blocks from the foster home and remove a few layers of clothing from little Ayla.

I also learned to lock my passenger-side door so that Michelle couldn't reach in to take Ayla out of her car seat as soon as I got there. I learned that lesson the hard way on my first visit, when Michelle frantically lifted Ayla out of the car, smacking her head mightily on the door frame. The second time we visited, I had the door locked, giving me time to walk around the car, stand next to Michelle, and caution her to protect Ayla's head. It didn't work. It didn't even work when I used my hands as a buffer between the door frame and Ayla's head. It was awful to see Ayla get hit in the head like that, of course, and it was also awful to see Michelle's disappointment at not being able to reach in and scoop her baby out of the car seat. She always greeted

Ayla's arrival with such unbridled joy, and I always had to start the visits out by stifling it.

These visits were heartbreaking. By about the fourth one, Ayla—normally an easygoing baby—started to cry at the first sight of Michelle. Possibly it was due to the memory of head bumps, although I think it was a more basic response to Michelle's intensity and aggression. By contrast, I found my own response to the chaotic energy emanating from Michelle to be overwhelming sleepiness. The visits were almost always in the mornings, but no matter how well rested I was when I arrived, fifteen minutes with Michelle affected me like a drug and I had to struggle to stay awake. I brought this up with a psychiatrist we consulted and she explained that my reaction was just a way of trying to escape the stress of the situation.

It soon became evident that Michelle didn't have even the most basic skills she needed as a parent. She was simply too impulsive and volatile. It was also clear that there wasn't another family member in a position to raise Ayla. Michelle's grandmother was not only quite old but also unable to assert any more authority over Michelle than she'd asserted over Michelle's mother when Michelle was a baby. There was no question that Michelle loved Ayla and wanted to be able to raise her, but it was no less true that Ayla wouldn't be safe with her. The only option for them would have been a living situation in which Michelle could be provided training and supervision around the clock while she tried to acquire basic parenting skills. And this was simply not available. So, our mandate to reunite the family notwithstanding, I felt I had no choice but to file for termination of Michelle's parental rights.

During the court hearing, Michelle's tragic mental state spoke for itself, making it easy to build the case against her. The whole proceeding was terribly sad, with Michelle alternating between angry outbursts and withdrawal. I don't think she fully comprehended what was happening, but she knew that Ayla wasn't being returned to her that day, and she was enraged. Her grandmother, on the other hand, understood everything, and sat through the hearing wordlessly except for an occasional "Harrumph," taking in the testimony from various experts about Michelle's difficulties along with my recounting of my experiences with Michelle and Ayla during our visits. Ultimately, it was Michelle's own statements that convinced the judge to rule against her. Everyone in the room could see that the judge had no option other than to terminate her parental rights—which made it all the more startling to find Michelle's grandmother immediately after the hearing telling me in no uncertain terms that God was going to punish me for what I had done. In her view there was simply no justifiable reason to take someone's child away. Period.

I know that my efforts to terminate Michelle's parental rights were based on my conviction that it was the only course of action available at the time that would give Ayla a chance at a normal life. Ayla would still have to contend with a genetic predisposition toward mental illness, but at least we could spare her years of upheaval and trauma that would increase the odds against her. Ayla's visits with Michelle no doubt caused her suffering, but they were relatively short-lived. Before she was three, she was adopted by her foster parents, and I am certain that the love and stability they provided gave her the best possible chance of avoiding the problems crippling her mother and grandmother.

I was tremendously happy that I could play a role in giving Ayla a better life. But I was also tremendously sad knowing that not so many years earlier, Michelle had been the baby being mistreated and needing rescue. She had suffered throughout her childhood and was still suffering as an adult. Now it seemed as though we could stop this cycle of dysfunction only by making Michelle suffer even more. I wished that Michelle's grandmother could understand why I didn't believe that God was angry with me. From my perspective, I was the one who was angry on Michelle's behalf.

6

Boy Troubles

B Y MY FOURTH YEAR AT DSHS, now considered a seasoned veteran, I was assigned a job that, in retrospect, required a lot more expertise than I actually had. I was sent down to Texas to see how two boys from Michigan were faring in their residential placements there: one in a large city and the other in the desert about three hours to the north.

Today, the words "residential placement" and "boys' ranch" set off alarms for me, but that wasn't the case when I was twenty-eight.

The boys in question were seventeen-year-old Jesse and sixteen-year-old Cole. I had known Jesse for three years and had watched his inexorable slide toward Michigan (or Jackson) State Prison, all the services the state of Michigan could offer notwithstanding. Imagining the treatment an appealing eighteen-year-old boy would get in that place had me terrified for him, my fears stoked all the more by a graduate school friend who had done an internship at Jackson and told me about hearing the screams of inmates being beaten and raped while guards stood by doing nothing.

Jesse was fourteen and had been in foster care for many years by the time I met him. His case file was a drearily familiar recounting: hardships he had faced, behavior problems he had developed . . . and one stand-out section in which the previous caseworker, Lou Ann, had written about his proclivity for stealing women's underwear. Beginning at about age twelve, Jesse would periodically break into neighbors' homes and abscond with as much underwear as he could find—a practice both unsettling and inconvenient for the neighbors. Every so often, Jesse's foster mother would retrieve the loot from his hideout—a rusty old car sitting on the edge of their property—and invite

Boy Troubles 39

the neighbors over to reclaim what was theirs. The victims adapted to the routine, apparently willing to tolerate it because they knew that the foster parents were good and responsible people who were trying their best to help a child in need. And they all liked Jesse—as I said, he was quite an appealing kid.

Other than the underwear thefts, Jesse didn't get into too much trouble. He was in a stable home with experienced and dedicated foster parents, and my job consisted of periodic visits and maintaining the necessary paperwork for his care. Nothing much happened for three years, until the day my supervisor, Jim, decided to accompany me on one of these visits. Jim had also worked with Jesse; he wanted to come along to say hello to him and his foster mother and see how they were doing. We got to the house, sat down in the living room, and had been chatting pleasantly for awhile with the foster mom when Jesse appeared in the doorway with a rifle. Being clueless, I didn't know how to respond, but Jim—an African American New Yorker—rose to the occasion and immediately started trying to talk Jesse into putting down the rifle, which, in time, he did. We left soon after, with Jesse in good spirits and the foster mother seeming concerned mostly about the lack of hospitality he had initially shown. But Jim took the incident seriously, and not long after, Jesse was on his way to residential treatment in Texas. Our hope was that his stay there would let us make the most of the time we had left with him before his eighteenth birthday, when he would age out of the state foster care system and be released into the wild.

The second boy was someone I knew only from newspaper reports about his high-profile crime. Like Jesse, Cole had had access to a gun. Unlike Jesse, he had fired it, severely wounding a child and the doctor who had run to the child's aid, ending the man's career as a surgeon and leaving the child in a wheelchair. Cole's shooting spree had terrorized the neighborhood for a period of time before the police were able to talk him down. His rampage was deemed an expression of his feelings about breaking up with his girlfriend, but there doubtless were other contributing factors.

Cole was just short of his sixteenth birthday and had had no serious difficulties with the law. He, too, was an appealing boy and, despite the enormity of his crime and the corresponding outrage in the community, his youth was taken into consideration and he was sent to a boys' ranch in Texas rather than to jail, on the theory that he was a good candidate for treatment. My assignment was just to see how he was doing and report back to the court.

My first visit was to Jesse's school. He was especially friendly and seemed comfortable there. He was happy about the fact that there were lots of girls at his new school and proud that one of them was his girlfriend. The school was a well-established institution with lots of rules—something I wouldn't have predicted would sit well with Jesse, but he seemed to be adjusting well. I met with his various counselors, who expressed neither grave concerns nor a whole lot of optimism about being able to set him on a path to success. There was nothing remarkable about any of this, and nothing further for me to do for Jesse other than write my report.

I had dinner that night with the director of the boys' ranch where Cole was staying and his wife at a charming restaurant in an upscale part of the city. They were both good company, and he was particularly outgoing and charming and seemed intent on ensuring that I had a good time. The next morning, I set off for the ranch, which was about one hundred fifty miles away, via a dirt road after the first hour. Eventually, in the middle of nowhere, the ranch emerged. I don't know what I was expecting, but I was pleasantly surprised: it looked like a summer camp with airy, fresh, pine cabins and quite a few large trees—an oasis in the desert. It struck me as remarkably clean and peaceful.

The plan was for me to meet with Cole, then talk with the director. Cole knew I was coming to see him, but since we'd never met, I doubt that he had any particular expectations other than that the visit might be interesting. He was polite and subdued, and his words seemed overshadowed by a sort of stunned disbelief, as if he was expecting to wake from a nightmare. He had no complaints about the ranch and appeared to be resigned to being there until he was eighteen. Cole must have realized how tremendously lucky he was to have been so young when he committed his crime. Not too many months later and he might have faced a long prison sentence instead of a few years in Texas.

When I met with the director, he was just as jovial as he had been the night before. He was obviously proud of the ranch, and I was an interested and appreciative listener as he told me about all of their successes. Sitting in his office and looking around at the pictures on the walls, it occurred to me that the boys at the ranch were an unusually good-looking bunch. The pictures weren't simple snapshots—many were professional-quality enlargements. I commented on how great all the kids looked, and it turned out that the director himself was the photographer. "How nice," I thought. "How nice that not only do the kids who come here get healthy and beautiful, but their parents get visual evidence that their kids are thriving." Impressed, I left that ranch thinking that they must have discovered a formula for success . . . and, in retrospect, I very much hope that they had.

Now fast-forward to a time many years later when I was working as an adoption counselor. I had been asked to complete a home study for a single man in his late forties who wanted to adopt an eleven-year-old boy he had met several years earlier while traveling in South America. The boy's aging grandmother felt unable to continue caring for him and apparently wanted her grandson to be adopted and come to the United States. The man, Geoff, presented himself as someone motivated by the desire to give this particular child a good life. Geoff stated that he was wealthy by inheritance and did not need a paying job, although he had a history of sporadic work as a teacher and coach.

Policy at the time required single male applicants to go through an additional step that was not required of couples or single women: a psychological evaluation to determine their fitness as parents. It was widely assumed in those days that single men who wanted to adopt might be up to no good, and that a psychological assessment could ferret them out.

During the home study interviews, Geoff was talkative and seemed forthcoming. He was a bit older than most applicants, had a lot of life experience, and was open about sharing his biographical information along with his views about parenting, cultural identity, and other topics covered in a home study. Geoff was articulate and sociable, and we discovered we knew a number of the same people since he had been a youth coach in the community where I grew up. I also discovered that Geoff was quite a name-dropper, but I just chalked this up to his wealth, reasoning that if your friends actually are powerful and famous people, it isn't name-dropping to say so. The only thing that struck me as "different" about Geoff was the way his office walls were lined with photographs of boys—not just sports-team pictures but individual portraits. There was virtually no uncovered wall space, all of it being taken up by these photographs; and there were photographs of boys I had known in high school.

I submitted my report with glowing letters of reference from Geoff's friends in high places and his favorable psychological evaluation, and eventually the child arrived. I visited with Geoff and his new son three times, as required, over the next six months and noticed nothing amiss. Geoff seemed to love being a dad and showering this child with all the trappings of a wealthy American lifestyle. Other than the fact that the boy put on weight at a rapid rate (not unusual when a child comes to the United States), he seemed to be in excellent health and adjusting well. I saw no cause for concern.

Not too long after the adoption was finalized, Geoff called to say that he wanted to adopt another child. He looked through an agency's list of waiting children and eventually settled on two brothers, also from South America. I updated the home study, which now included lots of information about how well he had done with the first child, and in about eight months Geoff became the father of three boys between the ages of ten and fourteen. Once again, I visited with the family three times over the next six months, and everything seemed to be fine. Geoff didn't appear to be at all overwhelmed by the dramatic changes in his life, probably in large part because he hired a Spanish-speaking housekeeper to manage a good portion of the workload. I honestly felt that things were going well for everyone in that family.

But the past caught up with Geoff one day when he decided to accept a substitute teaching position in a high school class that included a child he had molested some years earlier. This boy, more confident now, was shocked when he saw Geoff and went straight to the principal. He implicated Geoff and one of his high-profile references as well. Once they started investigating, the police had no trouble finding all the evidence they needed against these men. The friend was sentenced to five years in jail. Geoff and his sons, whose adoptions had long been finalized, fell off the radar, and I was told they had left the country. Meanwhile, I went searching for answers to the question of why I never saw through his façade.

Eventually I found a training manual for police officers that proved extremely specific and extremely surprising. Although people are better educated about child molestation these days, the things that really jumped out at me in this manual would still come as a surprise to most. Even more disturbing, it wasn't any one specific behavior that would pinpoint someone as a pedophile—rather, it was a number of things that, taken separately, would never be viewed as evidence of deviance. The list included a history of volunteer coaching, a history of mentoring disadvantaged children, financial security despite long periods of unemployment, never having been married, and various other normal and benign characteristics. Geoff had all of them.

The list also included such things as frequent name-dropping, concern with social status and appearance, concern with presenting oneself as charming, and (drum roll) owning lots of photographic displays of children. In short, everything on it described Geoff perfectly.

Reading this, my mind flashed back to the pleasant memories I harbored from my visit with Cole at the boys' ranch in Texas. How would I have felt about that situation if I'd had this training manual back then?

I don't know what ultimately happened to Cole; I do know that Jesse ended up serving time in Jackson Prison. Shortly after his eighteenth birthday, having aged out of the foster care system, he felt compelled to firebomb a convenience store when the owner refused to give him money for his nonreturnable bottles. True to form, he had an explanation that elicited a bit of head-shaking affection along with dismay. "It's not my fault!" he said, all innocence, "I've got no impulse control!" I guess that's what he learned at his school in Texas.

Geoff, of course, denied abusing any of his children, and I would love to believe him. My hope is that the ratio of three boys to one adult, plus the constant presence of the Spanish-speaking housekeeper, may have served to protect them. But I know that is wishful thinking. I just hope it's not also wishful thinking to believe that the charming, outgoing, photography-loving ranch director was exactly who he seemed to be.

7

Termination of Parental Rights

THERE ARE THREE GIRLS—sisters—who have always weighed most heavily on my mind. I met them when they were nine, twelve, and fourteen; the state removed them from their mother's home because of her severe alcoholism and allegations of neglect and abuse—including sexual abuse, which the girls at first vehemently denied had ever happened. There wasn't room for three new girls in any of our available foster homes, so the oldest sister was placed in one and the two younger girls together in another. Grace, the oldest, lived with a young couple in a rural area and seemed to adapt well to her new, quieter lifestyle. Next door to her foster family lived a dynamic woman with four teenaged daughters, one of whom was a foster child on my caseload. The woman happily served as a parenting mentor to the young couple, and her daughters befriended Grace and helped her adapt to her new school. All in all, things went pretty well for Grace, despite the fact that she had learning difficulties, struggled academically, and struggled with some aspects of day-to-day life.

Overall, Grace was pleasant, but passive to the point of seeming almost defiant at times. Since her foster home was about thirty minutes from my office, she and I had lots of time to talk as I drove her to and from various appointments. After we had accumulated some twenty hours of driving and chatting time, she finally worked up sufficient nerve to tell me that she thought I drove too fast. (I slowed down.) She never was able to get comfortable enough to tell me about the abuse she endured. That information came from Jessica, the twelve-year-old.

Jessica and their other sister, Annie, lived in what appeared to be a happy, stable foster family. The parents seemed kind and easygoing, the mom was especially easy to talk to, and the couple's other kids were friendly and well behaved. The house was ramshackle, and it was clear that the family was struggling financially, but the girls were welcomed enthusiastically. All the kids seemed to get along and Jessica was able to assert authority over the family's oldest child, a boy who was only a year younger but was much smaller than she was and less socially dominant. I visited the girls regularly but didn't have the one-on-one conversations with them that I had with Grace on our drives.

As time went on, Jessica and the foster mother developed a bond, and Jessica began to share some information about the history of abuse she and her sisters had endured. The girls started therapy and, little by little, Jessica revealed the extent of the sexual abuse, which amounted to (according to Jessica) Grace and Annie having been prostituted by their mother in exchange for alcohol. After this became clear, I felt I had the information I needed in order to try to terminate Sandra's parental rights. At about the same time, I discovered that I was pregnant with my first child.

The girls remained in their respective foster homes, and everything seemed fairly stable, while I built the legal case to terminate Sandra's parental rights. The case was based primarily on her untreated alcoholism and the therapists' and Jessica's testimony. Grace's learning difficulties and general passivity made it hard to communicate reliably with her, and Annie was too young and too traumatized to be put through the ordeal of testimony. But Jessica, who was now thirteen, was bright, socially adept, very beautiful, and somehow possessed of the strength and commitment needed to tell their sad story to a judge.

The effort took a long time and many months went by. Terminating someone's parental rights is (as it should be) an extremely painstaking and thorough process, and Sandra had to be given every possible chance to get help and change her ways. My service plan for her included getting counseling and treatment for alcoholism, neither of which she was able to do. I was also required to arrange for regular visits between her and the girls. She had been informed that there would be a termination hearing if she did not make the necessary changes, and presumably her attorney had impressed upon her that the stakes were now extremely high. My own relationship with Sandra was obviously damaged by my having filed for termination, but she continued to treat me with the same sort of jovial disdain she always had—an obvious mask of her true feelings. She wanted nothing to do with me or any other social worker, but she had to put up with me pestering her about visits with her daughters. At last, she agreed to schedule a visit for a weekday evening, and

I gathered up the girls at their foster homes for the trip to see their mother. Jessica and Annie were happy to see Grace, and all three girls shared stories about their foster homes on the drive but then fell silent as we neared the house where Sandra was staying.

Sandra moved a lot, and this visit was to take place at the home of her current boyfriend—an elderly-looking man who seemed pleasant enough. He ushered us in, and I helped him gather up chairs and arrange them so everyone would have a place to sit while we waited for Sandra to appear. When she finally came into the room, she didn't say anything or make any gesture of greeting, and I could see the girls slump with the realization that their mother was drunk. I tried to get them talking, but they were too distraught to give more than one-word responses to whatever I brought up, and Sandra wasn't saying a word. The boyfriend and I just ended up making small talk for a while.

After ten minutes or so, Sandra started muttering. Then the mutters escalated into veiled threats to "do something" to me, then into very specific threats about getting a knife and "killing you and that baby." The boyfriend, a frail man who was clearly no match for Sandra, kept yelling at her to shut up, which only intensified her anger. The girls were giving me ever-more-frantic looks, but I was trapped at the far end of the room, away from the door, with no idea of how to extricate us from the situation. Making a run for it at eight months pregnant seemed unwise, and telling the girls to run was likely to increase the danger to them, the way fleeing from someone triggers the chase. So the four of us sat stock still while Sandra ranted and threatened until she wore herself out. When the vitriol finally decreased and there was enough time between outbursts, I managed to shuffle the girls and myself out the door while the boyfriend distracted Sandra.

The whole episode lasted about thirty minutes, but of course it felt like hours.

As soon as we were safely in the car, I told the girls that I would never put them or myself in that situation again. If there were to be any further visits, they would have to be in the office, with adequate supervision and with the assurance that their mother hadn't been drinking. We were all frightened as I drove them to their respective foster homes. Seeing their mother drunk and making threats was nothing new to the girls, but I had just shown them that they weren't safe even when they were with me. Of course they already knew that—no one had ever been able to keep them safe from her. I was the one with delusions.

Sandra never took us up on the offer of supervised office visits. The next time the girls and I saw her was many months later in a courtroom, at the hearing to terminate her parental rights. But I could never get her out of my mind. I found myself routinely looking for escape routes wherever I happened to be, just in case she suddenly appeared with a knife. After that frightening visit, I devised a bizarrely comforting plan to push a dresser in front of my second-floor bedroom door and escape out the tiny window onto the roof if I heard Sandra coming in my front door. Dubious as that plan sounds, it reassured me—but only until my daughter was born. After that, I had to realize that I had no plan that could extricate us both from the Sandra-delivered dangers I imagined. My baby and I were simply vulnerable.

I was a very happy new mother, but also a worried one. During my daughter Erin's first year, I spent a great deal of my time either focused on protecting her or on terminating Sandra's parental rights—trying to protect those daughters as well. But I was also very much aware of the inequities between my life and Sandra's, and now that I was a parent, my attitude toward my clients grew more complicated.

I remember the first time I transported a baby to foster care. She was a darling, quiet eighteen-month-old whose mother had been extremely neglectful; I was a twenty-five-year-old who hadn't even done much babysitting. Even with my advanced degree, I knew very little about child development or attachment theory. So I assumed that since the baby never cried, she must not be suffering too badly. I also assumed that the people who designed the foster care system knew what they were doing, and I could just blithely carry out my job. Not until I had my own child did I grasp how devastating it is for children to experience a break, let alone repeated breaks, in their attachments— especially in the first years of life. When I became a mother and learned about what is normal for children, I began to understand the enormity of the consequences of my clients' abnormal lives. I found it heartbreaking to have to place an infant in a foster home knowing that (at the very least) that child would remain there during the crucial months when it should be bonding with its parents. If the baby was later returned to its parents, the bond it had formed with the foster parents would be broken. Either way, the child was harmed, sometimes irreparably, if the pattern of broken attachments continued, as it often did.

When my daughter was born, I was overwhelmed by her unscathed perfection and by the fact that I had the responsibility/power to do everything possible to make sure that life continued to be good for her. I wanted someone to have that same responsibility/power to make good lives for the children on my caseload, and I had to admit that that was a far cry from what I was doing. I was, for the most part, just maintaining a dismal status quo.

As my daughter got older and I became more attuned to children who were her age, I found it increasingly troubling to drive them to and from visits with their parents. I would never have allowed anyone to take my child away, yet I was routinely doing that to other mothers. And worst of all: generally, neither the child nor the parent seemed all that upset about it. There were rarely tears or protests by parent or child. I tried out the idea that perhaps these parents didn't love their children as much as I loved mine, as proved by their lack of emotion over these forced separations and by their not doing what the courts required them to do in order to regain custody. But the reality was much more complicated, and much more painful: I think they allowed and endured separation from their children because they truly believed that they had no other option. They couldn't grasp the concept of actually having enough control over their lives to prevent, or fight back against, misfortune. They felt completely powerless—as, soon enough, did their children. After enduring a few months of abuse or neglect, and the severing of their emotional bonds, the babies developed that same hopeless outlook. Why cry if no one responds? Why fight against something when doing so is futile? That quiet baby I was transporting—and who came to symbolize my entire caseload of children and adults—was placid, in other words, not out of contentment but out of despair.

More than more in my work, I found it impossible to find a reasonable way forward for the kids on my caseload. Do we risk leaving them in dangerous situations in order to preserve their bonds to abusive parents? Should we immediately terminate parental rights when a baby is born to a mother whose long-term mental illness makes it impossible for her to safely parent? Should we set rigid rules about just how long a baby can be in foster care before the parent's rights are terminated? And what would the magic number of weeks or months or years be before too much harm had been done? For that matter, how would we decide how much harm is too much? I came to understand that even if I could have fully understood/answered these questions, it still

Becoming a parent made my views about foster care much more radical. One would think that a new mother would have an increased awareness of the inviolability of the bond between mothers and babies. And I certainly "got that" on both an intellectual and an emotional level. But I was also struck by the realization that everything that happens to a baby has an impact not just on how well the baby is doing at that moment but on the rest of its life as well. Babies thrive in all sorts of situations, and there is no one best approach to child rearing. There are many and diverse ways to be a good parent, but the core of all good child rearing is allowing for the development of strong and consistent bonds with caregivers. And while there are many successful variations in caregiver relationships, and they don't have to be between biological parent and child, they do have to be consistent. Babies need consistency in order to learn to trust the world, and children need continued consistency in order to keep that trust alive.

More and more in my work, I found it impossible to find a reasonable way forward for the kids on my caseload. Do we risk leaving them in dangerous situations in order to preserve their bonds to abusive parents? Should we immediately terminate parental rights when a baby is born to a mother whose long-term mental illness makes it impossible for her to safely parent? Should we set rigid rules about just how long a baby can be in foster care before the parent's rights are terminated? And what would the magic number of weeks or months or years be before too much harm had been done? For that matter, how would we decide how much harm is too much? I came to understand that even if I could have fully understood/answered these questions, it still wouldn't be possible to eliminate the damage done by the disruption in the parent/child bond that is inherent to the foster care system. The history of child welfare work is littered with new theories, new approaches, new answers, but there seldom seems to be any truly significant improvement for the children and parents who are most in need of help. Some things just aren't fixable.

Eventually, Sandra's parental rights were terminated. Jessica reduced everyone in the courtroom, except her mother, to stunned silence or weeping when she described how Sandra would tell whoever the current "boyfriend" was to "use Grace or Annie" when she wasn't interested in having sex herself. Jessica, whose beauty couldn't have been an asset in that life, could never acknowledge that she had been the victim of any abuse herself, but her testimony left the judge with an easy decision. I was ecstatic at the knowledge that the girls would never have to return to Sandra's "care," but I was also aware of the loss they all suffered. Despite her extreme cruelty to them, Sandra had somehow managed to nurture an abundance of lovely qualities in her daughters; it made me believe that she must have done at least a few good things as a mother.

Shortly after they became free for adoption, Jessica and Annie went to live with a couple who hoped to adopt them both. Annie had developed a chronic medical condition that the foster family didn't feel capable of handling, so they were not considered as an adoptive home for the girls. Sadly, after only a few months in the new home, Jessica, who was now fourteen, decided she couldn't make the adjustment to this new sort of life. She asked to return to her foster family without Annie, and not too long after that she became pregnant, presumably by her thirteen-year-old foster brother. Years later I learned that Jessica had been sexually active with an eleven-year-old boy who had also been placed in the home and that he could have been the father of her child as well. Grace became pregnant at sixteen, married the baby's father, and set up housekeeping with the help of her foster parents. Things went relatively well for her for at least a few years. Meanwhile, I watched in awe and delight as Annie transformed into the beloved child of two of the most amazing people I have ever met.

But the crushing odds against the children on my caseload taught me not to trust foster care stories with happy endings. Now, almost forty years later, Google-empowered, I tried to find out what happened to Annie and her adoptive family without being intrusive. (Grace and Jessica, no doubt now with different names, proved impossible to find.) Although I found many entries about Annie's parents and their good works and successes, which are truly impressive, there is no mention that they have a daughter. And I am just flat-out terrified to find out why.

8

Making My Escape

WORKING WITH CHILDREN WHO were in the foster care system was over-whelming. I was always aware of how lucky I was to have work that was rewarding, meaningful, and virtually never boring or pointless. It mattered a great deal to me that my efforts actually made a difference in someone's life, and I was grateful to have work that felt useful. At the same time, the job often left me awash in heartbreak and frustration. After my daughter was born, I found the disparity between her life and the lives of the children on my caseload truly distressing. I spent my time with my own child making sure that her life was just the right combination of comfortable and stimulating. I made sure that her clothes were of the softest fabrics and her baby books had the sweetest illustrations, and I was vigilant about protecting her from any possible discomfort, let alone harm. And my husband and I delighted in everything she did. Meanwhile, at work I was faced with children whose troubles seemed bottomless: an eighteen-month-old whose mother routinely pulled out all of her teeth as they came in, a ten-year-old whose mother prostituted her for bottles of beer, and the older siblings of a three-year-old who had starved to death. Most of these kids' best hope was just to avoid attracting parental attention (although I guess the three-year-old might have benefitted from any attention at all). Certainly, no one seemed to have been delighting in anything the children did—at least not in any appropriate way. Any normal person had to fight the urge to scoop them up and head for the hills.

Truthfully, though, I wasn't going to head for the hills and complicate my happy, easy life for these kids, except in theory. In reality, I needed to keep some distance. The toddler with golden hair, bright blue eyes, and no teeth also had numerous broken bones and cigarette burns. The rail-thin older siblings of the starving three-year-old had suffered years of neglect, had significant developmental delays, and were unlikely ever to be able to form normal relationships. The ten-year-old was an incredibly brave, endearing and stoic little girl. Their lives, and the lives of all of the other children who were entrusted to my care, were filled with enormous suffering and turmoil.

With my new baby daughter and my bizarre escape-from-Sandra scenarios running through my mind all the time, I began to feel more and more that my work was distorting my life. This hit me with particular clarity one night at yet another party attended solely by my coworkers and our spouses. I was struck by how isolated from "normal society" I had become—how my social life was essentially a function of my social work, largely because the things I had to talk about were things only social workers could fully understand, stories that people from mainstream society would find profoundly disturbing.

I had now spent the first six years of my career focused on an area of social work that I had never intended to pursue. Against all my expectations, my desire to pursue any sort of career was being overshadowed by my desire to be with my daughter (a desire not unrelated to my hyperawareness of all the horrible things that can happen to children). I was beginning to look for an exit. And I wasn't the only one: in the office, we often talked about leveraging our skills and experience into finding a dream job—and the dream job we focused on was a school social worker position. The school social workers we knew seemed relatively stress free—and they had summers off. Every time one of these positions came open, several acquaintances of mine would apply, and, gradually, a number of them moved on to that happier world.

I was standing back at a party, watching the conversations, and thinking about how my little girl would be growing up in this isolated world of horror stories and moral distortion when I tuned into a story Lou Ann was telling.

Lou Ann, as it happens, had gotten one of those dream social worker jobs at a high school and was thus the envy of our group. The story she was telling was about one of the first kids referred to her in her new job. "He looked like a nice kid," she said, "He came in, sat down, greeted me politely, and waited for me to say something. I had looked over his grades and attendance and didn't see any reason for him to have been referred to me. 'You seem like a nice kid,' I said. 'Your grades are good, there aren't any attendance or behavior problems . . . Why are you here?'"

She paused, for dramatic effect, then delivered the punch line: "He answered right away: 'I fuck rabbits.'"

I don't want to say that that's what drove me out of Michigan; it was more that it kind of brought clarity and closure to a debate I had been having with myself for a while. By the next morning, I was talking seriously with my husband about moving back to Seattle, safely removed from the Sandras in my life. It wasn't much longer before I decided to leave foster care behind and try to start a new career in the happily-ever-after world of adoption, and to do it in Seattle.

II
AGENCY ADOPTION

9

The Home Study Process

RETURNING TO SEATTLE WAS wonderful. But as nice as everything was, it took me a while to adjust to my new life. I'd grown so accustomed to the sort of hypervigilance that my previous job often demanded that normal, peaceful living didn't come naturally to me anymore.

It's hard not to get jaded when you work in the foster care system. It happens almost imperceptibly, as the horror stories mount and you begin to find that you aren't as horrified by them as you used to be (and should be). For me, cynicism filled in for the missing horror, along with the conviction that danger could lurk anywhere or under anyone's pleasant surface. It wasn't a good state of mind and it wasn't exactly realistic, but it got me through those years with the Department of Social Services. I wasn't even aware of how much I'd changed until we were back in Seattle and, slowly, the tension eased, and I began to see the world as a more benign place. Once we left Michigan, I no longer felt nervous about running into my clients on the street or seeing their names in newspaper articles about awful crimes. I no longer drove by houses where I knew children had been abused and were likely to be abused again, and it was no longer my responsibility to try to figure out how to help them.

Before we left, I contacted an adoption agency in Seattle about a job. I was hoping for part-time work, and an interview was scheduled shortly after we settled into our new home. First I met with the director, and a couple of weeks later, I met with the real power players in the agency for further screening. These were two women who were technically volunteers but whose collective energy, charisma, and commitment overshadowed everyone else. They were especially effective at hosting informal introductory meetings for prospective adoptive parents; the fact that each of their lovely homes was full of thriving and adorable children, most of whom they had adopted, made them that much more effective at creating an extremely desirable picture of adoption.

The agency was growing rapidly in the early 1980s, and several other counselors were hired when I was. We had a few group training sessions and then were sent out to meet with families. It wasn't hard to follow the format for interviewing and writing "pre-placement reports" (the official name for home studies), which all families need in order to be approved for adoption. Also, there were regular meetings and training sessions, so I soon felt competent. I was able to arrange my schedule so that I worked primarily in the evenings and on weekends, while my husband worked from a home office, for the next four years. It was tricky financially for a while, but in every other way, it was fantastic. We reveled in parenthood, and a second daughter, Caitlin, was born just before Erin's third birthday.

My new employer, an adoption agency called the Washington Association of Concerned Adoptive Parents (WACAP), soon to become the World Association of Children and Parents, had been started in the 1970s by a group of activist adoptive parents who wanted to take greater control of the adoption process. Historically, the majority of adoptions had been handled by the state, by church-affiliated agencies, or privately by doctors and attorneys. The notable exceptions were agencies (Holt Children's Services being one example) that had been founded expressly to facilitate international adoptions—in Holt's case, the adoption of Korean children in need of homes after the Korean War. Other private agencies that focused on international adoptions emerged over the years, often as the result of a connection with a particular "placing" country or, as with WACAP, by founders who hoped to make use of, and improve upon, what they had learned from their own adoption experiences.

Although WACAP was created by adoptive parents, its mission was always to find homes for children rather than to find children for families. The agency's vision, as stated in their promotional information, "goes beyond traditional adoption services to include child assistance and sponsorship."[1] WACAP grew rapidly and dramatically over the years and became one of the largest and most highly respected adoption agencies in the country. Current statistics show that the agency has placed over ten thousand children in adoptive homes and has provided assistance to another two hundred thousand children.

My job as an adoption counselor with WACAP started in 1981, and I stayed with the agency for the next ten years. Most of the families I worked

---

1. www.wacap.org/AboutUs.

with were adopting internationally, with the majority of children in the early years coming from Korea, India, or Colombia. The agency also handled in-country placements of children coming out of the U.S. foster care system, and there was an innovative infant placement program, Options for Pregnancy, that provided counseling to pregnant women who were considering adoption for their babies. During my last four years with the agency, I took on a supervisory role in the Options program.

The agency was a wonderful place to work, and the prospective parents I met were polar opposites of the parents I had worked with in Michigan. I had long been fascinated by adoption and was happy to have the opportunity to work with families who were undergoing this exciting process. The job was especially rewarding after a family's child arrived; I was responsible for monitoring their progress for six months. Most of the time, this meant listening to the parents talk about how wonderful their new child was. These happy, loving families were the perfect antidote to the depressing cynicism I'd developed in my previous job.

Being an adoption counselor suited me temperamentally as well as professionally. As a young mother, I used to go for walks in our neighborhood in the early evenings. The baby in the stroller provided an excuse for meandering rather than walking briskly, and I soon discovered that my enjoyment came not only from the fresh air and exercise but also from getting a glimpse inside neighbors' homes. I loved to walk just as the sun was going down, when people were getting home from work and families were coming together again after their day apart. It wasn't yet dark enough to pull the curtains, but it was too dark to be inside without turning on the lights. That combination turned the little houses into cozy fishbowls and brought out the voyeur in me. I thoroughly enjoyed these snapshots from the lives of these not-at-all rich or famous families. In much the same way, I thoroughly enjoyed the detailed snapshots of people's lives that I was granted when writing pre-placement reports.

Thirty-five years later, I still write pre-placement reports and still enjoy the process. The requirements remain essentially the same. All prospective adoptive families in Washington (and most other states) must have a pre-placement report before a child can be placed in their home. The purpose is to assess the adopting parents' suitability for adoption, and to educate them about the adoption process and issues related to raising an adopted child. The counselor's approach and the form of the report vary somewhat depending on the type of adoption being anticipated. In a private (also called "independent") adoption, usually of an infant or very young child, legal custody goes directly from the birth parent to the adoptive parent. Standards for pre-placement reports for this type of adoption are established by the state. Agency adoptions generally require that state standards for the pre-placement report be met and also have additional requirements specific to the type of adoption being done. For example, if a family is adopting a child from China, the report will need to address cultural issues and explain that the adoptive parents thoroughly understand the process and the importance of helping the child learn about and value her Chinese heritage. Pre-placement reports for families who want to adopt children coming out of the foster care system must address concerns about the special needs and adjustment issues these children are likely to face. The length and thoroughness of pre-placement reports vary greatly, but the basic components are usually the same. They all require extensive background checks, medical reports, income verification, marriage licenses and divorce decrees, birth certificates, and letters of reference. The interviews cover biographical information, marital history, attitudes about child-rearing, attitudes about adoption, and much more.

Working on a pre-placement report provides me with the perfect excuse for asking people all sorts of questions about their lives. I've never grown tired of hearing about things like where they have lived over the years, what jobs they have held, what activities they enjoy, and so on. Each person is new and interesting to me, and I feel privileged to play a role in helping people find their child—as important and exciting an effort as I can imagine.

The stereotype about home studies (I'll call them that now since that's what most adoptive families call them) is that they are unnecessarily intrusive, time-consuming, annoying, and possibly even insulting efforts to weed out all but the most perfect (according to some secret standard) candidates for adoptive parenthood. The stereotype about counselors who do home studies is similarly negative: they are humorless, judgmental, and in search of reasons to turn down prospective parents. I have tried mightily over the years to change that image—as have most of the adoption counselors I know—but there is often still a degree of tension between a prospective adoptive family and the person who does their home study. And that is perfectly understandable.

The majority of adoptive families quite naturally feel anxious about the home study. They assume that it will be an ordeal during which they might be judged harshly and possibly even denied the chance to have a child. I do everything possible ahead of time (even addressing that issue in my introductory cover letter) to reassure families that failing a home study is extremely rare, but people can't help but worry. I am amazed and dismayed when, after I've spent many pleasant hours with people and am getting ready to leave their home, they say something like, "So, do you think we'll pass?" It's usually said lightly, but the anxiety comes through nonetheless and the air is heavy for just a moment. I say, "Of course," and we all laugh, but it is clear to me once again how emotionally fraught the situation is.

I remember one incident in particular that highlighted this for me. I was at a meeting where adoptive parents were comparing notes about their home study experiences, and one parent advised others to be sure to empty their homes of beer and wine before the counselor's visit. I pointed out that this was unnecessary, then was shocked to hear a woman whose home study I had recently completed say, "But, Anne, you checked *my* refrigerator!" When I looked confused, she said, "Remember when I asked if you wanted cream in your coffee and you were standing by the refrigerator and offered to get it? I just assumed that that was your way of checking for beer and wine." Until then I had assumed from how friendly the woman and her husband were throughout my meetings with them that we were comfortable with one another and were communicating well. Now I saw instead that they saw me as sneaky, even dishonest, and it seemed to me that the other adoptive parents in the room were more inclined to believe their version of reality than mine. So much for my conviction that I'd been doing a good job of dispelling the stereotype of the adoption counselor.

Most families aren't quite that suspicious, but plenty of people are noticeably wary about the home study. Some of my favorite times have been when a person who starts out feeling unhappy and nervous discovers that the interviews actually aren't so bad. It's almost always a man—a man of few words who isn't used to talking a lot about anything with anyone. The idea of being required to discuss such personal matters as his family, his marriage, and his ideas about raising children with a stranger is annoying and intimidating. Often in these situations, I get a series of phone calls from the wife ahead of time, with lots of questions about just what it is that they are going to have to talk about. She'll tell me that her husband doesn't understand why they have to go through this process. Basically, she is warning me that he is likely to be less than forthcoming when we meet. But I've learned not to worry because, time and time again, I've found that once they get going, these men discover, much to their surprise, that a home study isn't so bad.

I usually start out with easy biographical questions about a person's childhood, and I can see people start to relax when they recall things such as where they lived, the people they knew, the activities they enjoyed, what they liked or didn't like about school, and so forth. I ask them to speak chronologically, and I rarely have to prod them with much more than, "And then what happened?" Sometimes the normally quiet men go on and on while their wives sit in amazed silence. When they have completed their story, they usually say something like, "I don't usually talk that much." Or, "It was fun remembering that stuff. I thought I'd forgotten all that." My impression is that most people have a great time talking about themselves when given the opportunity.

But I'm not surprised that the majority of prospective adoptive parents, no matter how socially adept they are, feel some anxiety about the home study. It is inherently strange to have someone come into your home in order to scrutinize you, then render what feels like a life-changing verdict on your future.

I turned out to be as nervous as anyone. I had been an adoption counselor for three years when my husband and I decided to adopt, and I spent a week in advance of our home study scrubbing every inch of our house. Leaving no strategic detail to chance, I even made sure that cookies were just coming out of the oven when the counselor arrived. (It paid off: a description of "big, soft, warm peanut butter cookies" made it into the home study, presumably as another bit of evidence for what good parents we would be.) In truth, none of that was the least bit necessary. Houses don't have to smell of freshly baked cookies or be free of beer and wine. They don't even have to be particularly clean in order to impress an adoption counselor (particularly one, like me, who cut her professional teeth visiting pee houses). It actually is difficult, both ethically and legally, to deny a family the right to adopt a child. There is no end of ways to be good parents, and any worthwhile adoption agency or counselor understands this.

There has been only a tiny handful of people I was not able to recommend as adoptive parents. This is true in part because families do some self-screening before they even start the adoption process. Most people realize that if they have a history of child abuse, domestic violence, criminal convictions, untreated substance abuse, or untreated mental illness, they are not likely to be good candidates for adoption.

There are exceptions, however—that is, an arrest record in and of itself doesn't necessarily disqualify someone wanting to adopt. I remember running a criminal-history check on a prospective adoptive dad and getting back a rap sheet that made it appear that he had gone on an extensive crime spree across four states as a young man. He had been booked into jails in Montana, Idaho, Nevada, and California over a month-long period and ultimately ended up in Lompoc Prison for three years. His crime turned out to be driving a flower-painted van through Montana at a time when that sort of thing didn't go over well with the local sheriff. Unfortunately, he had also picked up a hitchhiker who was carrying some marijuana. The man's father, an attorney, decided to teach his son a lesson by declining to help with his defense. So the young man was transported in a rather leisurely manner from Montana to California by various law enforcement personnel and spent time in a number of small town jails along the way. Each night in jail was booked and duly recorded. The fact that he was ultimately sentenced to three years of hard time in prison came as a shock to his parents, whose definition of "tough love" was a little more benign. It struck me as incredible that this incident would come back to haunt him twenty years later, possibly denying him the right to adopt a child from Korea.

Another client's history was marred by a foolish and naïve encounter with the wrong people in his youth. While traveling, he agreed to bring a suitcase back to the United States for a friend of a friend with whom he shared lodging in a South American city. Two years later, seemingly out of the blue, his Seattle apartment was raided early one morning, and he was arrested and charged with drug trafficking and various other crimes committed by the suitcase's owner. A student at the time, he ended up accepting a sentence of probation for the trafficking offense; the other charges were dropped when it proved impossible to link him to the actual drug traffickers in any other way. The man went on to a successful marriage and career, and this episode was all but forgotten until he applied to adopt a child.

In both cases, the men wrote letters of explanation which, combined with their upstanding (and arrest-free) adult lives, satisfied the placing agencies that they were good candidates for adoption, and both men were allowed to adopt.

It is a more difficult matter when a troubling incident is not as far in the past. If, for example, an applicant has a relatively recent history of DUI, went through treatment and has had no further legal trouble, I still feel the need to have an expert provide an evaluation. I, and most other adoption counselors, have no expertise in the field of substance abuse and treatment and therefore don't feel qualified to make related assessments or recommendations. So before starting a home study in these situations, I ask families to seek an assessment from someone who specializes in substance abuse. If they can get a legitimate expert to determine that they no longer have a problem, I am extremely likely to accept that recommendation.

Sometimes, as the home study progresses, families will withdraw their application upon realizing that they won't be able to provide the court with sufficient reassurance about an issue in their history. But only twice in over thirty years of doing home studies have I felt that I could not recommend a couple as adoptive parents when they wished to proceed.

The first time caught me completely by surprise. The couple I was interviewing had told me about their concern in our first phone conversation, and I replied that I didn't see it as significant. The issue in question was age: the woman was twenty years older than her husband, and she told me that most people found this "unacceptable." I told her that I didn't see it that way (I have a brother-in-law who married a woman almost twice his age when he was twenty, and who is still happily married almost forty years later). But I eventually discovered that the age difference itself wasn't what was troubling about this couple. Rather, it was the secrecy around the age difference: she had adult children and grandchildren from a previous marriage who were not allowed to acknowledge publicly that they were her descendants. Her husband's family did not know that their new daughter-in-law had children and grandchildren. The woman had even gone so far as to train her toddler granddaughter never to call her "Grandma" for fear that others might overhear. The woman had told her neighbors that this little girl who visited so frequently was the child of friends.

Since it was obvious that this woman was a lot older than her husband—she was clearly in her forties, and he looked about fifteen—this behavior struck me as futile and troubling. The husband seemed to have taken on a peculiar caretaking role in this marriage, with his caretaking responsibility consisting primarily of frequent reassurances to his wife that she looked half her age. I suggested that we should talk about this a bit further, hoping that she could realize she didn't need to be so vigilant about keeping up the deception. I wanted to help her realize that if she could stop feeling defensive about the age difference, then her attitude would help others feel comfortable about it as well. While the husband was receptive, his wife was furious with me for not seeing that the problem was society's and not hers, and for not understanding that her secrecy was necessitated by people's unreasonable tendency to victimize her.

After a few more sessions with them, with my attempts to reason with her only making her increasingly angry, I told the couple that I didn't feel comfortable acting as their adoption counselor and I returned their fee. The woman concluded that I had misrepresented my true feelings and was just like everyone else in disapproving of their age difference.

The second couple was hoping to adopt a little girl from China. They were older than the average adoptive family and already had grown children and grandchildren, including a three-year-old granddaughter who lived with them because of her own mother's problems with substance abuse. Fifteen minutes into a scheduled two-hour session in my office, the husband fell sound asleep. Odd as this was, what seemed even odder was that his wife didn't think it appropriate to wake him. I decided that maybe he'd just had an especially hard day, and agreed to a second session, this time at their home, a few days later. About forty-five minutes after I arrived, the wife informed me that she had to leave to pick the granddaughter up from preschool and would be gone for about an hour.

Clearly, this couple didn't understand the need for them both to be present and awake in order for me to complete a home study.

With the wife gone, I kept talking with the husband. He said that he wasn't working because of health problems but that he and his wife planned to support themselves by opening an adult-care facility in their home. They had already completed their application and were expecting approval any day. He went on to say that they wanted to adopt an older child who could help with the caretaking. All this information was delivered in fits and starts, since the man kept nodding off while we waited for his wife to return.

The couple and their granddaughter lived on an extremely busy, four-lane thoroughfare with additional lanes for on-street parking. When I asked the woman how they handled safety issues, she told me that their grandchild was never allowed to go outside unaccompanied. No more than ten minutes later, during heavy rush-hour traffic, she sent the little girl, by herself, to get something out of their car—which was parked out on the street. The last straw came when I asked the woman about the adult-care license she and her husband were planning to get. She initially denied that they had applied for one, then lashed out at her husband for telling me about it.

She was self-righteously indignant when I declined to continue working with them, but I suspect the husband was relieved. And I was enormously relieved that no little girl from China went to live (and work) in that home.

It is sometimes true that people who should never have been allowed to adopt manage to find their way through the process and do great damage to the children entrusted to their care. It's not that hard for an applicant to keep up a reasonably good front during interviews with the counselor or to find people who will write good references for them. It occurred to me fairly early in my career that people who really were up to no good (probably, alas, like Geoff, the man who adopted the three boys from South America) would have tremendous incentive to present themselves well during the home study. Just as Geoff did, they would make every effort to be cooperative and engaging and to ensure that there were no grounds for denying them the opportunity to adopt. I remember that, despite the fact that Geoff had passed all the requirements of the home study, there was one woman in the office who said, "He makes my skin crawl." When questioned further, she could only add that she thought he was a snob and she just didn't like him. I agreed with her that he was a snob with some annoying affectations (like the name-dropping), but even if I had shared her instinctive dislike for Geoff, those feelings would not have given me adequate justification for rejecting him as an adoptive parent. Just as it is with birth parents, adoptive parents are allowed to be imperfect and annoying. Also, like some birth parents, some adoptive parents turn out to be bad people. I wish it was different for both types of parents—that there was a foolproof method for making sure bad parents didn't get to have children either by birth or adoption.

People who do home studies are being asked to pass judgment about the adoptive applicants they work with, but they are not—nor could they be—asked to provide assurance that these people will necessarily be good parents. It isn't realistic to expect that a counselor could proclaim with certainty that an applicant would be a wonderful parent. All the counselor can say is that the applicant has met all the requirements of a home study and appears to have personal qualities that would make them successful as a parent. That's a very different statement and doesn't make promises that the counselor is in no position to make.

The fact that a counselor or agency feels an affinity for an applicant or shares basic values or beliefs with the applicant should not affect her professional judgment about that person's ability to properly parent a child. This should hold true whether an applicant is rejected or welcomed. Surely, reasonable people can agree that there isn't one best way to be a parent and that a healthy society accommodates a variety of parenting philosophies and approaches. I certainly have my own opinions about a preferred parenting style, and I also have the widely held tendency to believe that my own views are "correct." However, my job has given me an unusual amount of information about how other people live their lives, and I couldn't have avoided coming to the realization that the world is full of happy, loving, successful families whose approach to raising children is nothing like my own.

10

Adoption Is the Good Thing That Happens

A FTER THE ADOPTIVE PLACEMENT of a child, a certain number of visits and reports are required from a social worker before the adoption can be finalized. With many international placements, the adoption is considered final in the placing country prior to the child's departure, but post-placement visits are still necessary in order to finalize the adoption in the United States. The purpose of post-placement visits is threefold: (1) to help the family with any adjustment issues or other difficulties they or the child might be having, (2) to report back to whatever entity placed the child, and (3) to reassure the U.S. agency and legal system that all is well and recommend that the adoption be finalized.

The period of adjustment for a child and family will vary depending on such factors as the child's age and previous living situation and how well the family has been prepared for the adoption. With international adoptions and children coming from the foster care system, it is typical for the placing agency to require three to six visits over a period of six months to one year. In private infant adoptions, the courts usually require only one post-placement visit, while families who adopt an infant through an agency can be required by that agency to have as many as four or five post-placement visits during the first year. Once the requirements for post-placement supervision have been met, the social worker can recommend finalization of the adoption, and a court date is set, at which time the adoption becomes final.

Obviously, one purpose of the post-placement visits is to make sure that the child is doing well, and most adoptive families assume that the written report will be an assessment of their abilities as parents. It does happen, though rarely, that serious problems are discovered during a post-placement visit, and a child placed with a family for adoption is removed from the home against the parents' wishes. Generally, this action would be taken for the same reasons that children are removed from the home of biological parents, such as physical abuse or mental-health concerns. When the problem is discovered prior to the finalization of the adoption, the placing agency retains legal custody of the child. The situation becomes much more complex with international adoptions, in which the adoption has been finalized in the placing country prior to the child's arrival in the United States. While the placing agency might be able remove the child from the home, the adoptive parents would retain legal responsibility for the child. Even in situations where the child has been removed from the adoptive home due to abuse, and against the parent's wishes, judges usually do not feel it is in the child's best interests to sever legal ties with that home until (and unless) there is another adoptive family ready to take over responsibility.

The period of post-placement supervision isn't simply a time in which the adoptive parents are scrutinized; it is also a time when they must decide whether to fully commit to this adoption and this child. There is a period of adjustment with all adoptions, and even with infant adoptions, the best course of action might not always be clear at the time of placement. For example, a child who appeared to be in good health and developing normally at birth might a short time later be discovered to have problems that the particular adoptive family does not feel capable of handling. Situations like this are tremendously sad, but the parents should not be judged harshly if they decide not to follow through with the adoption. It is important to remember that it is in the best interests of the child to be in a family that truly understands and accepts the situation and is prepared to provide the type of care the child needs. If the original adoptive family does not feel capable of providing this type of care, then they are not the right family for this child. Hopefully, they will be given understanding and support for knowing their own limitations and won't be pressured not to "give up," or criticized for doing so. In my experience, it has been far more common for adoptive parents to be the ones to decide not to complete an adoption than for agencies or the courts to force that decision on a family. Happily, both of these situations are extremely rare and the vast majority of post-placement visits are untroubled.

Due to the requirements for post-placement supervision, I have spent lots of time with adoptive families and children, and this has almost always been a joy. The families I serve in this capacity all live in western Washington, with the majority in the Seattle area. They have diverse socioeconomic backgrounds, but they share a general culture that is primarily Caucasian. Although their personal networks of family and friends are distinct, their wider communities—people like teachers, doctors, store clerks, and folks they pass on the street—are probably fairly uniform. I would expect that people living in the same sorts of communities would have similar experiences when they take their children out into the world, but the reports I hear from some adoptive parents would suggest that this is not the case.

When I meet with a family to complete a post-placement report for a child of a different race, the parents usually say something along the lines of, "We can't go anywhere without people stopping us to say how beautiful she is," or, "We never realized until now how many people are interested in adoption." They tell me about how much fun it is to go out with their child and that her presence and her race, which makes it apparent that she was adopted, get people talking to them in ways that never happened before. They probably don't realize that their experience is, in part, common to all new parents; babies in general tend to bring out the friendliness of strangers. But the important point here is that these parents enjoy the fact that their child attracts attention, and they interpret other people's interest in a positive way. They occasionally report that someone has said something awkward or insensitive and wonder how to best respond in these situations, but they see such comments as unusual and don't let them dampen their joy in showing their child off to the world.

A much smaller and far more vocal group of parents put the opposite spin on what appears to be the same experience. These parents tell me, "We can't go anywhere without rude people commenting on the fact that she is a different race," or, "We can't go anywhere without people asking us all sorts of nosy and personal questions about our adoption." I find this attitude unfortunate and largely unnecessary, and I feel bad for the children of these parents. It's hard for any child to have parents who see the world in a negative light, and it's even harder when the child suspects that a particular negative experience is somehow connected to them. The parents feel that they are acting as their child's advocate and protector by being vigilant about slights, but the child more likely will see only that there is something about them (race and adoption) that causes the parent distress. Even very young children can pick up on the tension when a parent responds defensively and, as children often do, they are likely to take it as evidence that they are somehow to blame for the problem.

This is not to say that adoptive parents don't encounter plenty of situations that require them to educate people about adoption or that parents should be passive in response to hurtful comments. All adoptive parents owe it to their children to take every opportunity to correct misperceptions about adoption, and parents need to help their children negotiate negative situations around adoption, race, or any other subject that presents concerns for them. But they need to do it in a way that strengthens the child and the family. Interpreting every problem the child faces as having its roots in adoption or racial difference is more likely to be confusing and troubling than enlightening or comforting.

I remember one mother of an Asian child, for example, who was convinced that a little boy at school was bullying her daughter because of her race. The children were in the second grade and the little boy, who sat behind her in class, was regularly pulling the girl's hair. The mother was frustrated because her daughter's teacher did not see this as racist and wasn't taking what the mother felt was appropriate action to educate the children in her class about racism. I don't know the motives of the little boy, but the little girl was a class leader, had many friends, and didn't seem particularly upset about the hair pulling when she talked with other children about it; there was no evidence of racial taunting or slurs. I suggested to the mother that the little boy may have just been trying to get her daughter's attention in the annoying manner of little boys since the dawn of time, but she didn't like that idea at all. She felt that her complaints about racism in the school were being ignored and she wanted something done about it.

The hair pulling soon stopped, but the mother's concern about it did not, and the most likely result was that this mother's preoccupation gave her daughter an unnecessarily fraught message about race. It likely also served to make the girl feel cautious about telling her mother anything that had the potential to be turned into an uncomfortably big deal. The mother thought her actions were empowering her daughter, but I suspect the opposite was true. I suspect it made the child wonder why the fact that she was Asian had so much power to upset her mother.

Another Caucasian family I knew had two children of Asian heritage: an outgoing and popular daughter, who seemed unworried about the racial differences in her family, and a younger son. The boy had just started high school and was struggling. His parents, who wanted to help in whatever ways they could, wondered if he was struggling with racial identity or adoption issues. Teenage adoptees in interracial families do indeed face racial-identity issues and continue to do so as they mature. However, after I met this boy it seemed far more likely that his sudden unhappiness was brought on by the onset of pretty severe acne and a delayed growth spurt that made him one of the shortest boys in the ninth grade. Both of those things were probably transitory (and shared by many teenage boys), and I suspect that they bothered this boy in the same ways they would bother a boy who was not adopted and not of a different race from his parents. The fact that the boy's self-esteem was at an all-time low seemed unlikely to be simply "an adoption issue."

Many adoptive parents reflexively wonder if a given problem of their child's is adoption related. It's hard to blame them. There are lots of books written for young children about adoption that suggest that kids commonly have negative feelings about being adopted. These books are upbeat and informative for the most part, but there is usually at least one page in which the child, or animal, who is the main character is shown to be sad, with the explanation being that sometimes she worries or is confused about what it means to be adopted. I remember one illustration of a little girl sitting on her bed, clearly in a funk. The narrative explained that she just needed to be by herself and feel bad for a while about being adopted. A parent reading this book might conclude that when his or her child was feeling grumpy or down, it could be attributed to worry about adoption or her birth mother. And it might be, but it is far more likely to be about something else: children, whether or not they were adopted, have all sorts of reasons for feeling grumpy.

Too many books meant to educate adoptive parents are guilty of perpetuating a negative image of adoption. This impression is often transmitted through the use of such carelessly broad statements as, "Children who are adopted are more likely to receive counseling than non-adopted children." Technically, that is true—but it is also misleading. The broad category of "adopted children" includes those who were adopted at older ages and suffered broken attachments, those who have come from traumatic circumstances, and those who have different special needs. Obviously, these children are going to have a higher than average need for various types of extra support, including counseling, but a child who has been placed in an adoptive home at birth has little in common with a child who spent his early years with an abusive parent and in a series of foster homes before being adopted. And abused children, whether adopted or not, share a common need for counseling. A child who is in need of counseling due to a history of abuse is far more likely to get it if he has been adopted than if he has continued to live with the abusive birth parents. While abused children who have remained with their birth parents are less likely to receive counseling, they are certainly not less likely to need it. This explanation seems obvious, but most people who are told that adopted children need counseling at a higher rate than non-adopted children don't stop to consider why this might be true. Instead, they assume that there must be something about being adopted that puts these children at greater risk for psychological problems.

I strongly object to the pathologizing of adoption, which is widespread in our society. It is common to hear adoption cited as the explanation for an individual's problems. People are likely to explain developmental delays or behavioral issues simply by saying that the child "was adopted," without taking note of such actual contributing factors as fetal drug or alcohol exposure, early neglect or abuse, traumatic experiences, institutionalization, frequent disruptions in caregivers, and other misfortunes well known to harm children. Instead, people simply characterize the struggling child as "adopted," as though that explains all of his or her problems and as though all adoptees are the same, whether adopted as a healthy infant or as a preteen refugee from a war-torn country. Media coverage of a terrible crime committed by an adoptee never fails to point out that the perpetrator was adopted, and we react as though that fact explains everything.

I find this pathologizing of adoption particularly frustrating because the general perception brought on by these attitudes—that adoption is risky business for both parents and children—is the opposite of the truth. For most children in need, adoption is the good thing that happens when the bad things are over.

11

Adoption Disruptions

UNFORTUNATELY, ADOPTION isn't always the happy ending everyone was expecting. When I worked in the foster care system, it was not unusual to get calls from beleaguered foster parents asking to have a child removed from their home. This wasn't exactly unexpected, especially when the child in question had significant behavioral problems, but it was usually extremely depressing for all concerned. If the child had been in the home for a while and/or if the placement had been expected to be long term, this sort of move was called a "disruption." The same sort of thing happens in adoptions, and while adoption disruptions are mercifully infrequent, when a child has to leave an adoptive home it is usually more accurate to describe the situation as *devastating* than *depressing*.

The first family I knew who had a disrupted adoption impressed me when I met them as not only picture perfect but perfect in more meaningful ways as well. There were two preteen sons who had been born to the parents, and the family had adopted three younger children, one of them a beautiful baby girl with serious medical special needs. At some point, the family had also adopted another boy, but I didn't know about him when I met with them to complete a post-placement report for the baby girl. I remember at one point in our conversation saying something boneheaded to the mother about how I didn't understand how families could just return children when things didn't work out, and she calmly replied that that had happened in her family. I was stunned. There was no way to undo what I had said, but I tried to suggest that perhaps it hadn't been a "real disruption" somehow. She wasn't buying it and didn't give in to the temptation to gloss over an awkward moment by agreeing with me that her situation had somehow been different. In fact, it had been a classic disruption and, although completely justified and necessary, it had left scars.

It was clear that the parents in this family were used to succeeding at whatever they took on and that they still felt a lot of regret over not having been able to be successful parents to this child. The boy had come out of the U.S. foster care system and was close in age to the older boys in the family and quite a bit older than some of the other kids. Over time, it became evident that he was victimizing the other children in the family in various ways. The parents were smart and experienced, they had tried everything they could imagine, including counseling, and they still didn't feel that they were doing an adequate job of protecting the other children. They made the decision that this child would have to leave their family because they were good parents to all of the children. Obviously, it was not good for the other children in the family to be put at risk, and it was probably even more harmful to the boy to be put in a situation where he was able to be abusive. Prior to this child's placement in the home, someone should have realized that a houseful of more vulnerable children was not an environment in which this particular child could be expected to succeed. It was more like a setup for failure. When even the most dedicated parents cannot keep everyone safe, either from being abused or from being abusive, it doesn't serve anyone's best interests to put any of the children at risk.

A family who adopted two children from Russia experienced a variation of this type of disruption. The first child had arrived at about a year old and had always been a gentle and sensitive child. His parents adored him and were eager to give him a little brother or sister, so they applied to adopt again from Russia when their son was almost four years old. They were delighted to receive a referral for a second son about a year later, and although they were a bit concerned that this child was only six months younger than the older boy, they eagerly went ahead with the adoption. But when the new child arrived, there was immediate trouble: although he was younger, he was bigger, stronger, and far more aggressive than the other little boy. Also, the new child had been living in an environment where he had to compete to get what he needed and wanted; as a result, he was easily able to dominate and overwhelm the older boy. This dynamic wasn't good for either child, and, understandably, the mother was finding it difficult to bond with a child who was making her beloved first child so unhappy. Worse still, when she expressed her fears to friends and family, some of them suggested that she was overreacting and that the boys would be able to work things out in time. This only added to her misery and strengthened her resolve to defend herself and her older child.

It may have been true that the boys would eventually "work things out" in some fashion (possibly with the older child always being subservient, the younger being a confused bully, and lots of resentment for everyone), but it wasn't the children's relationships with one another that was of greatest concern. More worrisome was the mother's attitude toward the younger child. It wasn't her fault that she found herself in this dilemma, but more significantly, it wasn't the new child's fault that his style didn't mesh well with his new family. In this family, his physical strength and assertiveness were interpreted negatively simply because, even as a three-year-old, he had the ability to frighten and threaten the older boy. If he had been placed in a family with children who were a few years older, he would not have been a threat to anyone. His behavior would not have been viewed as a problem, and his mother wouldn't have been busy protecting another child; she could have focused on nurturing him instead.

Happily, that is exactly what happened: the boy moved to a new family with much older and bigger kids who could easily handle his rough-and-tumble ways. I think the child suffered only moderately as a result of the disruption because it happened quickly, and he gained enormously. The first family continued to receive criticism for what most people saw as a failure, but they had no doubt that they had made the right decision for themselves as well as for their first child.

An extremely dramatic and traumatic disruption came to international attention in 2010 when an adoptive mother "returned" the seven-year-old Russian boy she had adopted by putting him, all by himself, on a plane bound for that country. I have no information about that particular situation other than what was available from the media, but I do have some insight into the struggles that children endure in Russian orphanages, how these struggles result in adjustment problems in the adoptive home, and how desperate that woman must have been. There is no excuse for the method she chose to try to extricate herself from any connection to the child, and the repercussions of that choice went far beyond what she apparently expected they would be. Surely, she didn't realize that she would be held responsible for the heartbreak of so many other adoptive families and waiting children whose adoptions were prevented when Russia claimed to be closing down all adoptions to the United States, supposedly in response to this woman's actions (though really in retaliation for United States imposed sanctions). This woman was thoroughly vilified and, although she should be held accountable for her cruelty and her astoundingly bad judgment, I suspect that there is a side to this story that paints her in a slightly better light. It's easy to say (and to believe) that we could never imagine giving up on a child, but is that really accurate? The adoptive mother claimed that the boy endangered the household because he lit fires, and she needed to protect herself and her other child from the possibility of a house fire. Assuming this was true, how do parents in these situations choose between the best interests, safety, and well-being of all of their children when these things seem to be in direct conflict? This question, and our inability to answer it satisfactorily, is often at the root of adoption disruptions. Things are further complicated in international adoptions, in which the adoption has already been finalized by the placing country before the child arrives in the United States.

Well-established and well-run agencies have procedures in place for dealing with placements that don't work out. Most of the time, when there is a disruption and a child needs to find a new home, it is possible for the placing agency to find a suitable family on their list of waiting families, and the re-adoption process can be handled without too much difficulty. But when a child's problems are severe, the task of finding a new home can be very difficult. Sometimes it's not even possible. Some children have problems that are too severe for any family to handle, and they require a different type of care, such as a group home or residential treatment facility—which are usually extremely expensive options. Then the problem becomes not only where this child should live, but also who should support him and for how long. Legally, when the adoption has already been finalized in another country, the adoptive family is held financially responsible for the child despite the fact that few families actually have the ability to pay for the type of long-term care that is needed. And is it really reasonable or ethical that the consequence to the family for failing at this adoption should be lifelong responsibility that is likely to deplete their financial (and emotional) resources?

The most troubling and urgent questions around a failed international adoption are, "What went wrong?" and "What can we do to prevent this from happening again?" As we often do when bad things happen, we want to hold someone responsible so we can believe (as people did with my grad school friend Miles and the little girl who died) that it all could have been avoided if only a particular person hadn't made a particular mistake. But it's likely that most parents in this type of a disrupted adoption are guilty primarily of naïveté or wishful thinking, rather than unkind or negligent behavior. In fact, there are more than a few child-placing agencies that actually seem to encourage wishful thinking in prospective adoptive families, along with the idea that a lot of love and prayer will fix most problem behavior. As a result, children are placed with families who are woefully unprepared for them. These same agencies provide little actual help in the way of post-placement services when families find themselves in situations they cannot handle and with children who bear little resemblance to the ones they thought they were adopting. While it's obvious that agencies that provide inadequate preparation and support for adoptive parents deserve blame for these ethical shortcomings, they are typically not legally responsible because the adoption has already been finalized in the placing country. Adoptive parents can find themselves very much alone in these situations; sometimes even their normal support groups (family, friends, church community, other adoptive parents) condemn their failure. That is harsh punishment for wishful thinking.

Countries that send their children to the United States (or another country) to be adopted want to be assured that the child is all right and is actually living with the family that adopted him or her. Post-placement reports usually provide this sort of evidence as long as everything is going well for the child and family. (They also help to counteract the recurrent rumors about children being put to use as domestic laborers or organ donors.) When there are problems with a placement, the placing country's concerns focus not only on the particular child but also on all the children it sends, or is about to send, to the United States. Problems serious enough to end in a disruption jeopardize other children's placements, the reputations of both the U.S. agency and the placing agency, and possibly the future of adoption between the two countries. Everyone works extremely hard to avoid and prevent disruptions for the sake of the individual child and family, and also for the sake of all international adoption. But it's important to keep in mind that in many cases a disruption is in the best interests of the child and doesn't need to be deemed a failure on anyone's part.

I was involved with one family who made the decision to disrupt and I couldn't have been happier. They were a couple in their late thirties who adopted a ten-month-old baby girl from China. I had not done the home study but was called on to consult with them when problems developed. Apparently, the adoptive mother had seemed fine during the home study but, as the previous counselor explained, it had now been several weeks since placement and she was not bonding with the baby. In fact, she was telling her husband and parents that she had decided that she didn't want a child after all. People aren't expected to bond immediately, especially if the child is also having a hard time and is rejecting the parent's efforts to attach. However, it is unusual for adoptive parents to express this degree of unhappiness when the child is so young and there isn't an apparent problem. So I went out to see what was going on and what could be done to help.

The family's house was a bi-level in a suburban neighborhood, and the living room was stuffed full of dark, oversized furniture, with the curtains tightly drawn, even though it was early in the day when I arrived. The baby was napping, so I had a little time to talk with the couple before meeting her. The husband seemed pleasant and made it clear that he was still hoping that I could convince his wife that she didn't really want this child to go away. I had thought ahead of time that the wife was probably having a version of "post-placement depression" and just needed some time to adjust to everything. It's not uncommon for adoptive mothers (like all mothers) to be hard on themselves in the first weeks, expecting complete bliss and finding worry and exhaustion instead. But after I met this woman, I came to a different conclusion. As she told me about the difficulties she was going through, I found myself cringing at the level of immaturity and self-absorption she was expressing. I felt thoroughly embarrassed for her and her husband, but she seemed to be completely unaware of how off-putting her comments were. In fact, she seemed to be expecting me to sympathize with her and to convince her husband that he needed to side with her against the baby.

It turned out that the husband was doing virtually all of the child care because the woman either was too tired or found it distasteful for some reason. There didn't seem to be any aspect of parenting or anything about the child that appealed to her. She didn't like diaper changing, feeding, or even holding the baby. The immediate problem was that the husband had to go back to work and no one, least of all the wife, felt comfortable leaving her alone with the baby. Her parents had offered to help, but they couldn't be there all of the time. The wife said she wasn't worried about hurting the baby but felt that being alone with her, and being expected to provide care, was just too much to ask. I think everyone else was worried about her hurting the baby, however, and her own fears about this may have been at the root of her detachment as well.

I expected the baby to be fussy, demanding, or somehow mysteriously unappealing, but that was not the case at all. She woke up sweetly and was all smiles as the husband walked into the living room with her in his arms. She was bright and engaging and adorable, yet the woman practically recoiled from her. On the surface, her reaction looked almost like jealousy, but I think it was closer to panic and that she had decided she wasn't capable of being a mother. She made it clear to me that she didn't want counseling. My job, in her view, was to help her husband and parents come to terms with losing the baby. As unsympathetic as this woman was, thank goodness she was honest with herself and everyone else about her reluctance to become a parent. Most people would have resisted acknowledging the feelings she expressed, fearing the condemnation of others.

The happy side of this story is that there is an abundance of eagerly waiting families for babies in these situations. These are families who are waiting to adopt and expecting to be called with referral information about their future child several months before they are actually allowed to travel to get him or her. Instead, they receive a call telling them that their wait could be a matter of days rather than months, and that their adoption will be significantly less expensive than anticipated since they might only have to travel across town instead of all the way to China, for example. The new adoptive family for this little girl was a couple in their early forties with an eight-year-old son from China; when I spoke with the mother, she seemed as different as possible from the first woman. She was talkative, self-assured, and interested in hearing every little detail about the baby and how to help her make a smooth adjustment to their family. Most importantly, she and her family were ecstatically happy that this baby was going to be joining them. As was I.

12

"Doing Good" Isn't Always Good

S OME ADOPTION DISRUPTIONS can result from the best of intentions; and adoption is rife with misguided good intention.

A few days after the attacks on the World Trade Center, an extremely intelligent and goodhearted woman called to ask what I knew about adopting one of the children who had been orphaned there. A Goldman Sachs orphan?

Such a call is not uncommon. When there is a large-scale disaster resulting in loss of human life (Hurricane Katrina, the World Trade Center attack, earthquakes in Haiti, tsunamis in southeast Asia), the phones are likely to start ringing at adoption agencies. True, the well-intentioned callers will be deeply affected by the suffering of others and want to help out, but the odd outlet for their concern is the urge to acquire the children of victims. With even a little thought and self-examination, it should become apparent that instincts leading people to help in this particular fashion aren't exactly selfless. If you doubt this, consider that families touched by the plight of children in Haiti would eagerly go into debt to come up with hefty adoption fees but would never send that same amount of money (or even a small portion of it) to a charitable organization where it could be used to benefit innumerably more Haitian children.

I think it is important for parents—both adoptive and biological—to recognize that the desire for a child is, at heart, selfish. People decide to get pregnant because they want a child, for whatever reason—but never out of a selfless conviction that a particular combination of egg and sperm deserves to be born. Parenthood certainly becomes a selfless undertaking once the child arrives, but the decision to become pregnant is not selfless. Similarly, it is important for adoptive parents to understand that their desire for a child, rather than their desire to "do good" (or look good), is the proper motivation for adoption.

Families who introduce themselves to me by saying that they want to adopt for charitable reasons are a challenge to counsel. I find it particularly difficult when they say that they are pursuing adoption because they "have a heart for children" or "feel called to help the children of Ethiopia," or some similar statement. They don't seem to recognize that most reasonably nice people are also touched by the plight of children in need. Families who feel that these sentiments set them apart can come across as naïve rather than generous and caring. It can be difficult for them to understand that what feels like uncomplicated goodwill on their part can look more like self-congratulatory pride to others, most importantly to the child who is on the receiving end of their charity.

Children should not be made to feel that their arrival in an adoptive family resulted from an act of charity, nor is it good for them to go through life with the idea that they are supposed to feel grateful to their parents for rescuing them. Birth and adoptive children alike ought to be grateful for the love and care their parents provide, just as parents are grateful for the love and care their children provide. Adoptive families feel grateful to God or fate or blind luck or whatever it is they believe brought them together in the same way that biological families feel grateful for one another. There should be no expectation of extra gratitude from an adopted family member. Sadly, parents who believe that adoption is an act of charity are in danger of creating distorted relationships with their adopted child. These are the parents who are hurt and astounded when, instead of being grateful, their children are resentful of their charity. And these are the parents who are likely to be extremely resistant to the idea that good intentions don't cancel out the damage caused by viewing adopted children as evidence of their parents' "good works."

Most traditional adoption agencies like to make it clear that their primary purpose is to find homes for children rather than to find children for adoptive parents. This distinction is especially noted when the agency handles international adoptions, older-child adoptions, or special-needs adoptions. There is no question that it is harder to find homes for some children than for others, and charitable instincts do sometimes play an important role in connecting a child and a family. But even when this is true, adoptive parents need to adjust their attitudes once they are actually parenting that child. Once the child is part of the family, relating to him or her as a recipient of the family's charity is inappropriate and undermines the development of healthy family relationships.

This is not to say that I am unmoved by feel-good stories about adoption. It is impossible not to find it heartwarming when, for example, a community or church group rallies to adopt a large number of suffering children. The children are sometimes survivors of a natural or political disaster and were in desperate circumstances before being brought to the United States and placed in adoptive homes. Happy as I am that these kids are now safe, I have a perspective different from the norm in that I see trouble lurking behind the assumed gratitude of the children and the shortsighted assumption on the part of some parents that all is now well. Sadly (and sometimes tragically), some of the families who adopt such a child are unprepared for the enormity of the child's needs and the task they have taken on. They may "have a heart" for the child, but they may also lack the considerable knowledge, skill, and resources they need to successfully care for him.

More than a few children who have been adopted in these circumstances do not end up staying with the family who adopted them. The happy ending to their tragic stories is never realized, and we need to examine the widely held assumption that life with an American family (any American family!) is the best choice for every child in need.

Consider the story of Rick and Betsy, who traveled to China to adopt a baby girl during a time when adoptions of children from that country were at their peak. While there, they also met a ten-year-old girl who melted their hearts. After their return home and several months of settling in with their new baby, they wanted to pursue adopting the unforgettable older girl. I talked with them at length about the difficulties of bringing an older child into a family with much younger children. But it is next to impossible to be hardhearted in these situations, and I knew full well that this girl might not get another chance to be adopted. I didn't want to be responsible for denying her this life-changing opportunity. I wanted to believe that this girl and this family could overcome the steep odds against them. I decided to recommend that the adoption proceed, out of the notion that the connection between the family and child, having occurred by happenstance, was "fated"—a common sentiment in this type of international adoption story.

The child arrived six months later. It was a disaster from the start.

I won't go into all the details about what was so troublesome; suffice it to say that this child who had lost every single thing that was familiar and comforting to her was distraught much of the time. The situation eventually became so dysfunctional that the mother and baby ended up leaving the home to stay with relatives. The ten-year-old, who was probably really several years older, repeatedly begged to go back to China, and the adopting parents wished for that as well. But the agency that had placed the child assured them that that was impossible, no matter what the child wanted. Even if returning to the children's home where she had spent most of her life seemed best for her, it would be a disaster for the delicate relationship between the U.S. adoption agency and its counterpart in China.

The parents sought intensive counseling, both for themselves and for a child who appeared to be in the grips of a developing psychosis, but were unsuccessful in finding someone with the expertise the situation called for. Everyone was in tremendous distress, and there didn't appear to be a way out for any of them. The placing agency was sympathetic but had no other appropriate family for the girl. In complete desperation, the father went on-line to research alternatives for treatment and discovered something called "rehoming" in which families who are seeking to relinquish an adopted child find families who are seeking to adopt such a child. On the surface, that seems like a reasonable idea. After all, it is not unlike the approach an agency would take in trying to find homes for a "hard-to-place" child. But in reality, the practice of rehoming has no legal, governmental, or professional oversight and is fraught with danger for the child.

The family did eventually find several families who could provide respite care for the older daughter and, after about a year, an appropriate adoptive family was apparently found. I hear from the first family that the girl is doing well now, and I certainly hope that continues to be the case. But questions remain in my mind about just how stable her situation really is, what the future holds for her, and whether it was really in her best interests to have left China. And I have to ask myself how I would handle things the next time a family wants to bring an older child into a family with a more vulnerable younger child. I would tell them what I have seen, I would caution them, and I would worry, and in the end I would probably decide they needed to find a counselor who felt less conflicted about this type of placement. I think I have finally come to the conclusion that I no longer feel comfortable being part of a process that puts children and families at risk in this way, but who knows how firmly I will hold onto that conviction the next time the situation comes up? Adoption counselors are just as tempted as adoptive parents are by the (sometimes misguided) desire to do good.

When people with younger children call me about adopting an older child, I ask them what they would do if they discovered that their older child was abusive to younger children in the family. Many people are shocked by the suggestion—pretty clear evidence of how unprepared they are for this type of problem—and some say they would get counseling for their children, as if that would necessarily solve things. Both answers suggest that the family intending to adopt has not fully thought through the potential issues in an older-child adoption. I believe that a child already in a family's home, whether by birth or adoption, has the right to feel safe in that home. That child also has the right to know that his parents will do nothing to jeopardize his well-being. No matter how goodhearted their intentions, parents who bring into their home a child who has the ability to significantly harm a child already there are taking a huge risk.

I know there are wonderfully capable parents who have succeeded in bringing older children into a home with younger or more vulnerable children, and there are plenty of examples of this type of placement working out well. I have worked with some of them, so I've seen firsthand how successful these adoptions can be. But I've also seen how completely unaware/disbelieving the parents can be, sometimes years later when the abuse is revealed, and I know of too many families for whom this type of placement has been disastrous. I also know that sometimes, despite everyone's best intentions, nothing could have been done by the agency or counselor to prepare the family adequately for the difficulties they would all face, which can be pretty unimaginable.

I would ask those who feel that I'm being unduly negative to consider who suffers when an adoption fails. The most obvious victim is the adopted child, who is now not only losing his home but also more of his self-esteem, his faith in other people, and his ability to form emotional bonds. The disrupted adoption has confirmed two of this child's basic beliefs: (1) that people cannot be trusted and (2) that there is something unlovable and unworthy about him. He has also suffered the loss of precious childhood time. He needs to devote every possible minute of his remaining childhood to learning how to form healthy attachments, and a disrupted adoption is a setback that is hard to overcome. Whatever time the child has spent with a family that ultimately decides not to keep him is time that has been taken away from him in a new family, and this child has no such time to spare. Chances are excellent that he has already endured a great deal of wasted childhood time prior to the unsuccessful adoption—time in which he was abused or neglected or suffered the trauma of poverty, social unrest, or natural disaster—and time spent trying to connect with a family that decides not to keep him immeasurably compounds his suffering and his loss, and can never be regained.

Parents, too, are victimized when an adoption is disrupted. Many of them take one of two harmful stances in reaction: either they vilify the child or they vilify the placing agency. As often happens with couples when a child dies, parents who have a disrupted adoption may find that they have very different, sometimes conflicting, methods of coping and of grieving and can be of little help to one another. For adoptive parents, there can be an added element of guilt and feelings of failure that are exacerbated by the critical—and often freely given—opinions of others. And if there is a younger child who has been abused, he may be happy and relieved that he no longer has to worry about being victimized but also feel that he was at least partially responsible for the failure of the adoption. That child may also hang onto the misguided notion, as so many victimized children do, that he was somehow partly responsible for the abuse.

My stance should not be taken as opposition to the adoption of older or traumatized children. What I object to is placing those children in homes where they have a seriously compromised chance of success. I'm afraid that parents who believe that they can always provide adequate protection for more vulnerable children in these situations are too often deluding themselves and are actually not a good resource for the older child. I am tremendously impressed by, and grateful to, the families who take on this sort of challenge and succeed at creating good lives for all of their family members. But I have also seen the families whose "success" is all for show, and if the surface is scratched a bit, layer upon layer of unhappiness and dysfunction is revealed.

International adoption of older children is sometimes driven by emotional responses that get in the way of the parents' ability to prepare themselves for the challenges inherent in these placements. I used to do home studies for families planning to adopt from Russia, Romania, Ukraine, and other Eastern European countries. In the early days of adoption from the former Soviet bloc, too many prospective adoptive parents clung to the idea that developmentally delayed children from these countries were "only" suffering from the effects of institutionalization and could be fed, loved, nurtured, and prayed into "normalcy," including the ability to form normal attachments with other family members. As time went on and these children struggled, people grew more informed about Fetal Alcohol Effect and the long-term, severe effects of early deprivation and institutionalization. Eventually, and very sadly, parents began realizing that a significant percentage of children from these countries had intractable problems that no amount of loving care or professional help could erase. Counselors were instructed by experts to inform prospective parents that approximately 25 percent of children coming out of Eastern European orphanages would have significant neurological damage. That's a staggeringly high number—yet it did not discourage many families from playing the odds in their effort to adopt a (Caucasian) child who they hoped would be without significant developmental or emotional problems.

As it turned out, some of these children, and the families who adopted them, found neither the happiness nor the permanence they were expecting adoption to provide. As a counselor in these situations, I felt that too many adoptive parents weren't fully comprehending the risks they were taking or the scope of the child's problems. They seemed to feel that the three-to-one odds against their child having significant problems meant there was a good chance everything would be fine. While that attitude might reflect a positive outlook, it also seemed to reflect wishful thinking, and some of these parents were not at all prepared for the consequences if they and their child did not, in fact, beat the odds. I found myself struggling to find the balance between adequately preparing people for the problems they might face and talking them out of doing this type of adoption. And I found myself increasingly uncomfortable in this position. I wanted to be able to be encouraging and supportive and to share in the family's happiness when the child was transformed and thrived. And if the child didn't thrive, I certainly didn't want to be the voice in the parents' heads saying, "I told you so."

There are no guarantees that parents will have a healthy child, whether through birth or adoption. All forms of parenthood involve a leap of faith into the unknown and a commitment to the child, no matter what problems arise. But in adoption, I believe that prospective parents have an added responsibility to be well informed about potential problems and to be completely honest about their own limitations in the face of these problems. Adoptive parents who indulge in a purely emotional response to a child in need are in danger of being dishonest with themselves about what they really have to offer that child. They are in danger of doing bad instead of the good they intended.

13

The Need for Open Adoption

Options for pregnancy was WACAP's in-country infant adoption program. Helen Magee, its first director, was an early advocate of open adoption and a tireless champion of the rights of pregnant women who were considering adoption (among other options) for their babies. For a period of time beginning in the late 1980s, with the assistance of a large federal grant, the Options program encompassed a five-state area and handled approximately one hundred infant adoptions per year. This was an impressive number at a time when it was becoming increasingly difficult to adopt an American-born infant. My job as a supervisor in this program was to provide ongoing training for the counselors and be available to them as a consultant. My work hours were usually pretty evenly divided between work as an adoption counselor and work with the Options counselors and their clients. The number of hours I devoted to my job, dictated by the needs of each situation, varied dramatically from week to week. There were some adoptions that consumed all of my attention, while others seemed to smoothly handle themselves.

The basis of the Options program's success was Helen's commitment to openness in adoption and to correcting the sins of the past regarding treatment of birth mothers. Options focused on ensuring that all prospective birth mothers were treated with care and respect, and were provided with the sort of counseling that would allow them to make fully informed decisions about their babies. The program's mission had been developed in direct response to the heartbreaking stories told by birth mothers from earlier times, when women were shamed into silence and submission by their pregnancies, and coerced into relinquishing their babies to anonymous adoptive parents. Birth mothers who had relinquished their babies in the 1970s and earlier, no longer willing to suppress their anger and sorrow, were finally beginning to speak out in numbers about what had happened to them. They wanted people to understand why their experience with traditional adoption, shrouded as it was in mystery, shame, and unanswered questions, had left them unable to properly grieve for, or fully recover from, their loss.

In the most unexpected settings, I will casually answer a question about what I do for a living and suddenly be confronted with just such an outpouring from a birth mother who needs this opportunity to express herself. I was once followed into a hotel restroom at a wedding by the maid of honor, who poured out the story of her teenage pregnancy for half an hour before another member of the wedding party tracked her down and hauled her off to the reception.

Another typical example from that era is the story of Monica, who talked nonstop for an hour one day when we met for lunch to discuss an unrelated matter. We had scarcely sat down and exchanged information about our lives and occupations when she—as she later apologized—"just spilled my guts all over the table."

When she was a fifteen-year-old devout Catholic who taught catechism classes on Saturdays, Monica had started dating a man who was six years older. There had been no discussion or instruction from her parents or anyone else about what to expect in this relationship and, not surprisingly, she became pregnant at age sixteen. Her boyfriend told her he would marry her but only if she got an abortion first. No one, including her parents, her boyfriend, and even Monica herself, felt that she was ready to become a parent. Monica stoically accepted responsibility for her situation, rejected the idea of an illegal abortion (it was 1966), and chose adoption for her baby. Her anguished parents, anxious that no one find out that their daughter was pregnant, sent her to what was called at the time a "home for unwed mothers," where Monica was effectively imprisoned with a dozen or so other pregnant teenagers until her baby was born. She remembers how unkind and judgmental the women who operated the home were and how they managed to make the girls feel thoroughly ashamed of themselves.

Monica never saw her baby, who was immediately taken from her at birth and turned over to adoptive parents. Everything was done in the strictest confidentiality in the belief that the less Monica knew, the more quickly she could move on with her life. She remained in the hospital for three more days, for some reason on the maternity ward, surrounded by women with their babies. On the second day of her stay, a cheerful nurse popped her head in the door and announced that it was "time for the babies to come." Monica remembers that she somehow found the strength to call back, in the most cheerful voice she could muster up, "I don't get to have one." The nurse ducked out and nothing further was said. No one in the hospital seemed to feel that Monica might need some extra comfort or support. Looking back now, her heart aches for that little girl who was so alone and who felt that it was her responsibility to reassure everyone else that she was just fine.

Monica went home from the hospital feeling "like damaged goods." She couldn't imagine going back home to live with her disappointed parents. She also couldn't quite envision what other options were available to her, so she married the father of the baby. They went on to have three more children over the next twelve years. There was no talk about the baby they had relinquished. It was an unhappy and verbally abusive marriage—and not a day went by that Monica didn't think about her first child.

Every year on the child's birthday, she would find herself depressed and consumed with worry about his or her (she didn't even know the sex of the child) well-being. Monica remembers being particularly depressed on the sixteenth of those birthdays. Her husband, normally inattentive to her emotional needs, finally felt compelled to ask, in an impatient and accusatory manner, "What's wrong with you today?"

"Well, there are two things," Monica replied. "First, this marriage is a disaster. And second, it's the baby's birthday and I was just wondering how that child is. Is it happy or healthy or even alive?"

After a long silence, her husband said, "I forgot that ever even happened."

His comment brought all the more to mind how lonely and isolated Monica had been in her grief. She separated from her husband shortly thereafter, and they subsequently divorced.

"The baby" (a daughter named Jane), meanwhile, had been on a years-long quest to find her birth mother. As a teenager, she had seen her original birth certificate, which included the city where she was born and her birth mother's surname. At age twenty-one, Jane married a man who was in the military and moved with him to his next posting, which was, coincidentally, in the town where Jane was born. She decided to do some research at the local library where she found a high school annual with a picture of a girl with Monica's surname who looked just like Jane. She also discovered that Monica's graduating class was about to have its twentieth reunion and was able to find out Monica's married name from an extremely forthcoming woman on the planning committee.

Now that she knew her birth mother's married name and phone number, all Jane needed to do was work up the courage to call. Monica remembers a very stressed and timid sounding voice on the line saying, "I don't know where to begin." Monica, who assumed the girl was a friend of one of her other daughters and was upset about something, urged her to just go ahead and tell her what was on her mind. Jane then asked Monica if she had given up a baby twenty-one years earlier. When Monica replied that she had, Jane said, "I am that baby." And the happy tears flowed.

Monica and Jane made plans to meet that afternoon. They spent hours together at a local restaurant getting acquainted and filling one another in on the events of their respective lives. Monica told Jane that she had three full siblings and Jane was excited to meet them and grateful that Monica was willing to share her family. The following day, Jane was introduced to her stunned siblings. Although they had previously known nothing about their oldest sister's birth and subsequent adoption, they were excited and very welcoming. Everyone was delighted and amazed to see that Jane not only looked just like Monica and one of Monica's other daughters, but also shared many personality traits, interests, and talents, and even had the same voice and distinctive bend in her little fingers.

This happened at a time when women were taught to be cooperative and passive above all else. When a young woman violated societal taboos by becoming pregnant, she was expected to accept the consequences as much-deserved punishment. Tragically, many a young woman in those days did not feel she had either the right or the power to object when others told her to relinquish her baby. She believed along with them that they knew and wanted what was best for her and for the baby. Inevitably, in the emotional aftermath, these people who were so sure they knew what was best became the focus of the birth mother's anger. They—most often the woman's parents or the birth father or various adoption professionals—were the people she held responsible for the loss of her child. Their insistence on telling her what to do forced her into the role of passive victim—an ultimately unsatisfying way for birth mothers to absolve themselves of responsibility for the decision to relinquish. Factor in the overriding secrecy and denial, and you have a perfect recipe for an eventual backlash.

By the late 1970s, many women like Monica were speaking out against this mistreatment, refusing to be silent and ashamed any longer. It was an exciting era of rapid change that resulted in an overhaul of adoption practices, with Helen Magee and the Options for Pregnancy program out on the leading edge.

An Options counselor's mandate was to provide unbiased counseling and support for whatever choice the woman made—whether adoption or parenthood. (Under terms of a Reagan-administration federal grant, Option's counselors were not allowed to talk with their clients about abortion as an option.)

Potential birth mothers were attracted to Options by the possibility of having a semi-open relationship with the adoptive family at a time when most agencies did not offer this type of adoption. Openness through the Options program generally meant that a pregnant woman would select the adoptive family herself and could meet with them prior to and/or at delivery, depending on the timing and logistics unique to each situation. After the baby was placed with the adoptive parents, openness generally took the form of having them send letters and pictures (usually through the agency) to the birth mother on an agreed-upon schedule, and sometimes included a visit or two after the adoption. Most prospective birth mothers believed that a couple's willingness to have this type of open relationship reflected their level of understanding and respect for her and for her decision.

Working as an Options counselor was a highly rewarding way to work with birth parents because in most cases the counselor was able to act as an advocate. Counselors were able to help women reach fully informed decisions and—if they opted for adoption—help them create an adoption that would leave them at peace. Of course, relinquishing a child was still going to be a heartbreaking loss, but the counselor could at least help turn it into a conscious decision made by the birth mother herself rather than a decision she was manipulated or coerced into making. It was also growing increasingly common for women with unplanned pregnancies to decide to raise their babies on their own—an option that Options' counseling encouraged women to fully explore as well.

These changes in adoption made my job as a counselor less difficult ethically but much more difficult logistically. It was easier ethically because I felt that birth parents were making their decision to relinquish out of selfless love for their babies and the realization that they wanted something for their children that they felt unable to provide. Rarely was the decision to relinquish made for practical reasons, such as age or income or single-parent status alone, as had seemed to often be the case in the past. Now it was more likely to be made because the birth parents didn't feel emotionally ready for parenthood and because the life they felt they wanted for their child was different from the life they felt they could give him or her.

The counselor's job was more difficult logistically because it now included a more complicated, open process that necessarily involved a greater number of people—all of them extremely invested in the outcome.

Helen Magee's inspired insight into the ethics of open adoption aside, there was also a simple law of supply and demand that influenced Options' popularity with birth parents. Because there weren't enough babies available for adoption to meet the demand from hopeful adoptive parents, birth mothers could start setting conditions for how they were to be treated and what sort of people they would consider as parents for their children. It should come as no surprise that they tended to prefer working with adoptive parents who weren't afraid or suspicious of them—people they could get to know during their pregnancy who would understand how much they loved their babies and who could be counted on to pass that message on to their children as they grew up.

One of the first birth mothers I encountered was an adorable seventeen-year-old. This girl, Ali, was extremely articulate, artistically stylish, and funny. Her boyfriend was the son of a prominent Seattle family and was definitely on his way to college rather than teenage fatherhood. Although this all happened a few years before the 1986 movie *Pretty in Pink* was made, the situation was as if the character Molly Ringwald played had gotten pregnant by the rich kid. Ali took part in a few birth-mom panels that were set up to educate counselors and adoptive parents about openness, and she did a fabulous job. She was smart and self-confident and knew what she wanted, but she was in largely uncharted territory in those days in regard to encouraging ongoing contact between birth and adoptive parents. Essentially, her goal was to help adoptive parents understand that they had nothing to fear from most birth parents, and she was one of best people I can imagine to relay that message. Ali was tremendously appealing, and she was also the essence of unthreatening. She would explain to the audience that she knew she wasn't ready to be a parent and that she and her boyfriend wanted their baby to have the wonderful, mature parents that they weren't yet able to be. But she added that she wished that she could be a fly on the wall in the nursery sometimes and just share in the joy that she knew her baby would bring to his parents. Ali's words were simple and her sentiment beautiful and clear: birth parents want to share in the joy that their children create, and openness in adoption makes that possible.

Like all parents, birth parents worry about their children and want the ongoing reassurance about their well-being that openness can provide. They worry about the child's basic health and happiness, and they also have worries that are related specifically to the adoption. The most complicated of these surrounds the fear that children will not understand why their parents chose adoption and will either be angry at having been "given up" or will believe that if they had been more worthy and lovable, their birth parents would have kept them. Birth parents want their children to be raised by people who will help them understand that their birth parents loved them and were motivated by the selfless desire to do what they felt was in their child's best interests.

Despite the fact that birth parents had eagerly embraced the idea of open adoption, the majority of families who wanted to adopt an infant in the 1980s and into the 1990s weren't as enthusiastic. Part of the problem was that some of the books and other sources of information about the benefits of open adoption were fairly terrifying to the average prospective adoptive parent. These books included supposedly reassuring examples of co-parenting arrangements that encouraged a high degree of interaction between the birth and adoptive families—examples that could seem anything but reassuring to uninitiated adoptive parents. Early advocates of openness, who could be overzealous in their enthusiasm, ignored the fact that many adoptive parents were already worried about not feeling 100 percent legitimate as parents. Expecting them to suddenly and eagerly embrace the idea that there would always be a second set of parents around, who would keep their fears fresh in their minds, was unrealistic. After decades in which vigilant secrecy was the accepted practice, people needed time to adjust to the idea of open adoption.

Of course, even when secrecy was the norm, confidentiality could be breached at some point in an infant adoption: names were sometimes not completely concealed on medical and legal paperwork; lawyers, nurses, and social workers made slips of the tongue despite strict prohibitions against sharing any identifying information; simple coincidences led people to conclusions about the identity of the birth or adoptive parents; or someone intentionally provided identifying information. In the era when Options for Pregnancy was most active, and ongoing contact (through the agency) was embraced, adoptive parents still usually planned not to share their full identities with birth parents. This created plenty of awkward situations and wreaked havoc with the notion that everyone was completely comfortable with everyone else. Occasionally, adoptive parents, at some point in the process, would just go ahead and reveal their last name. This might happen when, for example, everyone was sitting around in the hospital room after the baby's birth. In those intimate, emotionally charged moments, when the last thing the adopting parents want to do is upset or insult the birth mother, something would happen that would force them to decide in a split second whether to make a point of concealing their full identity from her.

More than a few times, I witnessed the following scene unfold: the birth parents, the new baby, and the adoptive parents are in the hospital room together, awash in joy and uncertainty as they ooh and aah over the new baby, the adoptive parents trying to conceal their anxiety over whether the birth parents will change their minds and decide to raise their child themselves. The birth parents are holding and exclaiming over the baby, and a nurse comes in with a form to be filled out. She asks the adoptive parents for their full names, and with barely perceptible hesitation, the adoptive mom says it out loud, spelling it for her. The birth parents, absorbed in their baby, say nothing—but I see the name register with them, and know they are filing it away, never to be forgotten.

Openness, while a simple, reasonable idea in the abstract, was (and often still is) tremendously complicated to put into practice. A counselor working with adoptive parents is asked to summarize and verify their "attitudes about birth parents and openness" in the home study. In order to do this, the counselor first must educate them about the benefits of openness, in the hopes that the prospective adoptive family will then decide that they are, after all, comfortable with openness and would welcome an open relationship with their child's birth parents. Obviously, adoptive parents who are working with an agency that encourages open adoptions can do the math: they understand that if they don't at least claim to embrace openness, they will dramatically reduce their chances of being selected by a birth mother. So, many of them grit their teeth, espouse beliefs they don't really share, and promise to do all sorts of things they hope never to have to actually do.

I have never been comfortable with a "one size fits all" approach to openness, with its assumption that everyone will act appropriately forever. I find it particularly troubling when birth and adoptive parents, with the help of attorneys and counselors, make decisions about ongoing contact on behalf of the child, expecting him or her to abide by whatever agreement they have reached. Obviously, it isn't possible to involve an infant in these decisions, but as soon as the child is old enough to have opinions on the matter, his or her wishes become significant. It is also true that no matter what adoptive parents say to me during their home study about their embracing openness, if they encounter real difficulties in later years, they will throw those ideals out the window and do whatever they feel is right for their child—exactly what I would expect them to do. Adoptive parents, like all parents, have the right to make decisions about their children. They also have the right, as do their children, not to be forced into making legally and/or ethically binding agreements about the relationships they will have in the future.

So I never find it reasonable to ask someone how they feel about openness in adoption without first discussing a lot of qualifiers. Is it going to be openness with someone they like and trust? Is it openness with someone their child enjoys being around? Is it openness with someone they like but worry about because she is in an abusive relationship? Is it openness with someone they like but who talks openly when they meet about regretting her adoption decision? Is it openness with someone who brought her drunk and aggressive boyfriend to the last visit? Is it openness with someone whose visits make the child sad? Obviously, a parent's level of comfort with openness changes in each of these situations, and it is completely appropriate for adoptive parents to modify their responses to questions about their comfort with openness to reflect that reality. I think the truest and most responsible answer for most prospective adoptive parents to such questions is, "It depends."

Still, I am a strong advocate of open adoption—with a few caveats. Ideally, the birth and adoptive parents can establish a comfortable and mutually rewarding relationship, and they and the child will naturally benefit from ongoing contact. One of my responsibilities as an adoption counselor is to help the birth and adoptive parents develop a "post-placement contact agreement," which specifies what type of ongoing contact they will have. Among other things, the agreement typically clarifies how many letters and pictures will be sent and how often, and in what form. It also addresses questions about visits, and it has become fairly common for birth parents to ask for (although not necessarily follow up on) a certain number of visits for a set number of years. When a child is very young, the parents make the decisions about these visits, but as the child gets older, I feel that his or her wishes become paramount. The adoptive parents might promise in the agreement to strive to create an atmosphere in which their child can develop a comfortable relationship with the birth parents (and often with other extended birth-family members), but it would be counterproductive to try to force visits when they make the child uncomfortable. I have seen this sort of discomfort develop, most often with sensitive children who find the birth parents' intense focus on them overwhelming.

Openness has enormous benefits for everyone in the adoption triad: the birth parents, the adoptive parents, and the child. Usually, what benefits one party also benefits the others because it increases everyone's overall comfort, feelings of security, and level of satisfaction. For example, when the birth mother is feeling respected and appreciated, the adoptive parents feel more secure and confident about her decision to place the baby with them, and the baby has a more relaxed and happy home. But there are times when the interests of the birth and adoptive families do not mesh, and there are even times when one person's desires might seem detrimental to the others. I knew one family with a bright and sensitive seven-year-old girl who had, for reasons unknown to her parents, grown uncomfortable about visits with her birth mother. The birth and adoptive families had previously enjoyed an unusually open relationship, visiting in each other's homes and even vacationing together. The parents sought help from a counselor who advised that they cut back on the visits for a while. The birth mother was understandably upset by this idea and by the child's reaction to visits with her. It would have been easy for her to blame the adoptive parents and assume that they had willfully turned the child against her. A surface assessment would suggest that curtailing visits for a while would sacrifice the birth mother's happiness to appease the child's possibly confused or manipulated wishes. Closer examination, however, allowed the child's intuitive discomfort with the birth mother's seemingly emotional dependence upon her during visits to become the catalyst for getting help for everyone: the child herself, her parents, and her birth mother. If the child hadn't been able to express her feelings or if her parents hadn't been sensitive to them, everyone would have continued enduring an increasingly strained relationship. The birth mother wouldn't have gotten the encouragement she needed to make some positive changes in her life, the adoptive parents would still be worried and confused about what they should be doing, the child would continue to suffer, and they all would have continued to grow apart. Fortunately, the birth and adoptive parents were perceptive enough to realize that their relationships were precious and well worth the effort it would take to preserve them.

Ideas about openness have changed a lot over the years. It is now common for adoptive families to share full identifying information with birth parents, often in their first encounters. In an effort to find a baby in an ever-more-challenging market, most families seeking to adopt an in-country infant post online profiles full of information about themselves, giving birth parents the opportunity to thoroughly scrutinize (and Google) them before any direct contact is made. There are ways for people to protect their identity, but the ways for people to get around those safeguards are ever multiplying. Given that reality, many adoptive parents accept the fact that confidential adoptions are largely a thing of the past.

For most people, this is a harmless trend, even a beneficial one. But there are some situations in which birth parents simply aren't emotionally stable enough for open adoption. It might seem that the best approach in these cases is a vigilant effort to preserve confidentiality, and this would indeed shield the child for a few years. But in the long run, it may prove harmful. Once the child is old enough to ask questions about his adoption or his birth parents, to realize that there are other adoptees who know their birth parents, and to learn to use a computer, the adoptive parents may find that they can no longer control the amount of information their child will be able to access. If they haven't created an atmosphere in which the child feels comfortable coming to them with questions about the birth family and trusts that they are telling the truth, then the child is likely to search for information in secret. Far better for the parents to share what they know and be as honest as their child's age allows them to be in talking about why they don't maintain contact with the birth parents. It is usually true that the unknown is scarier than just about anything else, so adoptive parents need to make sure that their child's imagination, and/or the "information" he finds out in secret, isn't more troubling than the truth would be. And in those situations in which the truth is just unavoidably troubling, it is all the more important for the parents to be the ones to talk with their children about it first.

When I worked with the Options for Pregnancy program, it was in the forefront of promoting open adoption. There were a few other agencies at the time that urged a much greater degree of openness, creating adoptions that seemed more like guardianship or co-parenting arrangements, but the majority of agency adoptions were still quite traditional. It was revolutionary in those days to allow birth parents to select adoptive parents, meet with them, have them present at the baby's birth, and maintain contact after placement. But change was happening quickly, and agencies that continued to operate under the old rules began to either adapt to some degree of openness or go out of the business of infant adoption. Those who chose to adapt were a cautiously excited bunch, feeling their way through new terrain.

Some years later, Patti Beasley—who had also worked at WACAP as an adoption counselor—and I had the opportunity to run our own agency, Adoption Connections. We decided to have a single counselor work with both the birth and adoptive parents. We had come to feel that conventional adoption social work practice was guided by the fallacy that birth and adoptive parents represent opposing sides in an adoption. What we usually found instead was that these were people who were working together to achieve the same goal; a happy family for the baby. Certainly there were times when people had differences of opinion about how some aspect of the adoption should be handled, and certainly there were times when a birth parent's requests exceeded a particular family's comfort level. But these were situations in which a counselor could either help them negotiate a solution or help them come to the decision that they weren't a good match for each other.

The adoption process is fraught with extreme emotions, and there are bound to be times of conflict. But when everyone stays focused on what is best for the child, there is strong motivation to work through these difficulties. The goal becomes larger than the straightforward one of finding a baby or finding an adoptive family; it grows to encompass the creation of a relationship that will demonstrate mutual care and respect between birth and adoptive families. This can happen whether people develop ongoing relationships or choose to meet only once. I have even seen it happen on the rarest of occasions—when birth parents have requested closed adoptions and asked us to handle everything confidentially. In all of these various kinds of arrangements, there is one common thread: everyone involved can say that they have done their very best for the child and for one another.

14

Finding Just the Right Home

NE SUMMER MORNING in 1985, I rode the ferry across Puget Sound to meet with an adoptive family living on Bainbridge Island, a thirty-five-minute trip from downtown Seattle.

The island proved to be bucolic; I drove past a charming little public grade school, thinking wistfully, "I wish my children could go to a school like that." The previous months had been spent trying futilely to figure out our six-year-old daughter Erin's school plans for the coming year. It was a particularly fraught time in the history of the Seattle school system, which a few years later would be given a total overhaul with major improvements that made the city a place where families once again wanted to send their kids to public schools. But that year was a bad one, and Erin was slated to spend two hours each day riding a bus to and from a dismal neighborhood where a little girl had recently been shot across the street from the school playground. We were not going to send our child there. The alternative was private school; the private schools in Seattle were proliferating like mad during those years. Erin had been going to a wonderful private preschool and kindergarten, founded by the University of Washington's Department of Early Childhood Development, for the past two years, and she loved school and thrived in that environment. But we had to look ahead, realize that private school fees were climbing every year, and wonder how we would be able to afford them in the years to come. We had two children to consider at this point (Erin and our younger daughter, Caitlin). We wanted a third, to be adopted from Korea, and there were considerable expenses attached to that decision as well.

As I watched the children playing happily on the grassy hillside playground, my thinking switched to, "Why couldn't my children go to a school like that?" As most parents do, I wanted my children to grow up in the best possible circumstances, and island life looked idyllic to me.

Our decision to move to Bainbridge was made in haste. A few days after my first visit, my husband and I returned to check out the housing situation—just an exploratory venture without any real thought or plan to move. By the next weekend, we had made an offer on a house, and two weeks after that we had sold our house in Seattle. Things happened so quickly that we couldn't help but wonder what we had done. We kept waiting for feelings of remorse to creep into our enthusiasm, but they never did. There was a brief moment of concern when we realized that there was no place on the island to get peanut M&Ms at midnight, but we adjusted.

When we moved to the island, the population was made up of newcomers (like us) and old-timers, meaning people who had grown up here, mostly Caucasian but including many Japanese and Filipino families who were early farmers and landowners. Bainbridge has always been a close-knit community—we quickly learned not to honk our horns or scowl at a stranger who might turn out to be your dentist or the parent of your child's new friend. The community's cohesion was never more evident than during the World War II internment of Japanese Americans. The local paper—the *Bainbridge Review*—was the first West Coast newspaper to editorialize against the internment, and islanders (many of them Filipino men who had come to Bainbridge to work in the lumber mills and the native American women they married) for the most part safeguarded the property of the interned until they could come back to reclaim it.

Bainbridge also had an artistic element that included lots of writers, painters, musicians, and a plethora of cottage industries. Many people on the island, including my husband, commuted to jobs in downtown Seattle, the ferry ride being a relatively quick, inexpensive, and extremely pleasant trip for a pedestrian. The commuters' days began and ended with a ride across Puget Sound and (when it wasn't raining) spectacular sunrises and sunsets that turned the sky and the snow on the Olympics and Mt. Rainier into gorgeous shades of pink, purple, and gold. On winter evenings, when the ride home was in the dark, even longtime commuters might take seats at the back of the boat to take in the dramatic sight of the city lights sparkling like countless jewels on the hillsides of Seattle and as they were reflected in the waters of Elliott Bay.

We moved into an old farmhouse at the end of a dead-end road with seven other houses, lived in by families with a total of thirteen children under age ten. Most of the houses had about an acre of land each, and the kids were given a degree of independence they would never have been allowed in the city. We were astonished by our good fortune at finding not only schools but a community and neighborhood that was everything we hoped it would be. Life on Bainbridge just kept surprising us in delightful ways. The nights were so quiet that we could hear seals barking on a beach a half mile away. We saw skies full of stars and meteors and experienced moonlight so bright it cast distinct shadows in the yard. The wildlife, including deer, raccoons, eagles, owls, and coyotes, was beautiful, exciting, and troublesome. The deer families that were so lovely to look at would regularly eat anything that blossomed, raccoons were ingenious at getting into the garbage, and eagles and coyotes made people's small pets disappear. Nevertheless, as long as our own small pets were safely inside, we were delighted by frequent visits from all of these animals. If the kids got to the bus stop a few minutes early in the morning, they could spend the extra time petting the horses pastured there, and sometimes as the bus drove past the bay, they would see a seal head pop up in the water.

I had been contentedly living on Bainbridge for about five years when I was contacted about working with a young couple from east Texas who wanted to find an adoptive family for their two young children—a two-year-old girl and a nine-month-old boy. Often, calls about wanting to place "older" children are a cry for help from someone who is feeling temporarily overwhelmed, and it is likely that the caller actually needs and wants assistance with some other aspect of life, such as finances or parenting, rather than with planning an adoption. Becca was seventeen years old (meaning she had been fourteen when she got pregnant with her daughter), and her boyfriend, Jarod, was eighteen. They lived together with their children, usually with one or the other of their parents, and, as Becca told me, they had so far been able to provide for their kids. Becca was a girl of few words, and I was having some difficulty figuring out why she and Jarod were thinking about adoption, especially since they had family support. She wanted me to tell her about adoptive families, however, so I did, and I also sent her some family profiles to look at.

Becca called again about a week later and said that she and Jarod were excited about one of the families they had seen and wanted to know if they could meet the couple. This time, Becca was more forthcoming in our conversation, and she told me that although nothing had happened yet, she wanted to find an adoptive family soon because both she and Jarod were on the verge of losing their tempers with the children. I asked her about leaving them with the grandparents when they were feeling stressed, and Becca told me she had the same concerns about the grandparents' lack of self-control. She assured me that the kids weren't in immediate danger, but in my experience, when someone expresses fear that a child "might" be abused, the abuse has often already happened. Becca denied that this was the case, but she was eager to proceed with an adoption.

The family Becca and Jarod wanted to meet was from Bainbridge Island. Within a week, they and their children had flown here and met the prospective adoptive parents, Mark and Elizabeth. The children were adorable and appeared to have been well cared for. Becca and Jarod were friendly and pleasant and straightforward in their explanations about why they wanted their children to have lives different from the ones they could provide. They talked about their hopes for the children's futures and also about hopes for themselves. They said they just needed a chance to grow up more before they would be ready to handle the responsibilities of parenthood. They were calm but not unemotional, and their resolve to do an adoption was clearly strengthened by meeting Mark and Elizabeth and being able to form an image of what life with them would be like for the children.

After the first meeting, which was at Mark and Elizabeth's home, we decided that the children would spend some time alone with them the following day while I took Becca and Jarod on a tour of the island. They were delighted by everything they saw. Becca, it turned out, was fascinated by sea life, so after showing them such things as the schools and parks, we headed for a beach. As we approached the water, Becca asked if we ever saw seals; I told her that there were lots of seals, that sometimes we saw otters and orcas, and that my daughters and their grandfather had once been no more than fifty yards away from a gray whale as they fished from the dock at this very beach. Becca then asked me about various types of sea life such as starfish, anemones, and crabs, and expressed amazement and delight when I told her that, yes, they were all here. But the thing that made her happiest was the sight of the zillions of little white clam shells that covered the beach. After exclaiming over their beauty, she asked if she might be able to take one home. Of course, I told her, "Take as many as you like." Then I hurriedly turned away to hide my emotions as Becca and Jarod filled their pockets with clamshells.

In a perfect world, Becca and Jarod would have suddenly aged about ten years, would have found jobs that allowed them independence from their parents, and would have then been able to raise their own children without fears about abuse. What really happened was that they returned to Texas a few days later and left the kids with Mark and Elizabeth, to grow up surrounded by sea life. My impression was that they hadn't wavered in their decision, which seemed clearly motivated by the desire to do the best that they could for their children. And, in this effort, Becca and Jarod appeared to feel well satisfied that they had succeeded.

III
ADOPTIVE PARENTHOOD
AND SISTERHOOD

15

Children Are Exactly
Who They Are Meant to Be

When a wonderful baby flies over the ocean
To come like a little bird, safe to this nest,
We'll surround her with all of our love and devotion
And give thanks for the child from the East who came West.

> By Jean Moehring, on the occasion of her granddaughter's arrival

I HAVE A DISTINCT MEMORY of the moment I first wanted to be an adoptive parent. It was 1964. I was thirteen years old and on a spring-break road trip with my parents and sister. We were driving across the country, stopping at various sites of historical significance along the way, but I just wanted to stay in the car and read. At one point in the trip, I was sitting in the car reading a newspaper article about a single woman (I believe she was a reporter) who had adopted a little girl from Korea. I think what made the story newsworthy was that the woman was a little famous and had managed to adopt as a single parent at a time when that was almost unheard of. But whatever the reason, I was fascinated—and could clearly see my future, most of which was extremely murky, as the mother of a Korean daughter.

Twenty-three years later, that future was realized in the adoption of our youngest daughter, Jocelyn, who arrived from Korea at three-and-a-half months old. My husband wrote a wonderful story about our adoption experience for the *Seattle Times*, in which he tried to explain why we had made the decision to adopt. As he told it, when I brought the subject of adoption up to him it didn't seem as though I wanted to start a discussion; it was more like I was announcing a pregnancy. And that's exactly the way I felt about it.

People were curious about why we had decided to adopt. We were already the parents of two daughters who had fulfilled our expectations of parenthood beyond our wildest dreams. The grandparents, especially, couldn't figure out why we didn't just have another child like the two we all adored so much. I would try to answer their questions logically, by saying things like, "Well, we just feel we've been so fortunate to have two healthy children and we don't want to press our luck with a third pregnancy." But that wasn't true at all: we wanted to adopt because it felt fated that we do so. I had known that little girl was coming for a long, long time.

I don't think it's necessary for adoption counselors to be adoptive parents—although many are—but there's no question that becoming an adoptive parent teaches you things you can't learn in any other way. And being an adoption counselor definitely helped me as an adoptive parent.

Jocelyn's adjustment to her new life as a member of our family was not easy for any of us. Although she weighed only ten pounds when she arrived, Jocelyn was a mighty force who immediately dominated the household with her distress. Erin and Caitlin, who were eight and five, were old enough to understand that she was, as her doctor so scientifically explained, "freaking out" about all the changes in her world. Most specifically, she was freaking out about the loss of her foster mother, and she wanted nothing to do with us—with the exception of her sisters, who could amuse her by day, and her new grandfather, whose broad chest could comfort her into sleep. Since Grandpa loved naps, this worked well for both of them when he was around. But the night times were dreadful.

Because I had known other babies who had similarly difficult adjustments, I took Jocelyn's unhappiness as a sign that she was smart and sensitive and, most importantly, that she had been able to develop healthy attachments in her foster home, along with the belief that her crying and protests would matter to someone. The babies who concerned me in my work were those who seemed not to have noticed that their lives had been upended, not only by new caretakers but by an entirely new world with strange sights, sounds, smells, and touches. It was common for me to do a post-placement visit in the first few weeks after a baby's arrival and then write a report stating that the parents described the child as calm and easygoing, noting that she rarely cried and was already sleeping through the night. On the surface, it looked as though these babies were doing well, and their passivity made the early adjustment period for their families relatively easy. But I think many of these "easygoing" children were actually so frightened and overwhelmed that they had retreated emotionally. Rather than register protest, they responded to the trauma with silence and complacency.

I remember one seven-month-old baby from Korea who carried this reaction to an extreme. She arrived bearing no resemblance to the child described in her referral paperwork. Her parents were expecting a child who was "smiling and babbling, sitting steadily and standing when her hands are held." Instead they brought home from the airport a silent and limp baby who seemed unable even to hold her head up. They rushed her to the doctor, assuming she was sick, but there was no indication of a physical problem. For two excruciating days and nights, the parents worried while the baby remained listless. Then, on the third day, she began to cry, and she cried for hours while her parents made futile attempts to soothe her. Finally, completely exhausted, the baby was quiet in her mother's lap. Then she slowly lifted her head, sat up straight and cautiously reached up a tiny hand to touch her mother's cheek. This child turned out to be exceptionally bright, and I think she had just initially "decided" that total withdrawal was an intelligent and sensible response to such a traumatic situation.

Jocelyn's adjustment period wasn't nearly as dramatic or as rapid, and it felt as though it took months before we figured out how to make her happy. Yet when I look at pictures of her first few weeks with us now, there is evidence of faint smiling, even then.

But she remained mysterious to us, and my husband and I had to relearn many of the things we thought we knew about parenting. For example, our tried-and-true methods for getting a baby to sleep, such as gentle rocking and quiet singing in a darkened room, seemed only to infuriate her. We finally figured out that what this baby found soothing was rigorous bouncing and distracting chatter, neither of which came naturally to our minds as methods for soothing babies. (When we met her incredibly vivacious foster mother thirteen years later, we finally understood why this behavior felt comforting and familiar to Jocelyn.)

I think the primary lesson that parents, whether by birth or adoption, need to learn is that it is their job to adapt to the child—not to try to make the child adapt to them. All children come to us as unique, distinct people, and it is the parents' responsibility—and joy—to discover how to help them thrive. This responsibility extends to everything from figuring out how to soothe them as babies to knowing how to steer them toward becoming independent adults.

When Jocelyn was a toddler, I was working as the Options for Pregnancy supervisor. I remember a training session for Options counselors that included a fascinating talk by a psychologist who wanted to give us tips about making the best possible matches between adoptive parents and babies. She told us about a study of adoptive placements whose authors concluded that the single most significant factor affecting long-term happiness in adoptive families was the fit between parents and children in what the psychologist called "energy level." She explained that a mismatch in the energy level of the parents and child was the most highly predictive indicator of an adoption disruption—meaning that the child ultimately left the family.

At first, this idea seemed preposterous. After all, there are plenty of birth families in which there is an obvious mismatch in the energy levels between parents and children, and they seem to have no more trouble getting along than do families in which everyone is similar in that respect. I also resisted the idea that families can be typed according to energy level and that family members necessarily resemble each other in this way. I found myself rejecting a lot of what the psychologist was saying, but as I thought more about it, I realized that Options and other agencies that encouraged open adoption were already doing a version of what she recommended. We weren't doing it deliberately—it was just a natural outcome of openness. When our birth parents searched for the right adoptive family for their child, they looked for people with whom they felt comfortable, and their (possibly unconscious) recognition of a shared energy level probably contributed to that feeling in subtle but significant ways.

When a child is born to a family, we assume that he or she will in some ways be a "chip off the old block." Children aren't clones of their parents, but they do share traits that go beyond height and hair color and include more nebulous areas such as talents, interests, and personality type. As someone who has worked with many hundreds of birth parents and adoptive families over a period of thirty-five years, I have been in a position to study the age-old nature-or-nurture question. I've watched in amazement as some children turn into the spitting image of their adoptive parents, even when they are of different races. I've been equally amazed by children who have had no contact with their birth parents but nevertheless grow up to share not only their physical traits but also their mannerisms, avocations, and dispositions.

I often thought about the psychologist's explanation of this "fit" between the energy levels of adoptive parents and children. She had used the example of the Thanksgiving dinner traditions of two large extended families. One family traditionally played football after dinner; the other played Scrabble. The kids in each family grew up knowing what was expected of them as they became part of the family tradition. For a high-energy kid in a football-playing family, everything feels natural, just as it does for a quieter kid in a Scrabble-playing family. But when you have a child who doesn't like to play football and is either forced to play anyway or is allowed to sit out (maybe reading a book), then problems can emerge. Other family members might interpret his behavior as being uncooperative and "not like us." Conversely, the kid who loves to play football would be just as noticeably different in the less energetic family. He would be squirming, unable to focus on the Scrabble game and dying to work off some energy—and the family might interpret all of this as uncooperative and "not like us." Of course the families still love their children, but there is an underlying recognition of difference, and when the different child is an adoptee, that can feel significant.

Then I started thinking about my own family, and the fact that there was a clear discrepancy between Jocelyn's energy level and the energy levels of the rest of us. Jocelyn is not hyperactive, and the rest of us are neither quiet nor sluggish, but there was a noticeable jolt of energy when she joined the family. My husband referred to her (with her "outsized zest for life," as he called it) as "the human plus sign," and she could be just as energetically unhappy when forced to do something that required sitting still. My husband and I were kept busy modifying our beliefs and approaches to what we had assumed was good parenting in order to accommodate the reality of this very distinct little person. With Jocelyn, good parenting meant things like understanding that a toddler—at least this toddler, unlike her sisters—just shouldn't be expected to sit happily at the table (not at home, not at someone else's house, and definitely not at a restaurant). Had my husband and I shared Jocelyn's energy level, we probably would have already known that.

Intellectually, I understand that high-energy children might fit better in a high-energy family and that the same is true for calmer children and calmer families. I also understand how completely appropriate it is for birth parents to pick adoptive families with whom they feel familiar and comfortable. It all makes perfect sense—except that if adoption agencies actually matched children with adoptive parents according to this metric, we would never have been matched with Jocelyn. And that makes no sense at all.

Before we adopted Jocelyn, I was part of an adoptive-parent support group made up of clients and fellow counselors. The group included mothers with children, aged newborn to six, who had been adopted from all over the world as well as through in-country infant adoptions. There were also a few birth children—including my two daughters—in the group. I thoroughly enjoyed socializing with these women and learned a lot from them and their children.

I also sometimes attended a larger gathering of adoptive mothers where speakers would share information and facilitate discussions. One discussion focused on the proper way to talk with a child about adoption—particularly about how to address your child's feelings of loss or confusion over not having "grown in your tummy." The consensus was that when children express this feeling, parents should soothe and cuddle them and tell them that they also wish that the child could have been in their "tummy." The mother and child could then bond over their shared loss. I wasn't an adoptive mom at that point, and everyone else seemed to be in agreement, so I didn't say anything. I had read similar things in books about adoption, and although the approach seemed a little odd, I couldn't explain why it bothered me.

Some years later, we adopted Jocelyn, and she grew into an energetic, outgoing, mischievous little four-year-old. She was not at all what I would call introspective and generally made it obvious when something was bothering her. Because of my work, we talked about adoption freely around our house, and we knew many other adoptive families—including our own extended family, with four of the eight cousins being adopted. (In later years, the number of cousins in the family would number eleven, with seven of them adopted and four of them Asian.) So Jocelyn just naturally amassed a lot of information about the subject.

Jocelyn knew the basics about where she had been born, how she had come to us, and that she looked different from the rest of us. The most complicated thing she knew was that she had a birth mother and that when she was born, her birth mother hadn't been able to take care of a baby and had decided on adoption. It was complex information for a four-year-old, and she didn't ask a lot of questions or express concerns until one day when she voiced the classic, "Was I in your tummy?"

I had always assumed I would say and do some version of what had been advised by other adoptive mothers. But the moment my daughter said that to me, I realized that telling her I wished that she had grown in my tummy was not only inaccurate but could be interpreted as saying that I wished she was a different child. The truth for her and for me was that her father and I had quite specifically wanted a daughter from Korea. We had made the deliberate choice not to have another child by birth primarily because I had always wanted to adopt a child from Korea. A child who had "grown in my tummy" not only wouldn't have been Korean—she wouldn't have been Jocelyn. I ended up telling her that she was exactly the child I had wanted and the child she was supposed to be. I also told her that I didn't know why it had happened that she had been born to her birth parents and then adopted by us but that, for us, it was exactly the right thing to have happened. And, most importantly, she was who she was, exactly the right person, because she had been born to her birth parents, not to us. There was a little further talk about how it was very, very hard for women who lived in Korea to have a baby when there wasn't a daddy around to help them, and that maybe her own birth mother had decided that she wanted her baby to have two parents to take care of her.

That sounds like a pretty complicated conversation to have with anyone, let alone a four-year-old, but it was actually quite brief, and off she went on her busy, independent way. There were no tears or cuddling—just big sighs of relief on my part for having figured out in the nick of time not to inadvertently make her feel as though I wished she was some other child.

About six months later, when she was five years old, I read Jocelyn *The Mulberry Bird*. We had already read lots of books about the process of adoption and had talked a bit about her own adoption, but this was the first time that the idea of birth mothers (in this case mulberry-bird birth mothers) was addressed in any depth. The book is about a young mother bird who is trying to raise her baby on her own because mulberry birds are the sort of birds where the father doesn't stick around. Although it is hard, she is doing well until a storm blows her nest to the ground, and she has to struggle to keep the baby warm and protected while also having to go off in search of food. Eventually, the baby gets sick, and the mother realizes that it will die if she doesn't get help, so she seeks advice from a wise owl. He tells her about some ground-dwelling birds that live far away (sandpipers, who according to the book raise babies as couples, so that one can look for food while the other stays and protects the baby), and she agrees to put her baby on the owl's back and let him fly the baby to them.

Jocelyn took in the story without question, no doubt registering the breaks in my voice and lengthy pauses while I collected myself. (I cannot read this book without getting emotional, even though there are some flaws in it, such as why not have the owl just fly the baby to a new nest, since single parenthood apparently works for mulberry birds most of the time.) I wasn't sure that Jocelyn even understood the book as a story about adoption because it doesn't actually use the words "adoption" or "birth mother." But when I was tucking her into bed, she told me that she thought that maybe now her birth mother "has a daddy and some other children." She went on to say "wouldn't it be nice of we could go and see her sometime and see her house and her beautiful garden." (It's all recorded in her "baby" book.) Jocelyn didn't say anything further that night about adoption, but she had clearly understood the essence of the mulberry bird's story. And she had clearly remembered our earlier conversations. At age five, there was obviously still a great deal she couldn't understand about the selflessness of a birth mother's love for her child (even when disguised as a mulberry bird). But I do think she got the message that birth mothers love their babies and that her birth mother had loved her. And that is a great way to start talking about adoption.

16

How to Talk about Adoption

TALKING TO CHILDREN ABOUT adoption is a lot like talking to them about sex: most parents find it stressful. This is largely because of our society-wide awkwardness about the subject, learned by adoptive parents along with everyone else. Although we don't usually think about it this way, our discomfort in talking about sex colors our conversations about adoption because adoption stories necessarily begin with the birth of a baby and the reality, no matter how heavily disguised, of people having sex. In a way, it can be easier for adoptive parents than for birth parents to talk to their children about "where they came from" because the abstraction of birth moms and dads "making a baby" is a step removed from the adoptive parents' own sex lives. But in other ways, talking with an adopted child can be more difficult, particularly when it evokes the suffering of infertility or other childbirth losses that the adoptive parents may have faced.

Adoptive parents often fear that they will make some sort of crucial mistake in the all-important conversations about adoption that will hurt or frighten their child, and possibly damage their relationship. Parents want specific instructions, preferably a script, to guide them through these talks. I don't have a script—there is no one-size-fits-all template—but I do have some suggestions based on things I have learned from the families I've worked with over the years and from my own experience as an adoptive parent.

1. Document the process.

Keep a journal during your adoption process. It does not have to be elaborate or eloquent; the facts will speak for themselves. When we were waiting for Jocelyn, I started a journal in which I would primarily record the various events along the way. It included such routine information as, "We sent in the immigration forms today" and "I made new curtains for your room," written as if I were talking to her when she would be old enough to understand. The journal also included more emotional entries, such as, "I stood over your crib for a long time today and imagined what it will be like when you are here." I am not usually a journal keeper, but I wanted Jocelyn to see that adoption wasn't simply a matter of the parents' putting their names on a list and then— voila!—a child appears. I wanted her to know how complicated and careful the process was, and how everyone involved was focused on taking such good care of the children. I wanted her to know how much we wanted her and how we thought about her every day of the wait. Not that I wrote every day—far from it—but I recorded the process faithfully. The journal proved to be far more important than I ever imagined.

When Jocelyn was a toddler, we would look at the journal and admire things like the pictures her sisters had drawn of what they thought she might look like and the cute invitation to her baby shower, without paying attention to the text. When she was about six years old—a non-mushy stage for her— we decided to read the book as a bedtime story. I read every word, and she paid attention to every detail. She heard about the preparation of her room, about all the interest and questions from friends and family, about her sisters' plans for her. She heard me say over and over again that I was so excited, that we were all so excited, that we could hardly stand the wait. She heard me get really mad when immigration lost our forms, and she heard me describe what it was like to see her picture for the first time. As I read to her, I realized that that little book, in all its mundane detail, was telling her how much we loved her. Normally, as a squirmy six-year-old, she wouldn't have allowed the expression of such sentiment, but she was all ears night after night. I had anticipated that the journal would be helpful in explaining the adoption process, but it was far more important than that: it was written-down, irrefutable proof of our love—any child could see that.

2. Create visual reminders/celebrations of the adoption.

These don't have to be elaborate in any way (although people are able to create fabulous personalized books these days). It will suffice to have a few pictures to look at and talk about together. Babies love to look at pictures of themselves, and I think the best, simplest way to introduce the word "adoption" to a child is with pictures. They could be pictures of the first time you held your child in the hospital, referral pictures from the agency, pictures taken at the airport when he or she arrived in this country, pictures of your family in the courtroom when the adoption was finalized, or pictures from a party celebrating that event. The important point is to have them available to your child and to display them where they can be appreciated. It will then be easy to make occasional comments like, "That was the day we finalized your adoption. We were so happy." That way, your child gets familiar with the word "adoption" before having any idea what it means and also gets the message that the word is associated with happiness. And you will never have to initiate the dreaded, "Sit down son. We have something to tell you" conversation.

3. Seize the moment, calmly.

The key to conversations about adoption with children is to be open, relaxed, and in the moment. It's almost never a great idea to sit down for "The Talk." That sort of approach just makes kids feel uncomfortable and tips them off that something awkward is about to happen. There are lots of good books about adoption for young children, but you have to be careful about your selections because there are lots of clueless books as well. My least favorite are those that reassure children that they're not flawed even though they were adopted. (It is amazing how many children's books have this slant.) They remind me of a book I saw once that was written for children who had been born by caesarean section in an effort to assure them that they were still normal. The book (and the parents who bought it) seemed to suggest that any "issues" the child might have were a result of their feelings of loss over not having had a natural birth experience, when in fact they were far more likely the result of being raised by neurotic parents.

Children typically don't have a great deal of interest in adoption until they have some idea about where babies come from or, in the case of interracial adoption, until they begin to notice that they look different from the other people in their family. The age at which they express interest varies widely, with some particularly sensitive and/or astute children asking questions almost as soon as they have the words to do so. The norm is usually between three and six, and the timing is greatly influenced by such outside forces as hearing about the arrival of another baby, either by birth or adoption.

The subject of adoption can also be brought up when your child listens to a book or sees a movie or television show that deals with adoption. Although not specifically about adoption, there is an abundance of children's movies in which the main character is a lonely child or animal in need of a family. Unfortunately, there is also an abundance of inaccurate and negative portrayals of adoption, and parents have to be careful—although even these can offer a chance for discussion and education. Often, it is helpful simply to say something like, "Wow, they sure got that wrong" when you see an incorrect portrayal.

The most important thing parents can do to encourage communication with their children is to create an environment in which adoption is talked about in a casual and informative manner, just like any other subject that is of interest to the family.

4. Prepare your child for conversations about adoption. (It's later than you think.)

Talk to your child early and give her the information she will need in order to be able to answer other people's questions the way she wants to answer them. This does not mean that you tell a young child all the details of her adoption story and then send her off to pass this information on to anyone who is curious. It's helpful to always keep in mind that your child's story is hers and that she alone should decide how and when to share it with others. Parents can encourage their children to be open and relaxed about the subject of adoption in general while still preserving the privacy of their personal stories.

A friend of mine who is also an adoption counselor told me about her experience with her daughter, who was adopted as an infant. When the little girl was about seven, the family moved to a new home, and she was outside playing with her new friends one afternoon. An older child apparently announced to the group that Julia was adopted—something that was not a secret. Then another child asked, "Why didn't your real mom want you?" Unfortunately, although Julia understood some things about adoption, she had no idea how to respond to this new idea that she had been unwanted or that her real mom was someone other than her mom. She came home crying, and her mother felt terrible for not having foreseen this situation, even though she regularly counseled other families about talking with their kids about adoption.

When adoptive parents talk about experiences like this, they usually focus on how insensitive other people can be about adoption. But we don't actually know that any of the children in this situation meant to be unkind. And even if they did mean to upset Julia, she was in a position to influence their attitudes if only she had known what to do.

I see at least two probable scenarios. The first is the one that resulted in Julia getting upset and the other children learning that adoption upsets people, specifically Julia. Now that the other children know how emotionally charged the subject is for her, they are likely to bring it up again, not necessarily because they are mean but because they are trying to figure out what the "deal" is with adoption. The second scenario is one in which the exact same things are said by the other children but Julia is able to respond to the question, "Why didn't your real mom want you?" by saying, "My birth mom was too young to take care of a baby." If she had had that answer prepared ahead of time, she would have been in a position to enlighten that whole group of children. If Julia hadn't gotten upset but simply answered matter-of-factly, the other children would not have come to the conclusion that adoption was an upsetting subject. Even if the other children were intending to be unkind, a calm response from Julia could have shown them that adoption was something she felt comfortable about, and it would have been eliminated as a subject about which they could tease her.

Clearly, it is asking a lot of a seven-year-old to educate the world about adoption and deflect possible bullying with one carefully chosen sentence. It is not, however, too much to ask of adoptive parents that they have conversations with their children that will help prepare them for people's natural curiosity about adoption. Even if Julia had been well prepared for this encounter, things might have turned out badly; but as it was, she simply had no tools to help her handle the situation.

5. All things in moderation.
Keeping the lines of communication about adoption open does not mean cramming the subject down your child's or anyone else's throat at every opportunity. It means that you handle the subject comfortably when it comes up, letting your child know that adoption is important and interesting to you but that you are not fixated on it. Most children don't like it when their parents make too big a deal about something, and they especially don't like being singled out or made to feel different. Artificially initiated conversations about adoption can trigger feelings of discomfort, and parents may mistakenly conclude that the adoption, rather than the parent's approach, is the problem. It is important to respect children's privacy and give them room to develop their own feelings about adoption and their birth parents. Parents need to understand that these issues can be quite separate from their own relationship with their child.

6. Silence is not golden.
Many adoptive parents tell me that their child has no interest in adoption because he never asks any questions. When the parents brought it up, the child seemed disinterested, so they now assume that if he wants to know more he will say so. I hear some version of this from all sorts of parents, including absolutely wonderful parents who would be happy to talk with their child if they thought he wanted to talk. I also hear it from parents who aren't comfortable talking about adoption, are clearly transmitting their discomfort to the child, and are relieved by the child's silence. But I do not believe that the silent children are not interested; I believe that they have gotten the message that something about adoption makes their parents uncomfortable, and they are nervous about finding out why this is true.

Adoptive parents should feel responsible for educating themselves, their children, and society in general about adoption. Attitudes have changed dramatically during my career, and they no doubt will continue to evolve. When I was a child, the whole subject of adoption was "hush-hush," the general feeling being that it was preferable for adoptive parents to avoid ever having to tell their children the (most likely shameful) story of their origins. I remember being about eleven years old and reading a "Dear Abby" column in which she controversially advised parents to be honest with their children about adoption, but not until they were thirteen and could handle the (again, shameful) truth. Any parent of a thirteen-year-old knows that that has to be one of the worst possible ages at which to confront a child with anything, let alone the fact that their parents have been lying to them about their origins for their entire life. Not only have they been lying—they also have been believing that adoption was such a painful, embarrassing, negative subject that they couldn't even acknowledge its reality to the child. The message the child eventually gets is that there is something about him (adoption) that is so bad that his parents couldn't even bear to tell him when he was younger.

What does a sensible child do after learning something like that? On the surface, he assiduously avoids the subject and shrugs off any further effort on his parents' part to engage in more conversation. Underneath, he has a million unanswered questions and worries. If the child is able to put on a good front, his parents will conclude that they have done their job, and he is just not interested in the subject. If he is less able to disguise his emotions, the parents will conclude that the child has been devastated by the fact of his adoption and will worry that their relationship has been damaged. And in a way it has—by their own prejudices and insecurities about adoption, which they have now passed on to their child.

7. Educate others, wisely.

When talking with people about adoption, it is worth keeping in mind two important points: (1) keep a sense of humor and perspective, and (2) take advantage of opportunities to educate.

While adoptive parents should be their children's advocates and defend them from harm, they also must be careful about assuming and handling insult. I remember one mom of four children of various races who talked about being in line at her local grocery store when the woman behind her said in what could have been a disapproving voice, "Are those children all yours?"

"Yes," she responded archly. "And they all have different fathers." The mother and the checker then laughed and the other woman said nothing further.

Depending on the intent of the questioner, that was either a brilliant riposte or a hurtful overreaction. If the other woman meant to be critical of

adoption or of interracial families, then the mother's response was an effective way to shut her up (and down) without encouraging further interaction.
But if the questioner's seeming disapproval was actually just awkwardly expressed curiosity, then nothing good was accomplished. By replying in a non-
defensive manner, the mother might have imparted a beneficial lesson to the
other woman. As it was, the other woman's embarrassment at this mother's
response might justify, in her mind, the feeling that interracial families are
unduly defensive or that mothers in these families are likely to have multiple,
short-term relationships.

In any event, a response generating more heat than light does little to
heighten people's understanding about adoption. My favorite image is of the
mother saying exactly what she did but then, after waiting a moment for her
comment to sink in, adding, with a smile, that she had adopted her children.
A good-natured response like that would have shown the other woman, and
anyone else who was listening, that she was secure in her parental role. Most
importantly, it would have shown her children that she knew how to handle
intrusive comments (whether or not they were intended to be offensive) in
a way that neither downplayed their importance nor let them escalate into
incidents that the children would find upsetting.

I know that most adoptive parents don't have a lot of extra time or energy
to spend on educating everyone they encounter who needs some educating
about adoption. We're generally much too busy to be able to drop everything
whenever the occasion arises in order to have the sorts of meaningful conversations that the subject requires. We have to pick and choose our moments
for these encounters, and we're not always going to have the right words on
the tips of our tongues. We're also not always going to have perfect control of
our emotions, and sometimes flat-out anger is both warranted and effective
in getting across the message we want to send—which is sometimes as quick
and unambiguous as, "Don't mess with me or my kid." Happily, overt public
disapproval of adoption isn't common, and people are much more likely to
find themselves in situations that are hard to read rather than clearly negative.

Adoptive parents need to keep in mind that these encounters can be used
not only to educate other people but to educate and strengthen their own
children and their own families as well. The parents' behavior and actions in
response to questions and comments about adoption will indicate to the child
how they should feel about these situations. If the parent assumes insult and
responds angrily or defensively, then the child gets a clear message that adoption is a subject that causes difficulty. If the parent assumes insult but reacts
calmly (though not passively), then the child gets the message that, while the
parent doesn't like what happened, the other person's behavior did not have
the power to threaten or anger the parent in a way that was upsetting to the

child. In other words, the parent retained control of the situation and of the message that their happiness and security as a family is in no way challenged by this person's ideas.

I don't want to give the impression that adoptive parenthood is beset by unpleasant encounters in grocery stores. I know there are many parts of the country where attitudes about interracial families are less favorable, but, happily, my family doesn't live in one of them, and we rarely encountered anything but approval. That doesn't mean there weren't opportunities to educate, though, even in situations that seemed benign. For example, one day shortly after Jocelyn's arrival, I took all three kids into a local children's shop. The women who worked there were always very nice and friendly and they gathered around to admire the new baby. It wasn't long before one of them said, "Oh, she's such a lucky little girl." Of course I knew there was no ill will in that statement, and the second-to-last thing I wanted to do at that moment was hurt the woman's feelings. But the last thing I wanted to do was miss the opportunity to say something that would help her avoid repeating that sentiment in later years, when Jocelyn was old enough to understand what it meant. I also wanted to correct the impression that we, or any other adoptive parent, had done some sort of favor for our children by adopting them. And I wanted to correct that misperception in front of eight-year-old Erin and five-year-old Caitlin in a way that was more meaningful than simply saying, "Oh no, we're the lucky ones."

So, much to the confusion of the women in the store, I went into a convoluted explanation about how I appreciated their intent but I wanted to let them know that it was important to me that they didn't see adoption as something that fortunate people do for unfortunate people. I went on to say (laughing) that if you wanted to get technical about it, the "lucky" children were Erin and Caitlin, who wouldn't exist without the assistance of their parents. Jocelyn, on the other hand, would exist and might very well have been sent to a much nicer family somewhere else.

It wasn't an unpleasant encounter, primarily because no one was acting upset, but I'm pretty sure it was a completely confusing encounter for those women. I don't think they really understood what I was trying to say, partly because I wasn't all that articulate and partly because the point is extremely subtle, but they were nice about it. To my mind, though, what was important had been accomplished; those women not only wouldn't say anything to Jocelyn about being a lucky little girl in years to come, but they would probably also think twice about saying it to other children who had been adopted.

Adoptive parents need to take extra care in educating extended family and friends about adoption since these people play an important role in their lives. With infant adoption, this can be done fairly easily. By the time the child is old enough to understand language, the various people who formerly said things like, "If her real mom could see how cute she is, she'd want her back" (with the implication that a birth mother could only relinquish an unattractive baby?) will have learned that this is not the way to give your child a compliment. This training can start even before you bring the baby home, with the simple use of a few key words. There's no need to introduce a lot of adoption jargon (which people, your child included, would no doubt find annoying), but you do need to advise people early and often to use "birth mother" (or whatever the favored terminology is at the time) instead of "real mother" or "natural mother" and to use "adopted" instead of "given up" or "given away."

It is usually sufficient simply to model the use of the words you want people to use, but if they don't seem to be catching on, you'll need to tell them directly what you want them to say. If they object or are forgetful, you can offer to lend them a good article or book on the subject. Remember that it takes time for people to learn new things, and others haven't been educating themselves about adoption the way prospective parents have been. But also remember that it is your job as a parent to do what you can to ensure that the people who are going to be part of your child's life will not say ignorant or hurtful things about adoption or race.

8. Honesty or protection?

Part of an adoption counselor's responsibility to the child being adopted is to elicit a promise of honesty from the adoptive parents, who are often asked to state in the home study that they agree to disclose the fact of adoption to the child and to give him or her accurate information about the birth parents and the circumstances of the adoption. Accepted policy is that all available information should be shared with the person who has been adopted at an age-appropriate time. Although families generally agree with this policy, there is no way to enforce their promise in later years or monitor the quality of the information the child is given. Like all other parents, adoptive parents are free to make decisions about how and when to tell their child whatever they want him or her to know, and I respect their parental authority, even though we may not always be in agreement about what is in the best interests of their child. The issue of full disclosure can be enormously complicated, and there are times when I have felt it did not necessarily coincide with the idea that "honesty is always the best policy." Honesty, and truth, can be elusive.

I had always assumed I was a proponent of full disclosure until the day I received a referral for one of my families, for a baby girl from Korea. A referral is the initial packet of information about a child that I would take to the prospective adoptive parents for review; it was thrilling, to say the least, to share their elation when they saw their child's picture for the first time. Normally, there is nothing worrisome in this information and everything in the referral packet can be happily shared with the child when she is older. Typical information in a referral would be about how the birth parents had not been in a good situation to raise a child and consequently had chosen adoption for a better future for their baby. But this referral said, "The young birth mother died in child birth while screaming in agony."

It was painful to read and hard to imagine any possible benefit in having this image forever embedded in the child's mind. It is enough simply to know that the birth mother died. I also came to realize that I didn't completely trust the information in those referrals. After all, most of them sounded practically identical; initially written in Korean and translated into awkward English, they sometimes contained judgmental descriptions such as "bar girl." The people who wrote them could make mistakes and misinterpretations just like anyone else. I rejected the idea that the few words that someone had written down about this birth mother should be seen as the absolute and overriding truth of her life, eclipsing all else in the child's mind. The person who wrote that statement hadn't been present at the birth, or the death, so what did he or she really know about the quality of the screaming? And why was it important to describe a birth mother as a "bar girl" rather than as a loving daughter, great cook, good storyteller, wonderful sister, beautiful singer, or any of the other qualities she might have had that would be far more important in letting the child know what she was actually like?

Another situation giving me pause about full disclosure involved a birth mother who said that she had been raped. She was Caucasian, married to a Caucasian man, living in a southern state, and expecting a biracial baby. I remember a discussion with the prospective adoptive parents about how one talks with a child about rape. And in that conversation, it occurred to me that we actually knew nothing at all about the father, not even his name. All we really knew was that the woman told us she was expecting a child that wasn't going to be her husband's biological child, and she wanted to plan an adoption and hopefully preserve her marriage. Given that set of facts, it seemed at least possible that the pregnancy resulted from indiscretion rather than rape. Of course, it is true that women who are raped sometimes do become pregnant. It is also true that women who want to plan an adoption and fear that the birth father will prevent them from doing so can avoid his legal involvement in the matter by saying that they were raped and do not know the identity of the father. Although it is illegal, and grounds for overturning the adoption if the father finds out what she has done, women who fear the father will cause them or the child harm or difficulty sometimes do take this approach. These two examples in which "full" disclosure was possibly less than the full truth are mercifully rare, and in most cases, honesty really is the best policy.

Adoptive parents of infants these days go through a home study process in which the importance of early and open communication is emphasized, and they are usually pretty well prepared to talk with their children about adoption when the time comes. This understanding and preparation is less common when a child is being adopted by a stepparent, primarily because the counselor's involvement comes after family relationships have been established—as has the story about how they came to be a family.

A too-frequent scenario when I'm doing a home study for a stepparent adoption is to be sitting in a kitchen with a couple in their early thirties, their one-year-old on the mom's lap and the seven-year-old boy—the one being adopted by the stepfather—coming in and out of the room. Three hours into the meeting, with the child now quietly playing nearby, we have gotten through the adopting dad's biography, the history of the couple's relationship, the circumstances of the seven-year-old's birth, and the couple's views on child-rearing. Now we start discussing one of the most important parts of this type of home study: whether, when, and how the family plans to structure the child's relationship with the birth father and other paternal relatives in the future; how to handle questions the child has if the birth father is absent from his life; and how to explain the adoption process to him. Parents sometimes tell me at this point that the child does not know about the adoption, and if he finds out the stepfather isn't his "real father," he will be devastated, and it will irrevocably change their relationship.

The parents seem oblivious to the fact that the child can't possibly have avoided hearing much of our conversation, and that even in the unlikely event that someone else hadn't already tipped him off, he now knows that the father he lives with is not his biological father.

Parents can be enormously clueless about what their children know, but in these situations, the desire to hang onto ignorance about this particular subject is astonishing. Parents convince themselves that they are preserving the child's innocence, even in situations in which everyone else in the family, including same-age cousins, knows that he has a different birth father. It is particularly odd when the stepdad didn't meet the child until he or she was about three or four years old. Yet I know many such families who cling to the belief that the child is unaware. It is delusional thinking on the part of the parents, and it can be extremely hard to convince people that they are not doing their child any good—rather, that they are doing a lot of harm by not talking honestly with their child.

I fully understand why a woman who was, say, in an abusive relationship with the birth father of her child would want to distance herself and the child from that person. And I understand why a loving stepfather would want to keep his family safe from the abusive birth father. But creating a false story is more likely to create difficulties for the family than to protect it. The first message the child should be given is simply that his birth father wasn't able to be a parent. As time goes on, and depending on what memories the child has and whether there is contact with the paternal birth family, the amount of information can be augmented. No matter how much or how little information about the birth father's situation or behavior is shared with the child, he or she needs to hear something positive about this person as well. Even in situations where the birth father is actually dangerous (and there will be no contact), it is usually possible to find something positive. The child has undoubtedly inherited admirable qualities that can be attributed to the birth father, even if they were all from recessive genes.

Parents can talk honestly with their child about a birth parent's problems without seeming to condemn him or her as a person. If the parents seem too harsh or judgmental about birth parents, they run the risk of inadvertently encouraging the child to identify with them and/or to feel the need to defend them. This can be a huge issue during teenage years when it is important that parents not set the stage, in essence, for their child to assert his or her independence by reaching out to a birth parent who is not a good influence. A primarily negative message from the parents about the birth parents can have an effect on the child that is opposite the hoped-for one. This does not mean that parents shouldn't be honest about problems. They do have to prepare their child for the reality of the birth parent's situation, but they should try to do it with compassion rather than condemnation.

Another area in which openness and honesty can get complicated for adoptive parents is when the child has memories of an abusive birth parent. I worked with one family who adopted a five-year-old and his two younger siblings, who had been voluntarily relinquished by their birth mother. She had been under scrutiny by Child Protective Services after several episodes in which one or another of the children suffered mysterious illnesses requiring hospitalization but defying diagnosis. The doctors suspected Munchausen's Syndrome by Proxy—in which a parent either causes, exaggerates, or invents symptoms of illness in a young child in order to get attention or sympathy or to feel superior to medical professionals—but they had no proof. That was provided over time by the five-year-old, as he grew to trust his adoptive mother. In her effort to help him adjust to his adoption, she had talked a lot about how his birth mother must have loved him a great deal to have made the decision to allow him and his brothers to be adopted. This adoptive family enjoyed an open relationship with the birth mother of another one of their children—a young woman they admired and respected—and they were trying to present the new birth mother in the same favorable light. But gradually, the little boy began to voice objections to the idea that his birth mother had been so loving. Eventually, he revealed that she had forced him and a younger sibling to drink dishwashing soap (so she could take them to the hospital with symptoms). Although the birth mother had told the boy that drinking the dishwashing soap was a punishment, and apparently he felt that he sometimes deserved punishment, he knew that his baby brothers did not, and he had come to his own conclusion that their birth mother was not, in fact, a loving person. The adoptive mother was horrified by what her child had gone through, but she was heartened by the fact that he felt comfortable sharing his feelings with her. She decided that honesty was the only approach that made sense in this situation, but she still did not condemn the birth mother as evil; instead, she talked about how the birth mother's behavior had been bad and how glad she was that the boy was now safe from that treatment.

9. Document contacts with birth parents.

In this era of open adoptions, a child is likely to have contact with the birth parents before he or she is an adult, and it is important that birth and adoptive parents who have an open relationship agree about which information is shared with the child, and at what age. Both the birth parents and the adoptive parents are entitled to privacy and autonomy in this matter. Just as biological parents don't share all the details of their own relationship with their child, so birth parents should be able to use their own judgment about which personal information they want to share, and when they want to share it. And adoptive parents, who know their child best, should be able to make decisions about how and when information is shared with their child when he is young, although at some point it will be important for them to step out of the decision-making role with respect to information and contact with the birth parents. Adoptive parents will need to use their best judgment to determine at what age they feel their child should have full access to all available information, including upsetting and possibly inaccurate information. It is not easy to decide the right time and the right way to share this sort of information, nor is it easy to find the right balance between protecting your child from painful information and always being open and honest with him. There are no hard-and-fast rules about exactly when and how to have these conversations since each child and each situation is unique.

In the past, it was usually fairly easy to establish a mutually comfortable level of communication between birth and adoptive families, and for both families to maintain control over their interactions. But the Internet has changed things dramatically. Now it is not unusual for adoptees and birth parents to contact one another via Facebook, and this can sometimes lead to difficulty. I was recently contacted by a girl whose birth mother I had worked with seventeen years earlier when the adoptee was a few months old. The birth mother had turned thirteen shortly before the baby was born, but she looked more like a frail ten-year-old. She and the baby were staying with an aunt and uncle and a number of cousins, all of whom were encouraging adoption, and the girl clearly had no ability to provide for herself or for a child. The baby seemed as delicate as a tiny bird, but she was alert and beautiful with enormous bright eyes. Because the birth mother was a minor, she was assigned a guardian ad litem and given legal representation, but even with that help, she was too young to fully comprehend the situation either legally or emotionally. Her aunt walked her through the steps of choosing a family, and she wisely selected an extremely kind and loving couple. After the placement, the birth mother returned to her family in another state and went back to middle school. She did not keep in touch with the adoptive family, although they would have welcomed an ongoing relationship with their daughter's birth mother.

Seventeen years later, when the birth mother was only thirty, she contacted the daughter through Facebook. At first, things went well, and the daughter enjoyed communicating with cousins and other family members as well as with the birth mother. But it wasn't long before it became obvious to her parents that something was troubling their daughter. It turned out that the birth mother had told the girl that the adoption had never been legal because the birth father had not known anything about it and therefore could not have given his consent. The implication was that the adoptive parents had taken part in a semi-black-market adoption against the wishes of the birth parents. The girl was understandably upset about this possibility; when she confronted her parents, it became clear to them that, even with their reassurance, their daughter still felt confused and concerned about how everything had been handled.

It was also clear that the adoptive parents had suddenly found themselves in an adversarial role with the birth parents, and that their daughter was essentially being asked to choose sides. Fortunately, the lines of communication in this family were wide open and included lots of talk about adoption. Even so, the situation was difficult and upsetting enough to make them seek counseling.

Happily, the situation was largely resolved when I shared my old case notes with the girl. They indicated that there had been phone conversations between me and the birth father, and also between the attorney and the birth father. It became clear that the man had known about the baby and had willingly relinquished his parental rights. The girl and I were also able to talk about the fact that her birth mother had been so young that she had probably not fully comprehended everything that had happened. Perhaps the birth father, who was in his early twenties at the time, had told the birth mother that he had had no involvement in the adoption in an effort to distance himself from any responsibility for his illegal relationship with a minor. The girl, her parents, her nice and reasonable boyfriend, and I talked for hours about various possibilities, none of which included either the idea that her birth mother might be trying to cause trouble or that her parents might have taken part in an illegal adoption.

I encourage adoptive families to keep copies of all correspondence with birth parents. Generally, this consists of letters or email messages the parents have sent to birth parents about the child's growth and milestones, what he likes to do, and how much he is loved, along with pictures of the child and of significant events in his life. These communications are full of the sort of detailed information (and bragging) that only people who love a child would be interested in. Put it all together and you have a thorough and thoughtful record of childhood that will be treasured by the child and adoptive parents as well as by the birth parents. It will also serve to let the child know that his parents were respectful and inclusive of the birth parents and will stand as a record if there is ever a dispute about this.

One couple I work with, Lucia and Scott, has been doing a fabulous job of communicating with their children's birth parents for the past nineteen years. Every six months since her now almost college-aged children were born, Lucia has sent a packet of pictures and a long letter to the four birth parents of her son and daughter. The twelve or so pictures are always arranged in order so that you easily see how the child has grown. They are also numbered and come with an attached sheet of paper detailing exactly when the picture was taken and what is happening. The letters are five or more handwritten pages that go into a lot more detail about the children's interests and activities. They are well written (Lucia is a teacher), but they aren't overly elaborate. Mostly, there are fun and interesting things to report, but there are also times when the letters share news that a child is struggling in school or with health problems. Lucia writes these letters exactly as though she were writing to a friend. And she keeps writing them despite the fact that she has heard back from only one of the birth parents, on only one occasion.

Lucia and Scott's adoptions took place before email and various photo-sharing websites made it a simple thing for adoptive parents to share information with a child's birth parents. These days, most people who have ongoing contact do so through texts and photo websites. Most families adopting now likely will end up sending far more pictures than Lucia has over the years, but I doubt any of them will do it with more care and goodwill. She could have switched to email a long time ago and saved herself a lot of time, but there would not be a handwritten "hard copy" record had she done so. There is something special about handling the actual piece of paper on which a letter was written. I feel certain that Lucia has created a family treasure for the birth parents, for her and Scott, and, most importantly, for the children. The letters make it abundantly clear that these children are well loved and that Lucia and Scott have done a wonderful job of honoring their commitment to the post-placement contact agreement. The relationship they have with their children's birth parents is right there in black and white, and there will never be any confusion about how honest, respectful, and caring toward everyone Lucia and Scott have been. What an amazing job they have done of talking to their children about adoption.

17

A Homeland Tour

Honoring Your Child's Heritage

WHEN JOCELYN WAS THIRTEEN, our family was able to take a trip to Korea. I told the girls ahead of time that this wasn't going to be a vacation (our vacations were typically weeklong stays at a hundred-dollar-a-week cabin on the wild Washington coast, extremely rustic and relaxing). This was going to be an experience.

What an understatement. There is so much to say about that trip, and my husband and middle daughter said most of it in articles they wrote for *The Seattle Times* shortly after we returned home. They did such an amazing job of capturing our "experience" that I decided to share some of what they wrote rather than recreate the story in my own words.

Here are excerpts from the article my husband wrote in October 2000.

Jocelyn's Family: A Journey

As our group of sixteen families made its way through our two weeks in Korea (looking almost constantly for faces that looked like our children's), a theme, of sorts, emerged: The more emotional and sentimental the parents grew, the less moved the children seemed to be. To judge from their outward demeanors, the kids were on a lark, their parents on a crusade. On our bus, the kids would sit in the back listening to music and chattering while the parents would be staring lugubriously out the window, memorizing the environment that had yielded their children.

We were driving, at one point, through the outskirts of Taegu, birthplace of Jocelyn and three other kids in our group, and I was lost in trying to imagine the lives and struggles of the people there when I heard a boy's voice from the back of the bus say brightly, "I'm really into Wu-Tang . . . hey—there's the bridge I was abandoned under . . . I'm really into Wu-Tang because. . . ." On several evenings, the families gathered in the hotel bar in Kyong-ju to take in a lounge act—two Asian singers singing American country and pop standards in English—and on one of those nights the kids were horsing around near the stage, while the parents sat at tables talking among themselves. Thirteen-year-old Julia Strang went up to the singers, requested a song, and rejoined the kids' party. No sooner did "Somewhere Out There" (the song her mother would listen to as she danced with Julia's referral picture and waited for her arrival) begin than her parents, Elaine and Bryce, and all the parents around them burst into tears as Julia resumed cavorting with her coevals.

It seemed that the Koreans we encountered often were as emotional as we adoptive parents were. Many of us were approached by Koreans asking us to tell the stories of our families, and explain why we had come to Korea. The story of Korean adoption is widely known—and widely debated—in Korea, largely viewed there as a national tragedy, part of the misfortune that unfolded after the nation's division in 1953. Those in Korea who believe that a stable, loving home, no matter where it is, is the most important thing you can give a child view Korean adoption as enlightened social policy; others in Korea view it as a shameful loss, akin to the forced separation of families in the wake of the Korean War. We were walking through an open-air market in Cheju City one afternoon when a woman with a little shoe stall looked at us, then turned to my wife, Anne, and asked, pointing at Jocelyn, "Daughter?" When my wife nodded, the woman ran over to Jocelyn, hugged her, and said in English, "Welcome back!"

By coincidence, we had arrived in Korea two days before one hundred people from South Korea, and one hundred from North Korea, were allowed to fly over the Demilitarized Zone and meet with family members from whom they had been separated since 1953, the year the Korean War ended and the border between the two halves of Korea was irrevocably sealed. For the next three days, Korean television broadcast reunion footage around the clock. It reminded me of the United States in the wake of the Kennedy assassination—every television everywhere was tuned into the reunion. It was a powerful context in which to be staging our reunions with Jocelyn's roots; we felt as if we were part of the same national story. And indeed, we were to find out later, we were: Calls to our adoption agency from birth parents seeking information on the children they had relinquished over the years increased by several hundredfold during the reunion days.

It was with considerably higher than expected emotion, then, that we boarded a bus one day for Taegu to meet a social worker from Holt Children's

Services, the agency that had arranged Huh Ok-Kyung's adoption. Our guide was scheduled to take us to the clinic where Jocelyn had been born. She met us at the Taegu bus station, introduced herself as "Mrs. Kim," loaded us into a waiting taxi van, and took us on a long drive through the city that culminated in a district called Bong Buk Dong. It is a broad, busy street lined with little shops and sidewalk vendors, with a cavelike labyrinth of an open-air market.

Mrs. Kim led us into a narrow alley and past a tiny restaurant, a tailor's, a beauty parlor, a dry cleaners and some other little shops, and brought us to a halt outside a tiny temple with a little metal gate. Here, she said, is the site of what had been a small obstetrics/gynecology clinic in 1986. It was here that little Huh Ok-Kyung had been brought into the world. I stared at the gate, then looked up and down the alley, videotaping, photographing, memorizing the sights, and trying to conjure the sounds of the clinic thirteen years ago, when the noises of traffic and marketing and bustling had been suddenly punctuated by our new baby's louder-than-life cry. I stood there stupidly, almost numb, not sure what it was I was feeling. Then I turned and looked at Jocelyn; she was blushing deeply and sporting a massive, hilariously outsized grin. It's the look she gets only when she is tremendously moved: a smile so much bigger than her face that it looks like something she's trying to hide behind.

By the time the day came for us to visit Holt's Seoul office and view Jocelyn's files, we all started coming down with the jitters. One of the older girls in our group had found her birth family and the reunion had been intense, to say the least. At the Holt's office we were ushered into a little room where we looked through Jocelyn's files, which turned out to contain nothing we hadn't already known. We added an album of pictures of Jocelyn and a letter for the birth mother to the file, in the hopes that someday she would be able to learn what had happened to her daughter, and might be reassured at finding what a happy and healthy girl she had grown up to be.

Then it came time to meet Jocelyn's foster mother, Shin Hae Soon, who had cared for her in her home for the first three months of Jocelyn's life. Huh Ok-Kyung had arrived in Seattle a clearly healthy and well-loved baby, and we had been anxious to meet Shin Hae Soon ever since we first laid eyes on our new little girl. When she walked into the room, Shin Hae Soon proved to be a tiny, shy woman who was clearly excited and moved at the prospect of seeing our Jocelyn. We noticed that she was carrying baby pictures that we had sent eleven years ago, and that she had kept them in pristine condition, like treasured relics. She came in and sat down, hugged Jocelyn, and began babbling and stroking and studying her hand as if it were the most amazing thing she had ever seen. Jocelyn had weighed only five pounds at birth, and now towered over her foster mother.

As she sat there fondling Jocelyn's hand and wiping away tears, we were told that only two percent of Korean adoptees ever return to Korea, and only one percent of them while still children. And Shin Hae Soon told us that Jocelyn was only the second to return among the scores of babies she had nurtured over seventeen years. When we gave her a photo album of Jocelyn's life, she hugged it as if it were Jocelyn herself.

Note to American adoptive parents of Korean children: Write to your foster mothers!

We were to spend the afternoon with Shin Hae Soon, first at the Holt offices, then during lunch at a nearby restaurant, then visiting her and her family in her home, where Jocelyn had spent her first three months. Jocelyn and Shin Hae Soon kept looking at one another and smiling fondly as if they'd spent the better part of Jocelyn's life pining away for one another.

The day proved to be an amazing, moving climax not only to our trip but to the journey we all had commenced the day Jocelyn was delivered to our home.

Back home a few days later, I found myself wondering what would stand out in Jocelyn's memory. Watching video of the trip that evening, we viewed again the face of the foster mom, Jocelyn's mother and sisters in tears, and Jocelyn with that massive double-decker grin. I looked over at her, covertly watching her watch the tape, and saw that same grin again. And I saw it then not only as an appropriately grandiose expression of her emotions about the trip and its revelations, but as a symbol as well: She is an American adolescent, rife with outsized emotions that she won't be able to articulate until she grows into them. Her heart and soul, like that great grand grin, are simply too big, at the moment, for the rest of her.

* * *

Jocelyn did change after that trip. It's not easy to be self-confident at thirteen, but she suddenly exuded a calm and self-possession that we hadn't seen before. Of course, part of it was the result of articles that appeared in the newspaper, her week as "cover girl" of *Pacific Magazine,* and the resulting "fame encounters," as she called them, when people she didn't know would tell her they had enjoyed reading about her trip. But I think her new attitude was more a result of her pride in discovering that Korea was an amazing country and that she had strong roots there.

Jocelyn's pride in her heritage was perfectly timed to correspond with her school's culture fair. She came back from Korea with a wealth of information and was eagerly looking forward to sharing it. We had been through the culture fair with Erin and Caitlin, each of whom had done a project on one of their great-grandmothers, and I had been extremely impressed not only by the presentations I had seen but by the fact that they seemed to have such a positive effect on the kids' self-esteem.

Jocelyn decided to do her project on her foster mother, Shin Hae Soon, and use this woman's story to talk about the Korean War and Korean adoption. Imagine her dismay when her teacher told her that she couldn't do it because Shin Hae Soon wasn't her relative. The teacher said that part of the project involved interviewing the subject (something our older daughters had never done with their long-dead relatives) and that Jocelyn wouldn't be able to do this with Shin Hae Soon. The teacher suggested instead that Jocelyn write about her mother, me, and my adoption experience. When Jocelyn told me about this, I decided there must be a misunderstanding and told her to go back and try again. When the second request was unsuccessful, I called the teacher to explain just how much this project meant to Jocelyn and why I felt it met the parameters of the culture fair. It was, after all, called Culture Fair, not Family History Fair or Appreciate Your Relatives Fair. The teacher still wasn't convinced, but did agree to discuss it with the department head. Incredibly, that woman agreed with the teacher and the answer was still no.

Finally, I wrote a detailed letter to the principal and school counselor explaining why it was so important for Jocelyn to be able to honor her foster mother and her own Korean heritage, and they gave her the go-ahead. We were relieved and happy but were also thoroughly dismayed by the fact that it had been so difficult to accomplish something that seemed so obvious and desirable. Jocelyn's project turned out to be a beautiful tribute to Shin Hae Soon and Korean adoption, and her report, along with the heartfelt comments people wrote to her about it, are among our most precious family treasures.

School projects that focus on genetics and heritage issues are often viewed as complicated for adoptive families, but they certainly don't need to be seen as embarrassing or confusing or in any way negative. Children who have been adopted don't relinquish their heritage in the process. These children and their parents should be encouraged to value and celebrate the "input" they have gotten from both their birth and adoptive parents. I suspect Jocelyn's teachers thought that her desire to do her project on her foster mother somehow dishonored her true family (us)—a sadly antiquated view of adoption that is still held by a lot of people.

People who adopt children from different cultures need to help them develop a positive identification with their country of origin. This isn't easy for the average American family because most of us have little opportunity to experience the child's original culture. As I explained in my letter to the school, "Our family was hugely blessed this summer by being able to take a trip to Korea. We were further blessed by meeting Jocelyn's foster mother and her family. Jocelyn fairly exudes pride in her cultural heritage these days. . . . We are absolutely thrilled that she wants to share her foster mother's story (and by extension, her own pride in having been part of such a wonderful family) with her classmates. What possible reason or benefit could there be for denying her this opportunity?"

No one at the school made any attempt to answer that question. I hope that the experience served to educate those two teachers, but I suspect that because we ultimately were forced to go over their heads, they were unhappy with us, and unmoved.

We encountered only a handful of awkward and/or frustrating situations over the years in dealing with our schools. Teachers and staff were virtually always helpful and reasonable—with one exception that is in retrospect, comical. When Jocelyn was going into first grade, we requested that she be assigned to a Japanese American teacher. Caitlin had been in this woman's class, and we knew she was a wonderful teacher, but that wasn't our most important consideration; the fact that she was Asian trumped everything else about her. Erin had been all the way through the relatively small elementary school by this time, and Caitlin was in the fifth grade, so our family was well acquainted—and extremely happy—with almost everything about the school.

I knew that requesting a specific teacher was a touchy subject, and that you had to have a good reason if you wanted to do this. You also had to phrase your request not by using the teacher's name but simply by describing the qualities in your child that warranted this special request. To me, the opportunity for an adopted child in a different-race family to have a teacher who shared her racial heritage was about as good a reason as any that I could imagine. So I wrote a letter saying that I wanted my child to have an Asian teacher. In response, the school social worker called me in frustration, saying, "Anne, you can't request a teacher by race!" The implication was that I was somehow gaming the system or perhaps was politically incorrect. I tried to explain how important it would be to Jocelyn to have a same-race teacher and how this was a rare opportunity for her to establish a meaningful relationship with an Asian woman at an especially impressionable age. Assigning Jocelyn to this woman's class seemed obviously and enormously beneficial, but the social worker wouldn't commit.

I suspect I would have taken this battle all the way to the governor if need be, but Jocelyn finally was assigned to the requested classroom (there was a one-in-three chance anyway), and nothing more was said about my inappropriate request. The following year, I requested another Asian teacher, by race, not by name, and Jocelyn was put into her classroom without comment. There weren't any more Asian American teachers in the following grade-school years, but those two women had done a fabulous job of being Asian at a time when that alone did Jocelyn a world of good. They were also wonderful teachers.

A final note: when Jocelyn was in middle school, the district hosted a conference on adoption, which the school social worker and I attended. I was heartened to discover that requesting teachers by race, for a child of the same race, was now accepted as not only legitimate but also enlightened policy.

18

A Sister's Journey of the Heart

AND HERE ARE CAITLIN's comments on the trip to Korea . . . and on her little sister. This article was published in the *Seattle Times* in 2003.

Coming Home: A Sister's Journey of the Heart
By Caitlin Moody

Hey, you. Hey, Joss, Jawz, Jossie, Joey, JoJo. Jocelyn Okyung Moody. Hey, pal. Jocelyn. The young one. The third one. The last one. After Erin, after Caitlin, there is Jocelyn. Okyung. The infant you. The Korean you. The you with a mysterious biology. Was your mother athletic, too? Did her eyes weigh with the same intensity? Or your father? Are those his broad feet? His thick, straight hair, whispering red in the summer, blue-black in the snow? Who gave you the dimple? The petite nose and tiny moles you so lament? Moody. A last name. A family name. Your family name. Not to mention a certain trait in each of us. The talking you, the hearing you, the reading, writing, singing you. Your humor and your laughter. Your poetry. Your temper, or at least the resulting flow of curse words. It's your "I love you."

Just like mine, your first word was "Mom." I taught you the alphabet on the same scratched, green easel during lesson after lesson of "school." In our living room. In our pajamas. You sitting like an eager puppy, brown toes tucked under your new big-girl pants. "A, B, C, G, L-M-N-O-P." Tripping over the same letters I frustrated Erin with so many times when I was the student. Different from the arrangements of lines, curves, dots and strokes they taught us, or tried to teach us, every summer at Korean Culture Camp.

Before you could speak, Erin and I were singing "Old MacDonald" in Korean, dancing in hanboks, and holding colorful fans. Looking at the camp pictures now, two white and fleshy faces pop out from the sea of smooth tan—a hundred Korean adoptees smiling back at the camera. We didn't notice then, never felt strange. Not at five or at eight. Did you ever notice it at that age?

I still think it's a little ironic you went to camp only a few times yourself. By the time you were old enough, I guess Mom had decided we'd all been sufficiently "cultured." Or maybe she was just tired of the long trip into Seattle. Either way, you seemed to be more than well-adjusted. We talked so often and so positively about Korea and adoption, you had taken to asking Erin and me about our birth mothers. Entirely confused by our answers, you would search us for the joke and then feign an understanding. It was evident from your look that you felt terribly sorry for us, either for being so ignorant or for truly missing such a crucial part of life. Sure we had Mom, but no birth mom? We even looked the same. How boring.

Mom may have been right about the TV. It did make us fight sometimes. But it did worse things than that. Erin was fourteen already; I was eleven. I remember a day near the end of summer that had us home while Mom was in Seattle. Erin was already immersed in *Jerry Springer* when we sunk down onto the other sofa, ignoring the grass stains on our shorts and the mud on our bare feet. Jerry was talking to members of the Ku Klux Klan. We sat and listened to a man in a purple robe and sorcerer's hat tell the audience about the natural superiority of his race, the white race. Uninterrupted, he told us of the hatred he felt—we should all feel—for less-evolved, inherently savage, dark-skinned races. I think you were too young to remember. "Caitlin," you were still looking at the TV, "does he hate me?" I hope you were too young to remember.

You started looking. In the Nakatas' grocery store you would tap Mom on the leg, "Look, Mom, an Asian like me!" So we all started looking. Everywhere we went. "Hey, Joss, there's an Asian. Oh, and over there, there's two." You loved it. It was like our own little road-trip game: Spot the Asians.

We talked about a trip to Korea the way we talk about everything else: "Definitely someday. Maybe after Dad's next book."

So yeah, I was as surprised as you were when we boarded the plane at Sea-Tac—taking you back. Taking us with you. Thirteen years after your first flight and thirteen hours before landing in Seoul.

You didn't sleep the whole way there. I know, because I couldn't sleep, either. Exhaustion made the experience of maneuvering through the airport just that much more disorienting. But you were wide awake.

In the city, we immediately drew stares. An American family strolling through the crowded streets, craning our necks, saying nothing. It was the ultimate Korean Culture Camp, and we were all there.

Our second day out, winding through stand after stand of fresh fruit and dried fish in the covered market, you accidentally bumped into an older man. He turned and began scolding you in rapid Korean as you stood speechless. Appearing terrified, you returned to where the rest of us were standing, then immediately erupted into a grin I'd never seen on your face before. "He thought I was Korean!"

Mom couldn't stop scrutinizing every face we saw. Looking for your features. Looking for you. She cried when we saw the building where you were born, back behind the fish market. It's now a Buddhist temple.

After a few days, you were moving easily through the sidewalks and market, floating ahead as if holding an invisible pass. Remember the woman in the Cheju market? We were walking together past her stand when she stopped us—stopped you. Gripping your shoulders, she looked close into your face, then looked over at Mom. "Mother?" she asked, and you nodded. Her eyes filled with a smile that took over her intense expression. "Welcome back!"

The next day was the reunion of one hundred North and South Korean relatives separated by the division of the country. Apart for nearly fifty years, this small sample of families was allowed to meet in the Demilitarized Zone for one day as a sign of good faith, before returning to their respective sides. Every reunion was being televised on every channel, and every South Korean was watching.

I was watching you. Family after family fell together sobbing, touching each other's faces, some fifty years older than their memories. Your eyes were attached to the screen in our hotel room, twenty stories above the traffic lights. I wondered if you were looking to find something familiar. I wondered if you knew the immensity of what you saw. I knew that you felt it. But were you feeling it because of history? Sympathy? Empathy? Biology? All of these?

Yes, when we met your foster mother, I could see that it was all of these. Sitting in the upstairs office of the orphanage, your orphanage, we waited with our photo album and gifts. Shin Hae Soon had arrived, they told us, but she was collecting her nerves and emotion before entering the room. Twenty-one foster children, and you were the first to return.

As soon as she stepped into the room, all her collecting was washed aside. Seeing you once, the tears took over. Her wiry four-foot-ten-inch frame taking you into her arms like the infant she remembered. She touched your hair, your face, your tummy.

She'd brought you that set of underwear—white with pink dots—the customary gift for a daughter on her thirteenth birthday. But American food had made you much bigger than the thirteen-year-old Korean girl she'd expected. Later, in the hotel room, we all laughed as you put the underwear on the only place they'd fit—your head. And we laughed harder when you put on your new hanbok, made of unbelievable silk with intricate embroidering, the underwear still pulled over your long, black hair. The perfect reconciliation: your body draped in exquisite, traditional Korean elegance; your head squeezed into a pair of cotton underwear, laughing to tears.

I had to leave the day you went to visit the Demilitarized Zone. I was flying straight to Los Angeles to start school, and wouldn't see you again until Thanksgiving. It felt strange leaving you there. I was boarding my second leg of the round-trip flight, but you had already completed yours. Your next flight would be another takeoff, another beginning. Walking away from you with my bags, I didn't turn to wave, wanting no one to see the tears that invaded my eyes for the first time, betraying my nonchalance.

Mom called me when you all got home. I was doing fine, a little fuzzy, but fine. I showed pictures of the trip to my new friends, but they were difficult to explain. I couldn't describe how different you looked in the pictures. How the quality of your expression was new, mature, fuller. I couldn't define it for myself, let alone for people who'd never known you.

When I came home for Thanksgiving, Mom had put the map of Korea on the kitchen wall next to the one of the U.S. We told aunts and uncles and cousins and grandparents stories from the trip while we stuffed ourselves with turkey, sweet potatoes and pumpkin pie. You can always eat the most pumpkin pie.

I still get to laugh occasionally when someone new sees your picture and, after pausing to be sure it's politically correct, they manage, "So she's adopted, right?"

"No," I begin, "it was the strangest thing"—but I never take it too far. Then I get to tell them how you're the only Korean varsity player in your basketball league, and fill them in on your musical aspirations as "Lil' Asian the Rap Sensation." You always give me good material.

So anyway, I guess I'll let you go. I just wanted to say hey.

Hey, you.

19

Awkward (and Worse) Encounters for Adoptive Families

ONE THING THAT CAN CATCH interracial adoptive families by surprise is the emergence of awkward misconceptions years later, when the adoption and the drama surrounding it are all but forgotten, and family members no longer expect people to remark upon it.

One lovely summer day, for example, Jocelyn, who was then twenty-one, and my husband took the ferry into downtown Seattle together. They were on their way to the Korean Consulate to get her a passport so that she could spend the summer in Seoul. It was the summer after her junior year in college, and she had gotten an internship with the City of Seattle Engineering Department. Incredibly, Seattle was working on a project with a professor at Seoul National University, and immediately upon Jocelyn's accepting the internship, her boss asked if she would be willing to spend it in Korea.

My fifty-eight-year-old husband (a man with such a kind face that he used to be told he looked like Jesus, and whose appearance once rattled a middle-aged golfer so thoroughly that she gasped at the sight of him and then joked about "meeting my Maker") was wearing jeans and a T-shirt, typical Northwest garb. Jocelyn, who was planning to meet friends for dinner in Seattle after the appointment, was wearing a bright red summer dress and sandals. As they boarded the boat, they noticed that a middle-aged woman was glaring at my husband. He turned in confusion to Jocelyn, to see if she noticed, and saw that she was barely managing to stifle a laugh. At which point my husband realized that the only reason this woman could imagine for a young Asian woman to be with an older Caucasian man was as his consort. She could not envision this lovely young woman as the beloved child that she actually was but instead saw her as the embodiment of exploitation.

Such stares, while not frequent, are certainly disquieting, and this proved not to be an isolated event. There were more such glaring incidents; and one day when Jocelyn and my husband ran into an acquaintance he had not seen for more than twenty years, the man asked, "Is this your wife?"

When Jocelyn was little, things were wonderfully different. When she rode the ferry with her father, they would both be bathed in the approving attention of strangers. The women who worked on the ferry dubbed themselves her "ferry godmothers" and would gather around to admire her whenever she was aboard. People didn't treat me that way when I was with her, but something about the father/charming daughter combination drew their affection. My husband used to joke that it was great for his ego to go out alone with her.

So it was a difficult adjustment to find himself an object of scorn, but, characteristically, easygoing Jocelyn thought her father's discomfort was pretty hilarious. Hopefully, the glaring woman figured out her mistake and learned something about pre-judging, even though, in truth, she was statistically more likely to have been right than wrong, and in that light, her disapproval was understandable, even laudable.

Uncomfortable encounters like these are inevitable, and adoptive families need to learn how to deal with them in positive ways. Ideally, their responses will serve to inform and educate others. It would have been great if my husband and daughter could have said or done something (like have her loudly call him Dad) that would have quickly clarified the situation and made everyone feel better. But one rarely has a great response available just exactly when it's needed.

During most of Jocelyn's childhood, people were pretty oblivious to her heritage. A favorite family story is about how her middle-school basketball coach, a Japanese American man who knew our family well, had a serious talk with her about her prospects as a ball player in high school. He concluded that her natural abilities as an athlete would be aided by the anticipated growth spurt "because your dad is pretty tall." Even after she started laughing, it took him a minute to understand what was so funny.

As with many interracial adoptees, it wasn't until she left home that Jocelyn started to really be identified primarily as Asian rather than as a member of our family or just as herself. She went to college in Massachusetts, where Korean adoption is less common than it is in Seattle, and discovered that no one, even upon learning her name, assumed that she was a Korean adoptee with Caucasian American parents. So she spent a fair amount of time educating the people she got to know about foreign adoption. One of her first stories along these lines involved the boyfriend of her first roommate, who recommended a movie to her one day.

"You'll really like it. It has all kinds of kung-fu fighting and stuff," he said. "Well, . . . I may look Asian . . . "

Things were weirder when she tried out a couple meetings of the Korean Student Association and discovered that she had nothing in common with the people there. In retrospect, this is puzzling, since she had been able to establish a number of good friendships with Korean women during her summer in Seoul, but it was nonetheless true, and she felt that her behavior and demeanor seemed boisterous and inappropriate compared to the other female students. (The fact that they were all engineers probably skewed things a bit socially.)

Jocelyn played soccer during her college years and was rewarded for her efforts with Most Valuable Player awards and team captain designation in her junior and senior seasons. She made close friends on that team and thrived on the competition of intercollegiate soccer. My husband and I took a five-day vacation to the East Coast each fall during Jocelyn's college years so that we could watch a few of her games. We were able to attend the last game of her junior season, against the team that led her school's division.

It was senior night for a number of the girls, there was some extra emotion on the field, and things seemed a little rougher than normal. Just before the end of the first half, which was scoreless, we were startled to see Jocelyn blatantly elbow an opponent and send her flying. The ball was nowhere near them and the referee apparently didn't see what had happened. There was some buzz in the stands, though, and we exchanged "What's up?" glances with the parents around us. A minute later, there was another ruckus on the field and this time the ref ejected one of the seniors on Jocelyn's team, a gentle girl who had played for four years without a single foul. She came off the field in a rage, and the whistle blew for halftime. The second half of the game was without obvious drama, but clearly something was amiss, and, although the other team won, they didn't seem to be celebrating their victory. Neither team was smiling.

The trouble had apparently started early in the game with a lot of trash talk, but the defining moment came when a pretty little blonde snarled, "Get off me, you Chink!" at Jocelyn, who reacted with the thrown elbow. She had then told an amazed teammate what had been said, and that girl had reacted with anger that quickly spread to the whole team. When I heard all this, I was furious and wanted to confront the girl, but Jocelyn assured me that that would be unwise. The tension was alleviated by an African American friend of hers, who ran up to Jocelyn as we were leaving the field, "You are so lucky! So lucky! I've waited all my life for someone to call me 'N*****' so I could take them out!" Jocelyn and the teammates around her laughed heartily, while the parents . . . well, none of us knew quite how to react, although the tension in the air had immediately lifted, for some reason.

Jocelyn's coach and the athletic director asked to meet with her the next day, after my husband and I would be on our way back home. Jocelyn called just as we were boarding the plane to tell us that the incident was being taken seriously, that a report was being filed with their athletic conference, and that the other school would be expected to discipline the offending player, who was also a team captain. Jocelyn was surprised—and, ultimately, gratified—at the response. Eventually, she received a letter of apology from the girl, who was suspended for the rest of the season—a suspension that may have caused her team, which had been favored to win that year's conference championship, to suffer a season-ending loss in their next game.

I don't know what sort of long-term effect these punishments had on that girl or on her teammates. I don't believe for a minute that she hadn't used racial slurs before, as she claimed in her letter, or that she wouldn't be using them again. But I do think that she and her teammates, as well as the girls on my daughter's team and any other soccer players who heard about the incident, would now think twice about using racial slurs in a college game. It also sent a message to anyone on those teams who might have thought that using racial slurs wasn't a big deal. And the aftermath meant a great deal to Jocelyn.

There were other lessons for her to learn as well. The nicest one was about how immediately and thoroughly her teammates, her coach, the athletic director, and various other friends and acquaintances had come to her defense. It was also nice to learn that those little platitudes the refs say before games about the importance of sportsmanship actually mean something. And it was nice to learn that, this time, bigotry and thoughtlessness were trounced.

But there was also a lesson to be learned that wasn't so nice, because most of Jocelyn's life won't be happening in a well-regulated soccer game. The next time someone says something rude to her, it's more likely to be on the street or in a bar. Not only won't there be a ref, but if she throws an elbow she'll be the one who ends up in trouble. Her friends will probably (and probably wisely) urge her to calm down, and there will be no procedure for airing her grievances.

We did not bring our daughter up to expect racist encounters, nor did we give her any more than the most rudimentary information or advice about how to handle them. As Caucasian parents, we know that we were limited in these areas, and our efforts no doubt fell far short of ideal. We had the good fortune to have been able to raise her in a community that valued her Asian heritage but, at the same time, rarely acknowledged it. She had to be the one to assert an interest in identifying herself as Korean, to embrace both the genetic and environmental influences in her life, and to understand that they have been equally important in making her who she is.

One argument against interracial adoption holds that Caucasian parents can't adequately prepare their minority children for life in a racist society—

and I agree that we have a deficit there. We don't have personal experience or family tradition from which to draw lessons. When I'm doing a home study for a Caucasian family who wants to adopt a child of a different race, they often tell me that they don't care about race or "don't see race." I know that they think they are saying that they are not prejudiced against any other race and that they will love and welcome any child they are fortunate enough to adopt.

I don't doubt at all that they will love their child, but families need to understand that "not seeing" race is not a quality that will make them good adoptive parents for a different race child, or good citizens in a multiracial society. It is vital that they not only see their child's race but also that they embrace it and understand that it is an important part of their child's identity. "Not seeing" race is essentially to dismiss its importance, a stance that may prove relatively comfortable for most of the family while the child is young but will be far less comfortable for the child as he or she interacts with the outside world—a world that does see race.

It's clear that the sort of counseling adoptive parents get about this issue, which is a required part of the home study, cannot possibly replace a lifetime of experience as a member of a racial minority, but it can help to make parents more informed and competent in the face of racial insult. Adoptive parents may not handle things in the way a parent of the same race would, but that doesn't mean their approach will necessarily be insensitive or ineffective. As is true in so many aspects of life, the fact that something is different doesn't make it inferior.

By this standard, I'm not sure how we measured up as parents. But Jocelyn did say something that seems both revealing and troubling in this regard. At the beginning of the conference process with the athletic director, while updating us on how it was playing out, she suddenly said, "They picked on the wrong Asian this time—the one with white parents." There are many layers of meaning to interpret in that statement, but she might also have said, "The one with white privilege."

20

Jocelyn's Birth Mother

JOCELYN IS NOW TWENTY-NINE years old, the same age her birth mother was when Jocelyn was born. The information we received from Korea in January of 1987 (Jocelyn's referral packet) contained information about her birth and her first two visits to the doctor. We were also told her birth parents' ages, level of education, and occupations, and there was a brief statement written by a social worker indicating that her birth mother had "parted from the natural father" and "relinquished her parental rights toward the baby, wishing to have the baby adopted into a loving family for the baby's desirable future."

This was all we knew until Jocelyn was six years old. She had developed pretty severe asthma at age five, and after one especially grueling period in which she had pneumonia seven times, we were desperate for any information about her health history. We had been told that if a child had medical concerns, the family could write to Holt Children's Services to ask if there was anything in the file about the birth parents' medical histories that might prove helpful. In response to our letter, we received half a page of additional information from Holt. We learned that the birth father was a reserved and quiet man with a roundish face, masculine physique, and a double eyelid. The birth mother was described as outgoing, with an oval face and medium shape. The agency could provide no medical history information, which was unfortunate, but what they did provide we treasured, and we accepted the idea that they had sent us everything they felt we should have from Jocelyn's file. This was confirmed for us on the trip to Korea when Jocelyn was thirteen and we were allowed to meet with a Holt social worker and review her file, at least the part that wasn't confidential.

Jocelyn returned to Korea by herself in the summer after her junior year in college. She had been hired by the City of Seattle Engineering Department and sent to Seoul National University for a summer internship. It was incredibly good fortune in regard to her career and an even more incredible opportunity to reconnect with Korea in a truly meaningful way. Her supervising professor and his staff were gracious and kind, and immediately included Jocelyn in their social lives. She was invited to go on long hikes (sometimes by moonlight) with the professor and his friends, most of whom were in their sixties and seventies and were still energetic hikers and climbers who had no trouble scrambling up the steep mountainsides near Seoul. Jocelyn also went on shopping trips with the young women she met and to restaurants and bars with a group of graduate students who socialized frequently. She played soccer with a group of international students (all men) and was disconcerted at first when she realized that people were stopping to stare at the spectacle. Jocelyn's women friends explained to her that they had loved to play soccer when they were young but had been forced to stop at puberty. They assured her that it was okay, if unusual, for an American to be seen playing soccer with men, but for Korean women, that sort of thing was out of the question. They didn't think that people were having any trouble distinguishing her from a "real Korean woman."

Jocelyn's friends at the university all seemed interested in her status as an adoptee, and one especially sweet and helpful woman offered to accompany her to the Holt offices and serve as a translator. Jocelyn was hoping to meet again with her foster mother, and she was wondering if there might be any other information about her birth parents that the agency was willing to share with her. Attitudes about birth parent confidentiality had changed a bit over the years in Korea, not as much as they had in the United States, but enough so that it was possible to raise the subject again without seeming disrespectful. At the very least, Jocelyn wanted to make sure that the agency knew that she was interested in contact if her birth mother ever sought information from them about her.

Jocelyn had a wonderful visit with Shin Hae Soon, her foster mother, who was delighted to see how she had grown and thrived and that she was now working with an esteemed professor at "the Harvard of Korea." The social worker at Holt didn't share any additional information but she did point out that among the information we already had was Jocelyn's birth mother's national ID number, a number we hadn't realized had any significance. She suggested that since there had been no contact from her since Jocelyn's birth, the birth mother might not welcome it now, but that if Jocelyn wanted to pursue the matter further she might engage the services of an investigator named Mr. Lee. The social worker told Jocelyn that although Mr. Lee was "a very diligent man," she would need to be patient.

The group of graduate students was hugely excited about this development, and some of them wanted to take matters into their own hands. They told Jocelyn that they knew people who worked for the government and could trace an ID number and urged her to let them help with the search for her birth mother. Wisely, she decided that she would not take them up on this offer, as well-meaning as it was. She felt strongly about following the proper procedure, as determined by Holt, and she felt even more strongly about not taking any action that had the potential to hurt or embarrass her birth mother. There was one person, an older friend of the professor's, who told Jocelyn that he felt that she should not try to contact her birth mother. In private, he explained that in his own family a child had been relinquished for adoption and, out of respect for his mother, no one ever spoke of it. The man had tears in his eyes as he talked about his younger brother, who now lived somewhere in the United States. It was obvious that he wanted very much to have information about his brother and to be reassured about his well-being, but it was also obvious that any discussion of this subject within the family was absolutely forbidden. It was slightly less obvious that this man, along with much of Korean society, still believed that this silence was for the best.

So Jocelyn waited. For the first few weeks after engaging the services of Mr. Lee, it felt as though news of her birth mother would come at any moment. But as the weeks turned into months, it became clear that the search wasn't going to be just a matter of connecting a name to an ID number. It was discouraging, and in an effort to amuse her little sister, Erin, disguised as Raymond Chandler, sent the following message to Jocelyn:

Lee sits at his desk in a smoke-filled office, smoking. It's night. His jacket is off, his sleeves rolled up to his elbows. He's diligent, but distracted. There's something in the air. He can sense it.

A shadow passes outside his door. It stops. It reads the lettering on the milky glass: Mr. Lee, Private Eye.

Lee waits. He takes a drag on his cigarette.

He waits some more. He exhales. He's diligent. Maybe too diligent. But he can't concentrate. Not like this. Not with that shadow, whoever it is, lurking outside. Come in or scram, he thinks.

Lee gets up. He walks to the door, opens it.

It's a dame.

She looks up at him.

She's young, a kid really . . . couldn't be more than 21. She looks sad though. She walks past him, into the office. Lee watches her back.

The quiet's getting heavy. Better break it, Lee thinks. "Why the long face, kid?" he asks. Most Koreans have really round faces.

She looks up at him, then away. "Funny you should ask," she says. Her voice is soft and low. The kind of voice dames have in the pictures. "That's what I'm trying to figure out."
Lee smiles. This one's a tough nut to crack. She's going to make him work for it. He likes that. Maybe it's his diligence . . . who knows? "You stick with me, kid. You stick with me."

Jocelyn sent it on to us in her next email along with her own message saying that the story had made her laugh so hard she cried. Over time, we all gradually stopped thinking so much about Mr. Lee and what he might be finding out.

After another eight months had passed, Jocelyn again emailed the Holt social worker, who wrote back to say that she remembered Jocelyn clearly and that she had been checking with Mr. Lee regularly. She told Jocelyn that Mr. Lee had contacted hundreds of people who could be her birth mother, mostly through letters and some phone calls, but no one had come forward. The social worker told Jocelyn that she had postponed writing back because "deep down, I wanted to believe that if I waited long enough, something new and interesting would turn up. Each time I have to share disappointing news with adoptees, it makes me feel bad (and sometimes sad)."

And that was that. There has been no further news, nor do we expect there will be. It is probable that none of the women Mr. Lee contacted was Jocelyn's birth mother, but it is also possible that one of them was and that she made the decision to remain anonymous. Perhaps she has decided that, for her, silence really is for the best.

* * *

Americans began adopting Korean children after the Korean War when stories about homeless and orphaned children began to appear in widely read U.S. news magazines such as *Life* and *Look*. The people featured in these articles were usually kindhearted soldiers and the adorable children they had befriended. Their stories were written in a manner meant to elicit sympathy from the American public and encourage them to send money and supplies to help care for the suffering children. But there was a backstory that didn't get much publicity. As has been true throughout history, when there is an occupying army, there are going to be sexual relationships (some consensual, some not, and many quasi-consensual when women are forced by poverty into prostitution) between the occupiers and local women. This was true for American soldiers after both world wars, but the offspring they left behind in European countries were able to be assimilated into their mothers' culture in ways that the "G.I. babies" in Korea were not.

Mixed-race children had no place in Korean society. They were outcasts, and their desperate circumstances were impossible for some of the American soldiers to ignore. Through the fence around their military bases, these men could see children as young as three or four years old in rags, digging through the garbage, hoping to find something to eat or something that could provide a little warmth or shelter during the cold Korean winters. (In one camp, the soldiers helped out by digging tiny individual foxholes in the dirt hillside for children to crawl into at night. One man recalled how both charming and heartbreaking it was to see their beautiful little heads pop up out of the holes in the morning.) The children's suffering was evident, as was the fact that their fathers were likely to have been among the warm and well-fed men inside the base.

As is also true with occupying armies, their leaders had no incentive to acknowledge the reality of the children their soldiers had fathered, and there was essentially no organized action on the part of the U.S. military to care for them. Fortunately, there were individuals who felt different about America's responsibility to these children, most notably Harry Holt, an Oregon farmer who, with his wife Bertha, was moved to take action that prompted both Korea and the United States to allow the Holts to adopt eight mixed-race Korean children. The Holts went on to establish an orphanage and adoption agency in Korea, change U.S. immigration law so that children could be adopted by American families, and set a precedent for international adoption that has been used (and sometimes abused) in numerous countries around the world.

I had been fascinated by Korean adoption since I was a teenager, but I didn't really know much about it until I started my job at WACAP in an era when the majority of international adoptees were babies and young children from Korea. After working in the foster care system, in Michigan, I had developed strong views about how harmful it was to allow children to spend so many years of their lives in uncertainty. I saw more than a few situations in which children were placed in a foster home at birth, returned to the birth parent periodically in hopes that things had improved, suffered years of abuse and broken attachments, and were rarely "freed for adoption" before age five. This was about as good as the system got in those days. People who asked me about my new job in international adoptions often wanted to know why Korea had so many children needing to be adopted. Why couldn't the country take care of its own children? I frankly hadn't thought a lot about the answer to that question and was just happy that it seemed the Koreans had figured out that it was in the best interests of all children that they be adopted as infants rather than as traumatized five-year-olds. In contrast to the U.S. system that practically mandated extended foster care, the Korean system looked like enlightened social policy to me.

But a commitment to "the best interests of the children" was not exactly what prompted the Korean government's support of international adoption. Korea was a patriarchal society in which the father's name established a person's entire worth, and there was no tradition of adoption of "worthless" fatherless children within the country. The Korean government's support of international adoption was largely fueled by attitudes about racial purity and a cultural unwillingness to accept mixed-race children as members of Korean society. It was also fueled by attitudes toward single mothers, their desperate financial situations, and the lack of any sort of social-welfare program or policy to help them. After the war, when the entire country was struggling, it was understandable that there simply weren't enough resources to help all the people who needed help. But as Korea regained its economic footing and then began to thrive, it was hard to understand why governmental and societal attitudes about helping those less fortunate, or about domestic adoption, hadn't evolved along with the economy.

In 1986, when Jocelyn was born, it was unacceptable for a woman in Korea to raise her baby as a single parent. An unmarried pregnant woman knew that not only was there no aid available from the government but also that she and her baby, and probably her extended family, would suffer social and economic hardship if she kept her child. This might come in the form of lost jobs, ineligibility for schooling for the child, and ostracism from other people in their community. It was simply true that women in this situation felt that their children would be better off in adoptive homes, and both the Korean and U.S. governments agreed with them. The idea that there should have been some sort of assistance given to these mothers, short of helping them to give up their children, seems to be a relatively recent concept to much of Korean society.

It is an unavoidable reality for adoptive parents that our families and our joy in our children are often made possible by their birth parents' sorrow. We are not only privileged to have become our children's parents, but we are also privileged to be in a position to provide the "loving care for the baby's desirable future" that their birth parents hoped they would find—just the sort of loving care that the birth parents would have provided themselves if they had been able. We hope they somehow know how treasured their children are and, as five-year-old Jocelyn said, we hope that their birth parents "have a daddy now and a beautiful garden" . . . or whatever the components of a good and happy life would be for them.

Jocelyn is married now, to a man of French and English heritage, and they hope to start a family one day. That mixed-race baby is going to be among the most eagerly awaited and well-loved children on the planet.

IV
ADOPTION CONNECTIONS

21

Our Own Adoption Agency

B Y 1991, I HAD BEEN WITH the World Association of Children and Parents
for ten years and was filled with appreciation for the agency and its accomplishments. For most of my years at WACAP, I believed that private—or
independent—infant adoptions, in which a family hires an attorney to handle
all legal matters, were likely to be less ethical than agency adoptions because
the lack of a counselor for the birth parents in the former suggested that their
interests might be overlooked. But as I grew more familiar with people involved in private adoptions (usually other adoption counselors and attorneys
I met at conferences on open adoption), my opinions evolved. I could see that
agency-versus-independent arguments were sometimes driven on both sides
by ignorance about how the other side operated and were likely to be fueled
by each faction's desire to discredit the other's approach and win clients at the
other's expense. I also came to understand that there was room for both types
of adoption and that there were pros and cons to each of them.

Formerly, it was believed that agency adoptions could provide a more predictable time frame and a safer process than could private adoptions, while
private adoptions were often faster, less costly, and more open. But as traditional agencies began to acknowledge the demand for openness, and as there
were fewer babies available for adoption, agency and independent adoption
grew more and more alike, with agencies being the ones to make the greatest
adjustments—particularly in regard to openness. Both types of adoption were
governed by the same laws and ethics, but now agency adoption was adapting
in order to stay in a game in which birth parents held most of the cards and

often saw no need for an agency's involvement. As birth and adoptive parents grew more comfortable with openness and with each other, independent adoption grew, making it increasingly hard for traditional agencies, with their set ideas and high fees, to compete—even though independent adoptions, lacking a fixed-cost structure, sometimes turned out to be even more expensive than agency adoptions. But the perception of lower costs, combined with greater control over the process, made independent adoption attractive to both birth and adoptive parents.

My time at WACAP and with the Options program had given me a solid understanding of birth-parent and adoptive-parent counseling and a rudimentary understanding of the business side of adoption. It seemed that the primary business-side problem at Options was that it had grown dramatically during five years under a federal grant, and when that source of funding expired, the program had to support itself by raising fees at a time when adoptive families and birth parents were being drawn to independent adoption. There just didn't seem to be a clear advantage to either birth or adoptive parents in working with a large adoption agency and taking on their part of the costs of maintaining it. While an agency's reputation might be reassuring, people were less willing to pay for that reassurance as stories of successful independent adoptions spread.

My concerns about Options and where it was headed came to an end when I accepted a position as social work supervisor for a new adoption agency that handled things differently. It had been started by two adoptive mothers (Dee Talarico and Nita Burkes) who had astonishing energy, good business sense, good timing, and chutzpah. The fact that one of them was a sculptor and the other a ski patrol volunteer, and that they each had two young children at home (one of them with significant special needs), hadn't deterred them from their goal of operating an adoption agency. They had adopted their children independently, had learned a lot in the process, had been informally advising other prospective adoptive parents, and had eventually decided they wanted to be getting paid for their work. Although it seemed improbable, given their lack of credentials, Dee and Nita kept plugging away and eventually obtained the same child-placing agency license as those held by large, well-established agencies.

Although their new agency, Precious Connections, was licensed as a child-placing agency, there was a crucial difference in their approach: legal custody of babies went directly from the birth parents to the adoptive parents instead of to the agency first, as was customary at the time. This distinction pleased both birth and adoptive parents and reduced the overall legal and financial risk to the agency. Legally, Precious Connections adoptions were handled like independent adoptions rather than agency adoptions. Families contracted separately with an attorney—usually one of four in Seattle, all of whom were members of the American Academy of Adoption Attorneys—and the agency handled all other aspects of the adoption.

Since Dee and Nita weren't counselors themselves, their license stipulated that they be supervised by someone with a master's degree and some years of supervisory experience. Ours was a fruitful partnership, with me benefiting from their business sense and willingness to rise to whatever challenge came along, and them benefiting from my professional experience and credentials. We operated as a team of three for several years. Then Dee, who had recently given birth to a third child, decided to focus her energies elsewhere, and another ex-WACAP counselor, Patti Beasley, became a co-owner of the agency, along with Nita. Some time later, Nita also decided to leave. I had never aspired to own an adoption agency, and I didn't see myself as having either the knowledge or the interest required of a small-business owner, but nevertheless was excited at the opportunity that had more or less dropped in my lap. In 1990, Patti and I renamed the agency Adoption Connections (no connection to the various other agencies with either identical or extremely similar names that emerged around the country in later years).

Our work with adoptive families generally started with the home study, the creation of the family profile, and then writing and placing ads in various newspapers around the country. In the early days of the agency, before the Internet, families placed ads in newspapers, and an investment of a few hundred dollars would often yield at least a few calls from prospective birth mothers. We placed most of our ads in free newspapers in states where adoption laws were favorable to independent adoptions. Often, the people who responded to the ads hadn't been specifically searching for an adoptive family by reading the newspaper, but a particular ad had caught their eye. If they were pregnant, or knew someone who was pregnant and didn't feel able to raise the child, the ad might start them thinking about adoption as an alternative.

Callers were usually women who had just discovered that they were pregnant and wanted to explore their options, or they were women who were in the later stages of pregnancy and had made up their minds (or thought they had) to do an adoption. Sometimes we would talk to callers and then not hear back from them and assume they had decided against adoption only to hear from them again late in the pregnancy when they were "ready to go ahead." One memorable call came from a woman who told me that she had seen a family's ad six months earlier, when she was newly pregnant. She hadn't been considering adoption at that point, but something about the ad prompted her to tear it out of the paper and put it in her wallet. Now she was calling to see if there was any chance that the family was still looking for a baby because she had made the decision to do an adoption and she was still thinking about them. Needless to say, that adoption felt fated.

You never knew at first where these calls would lead—to elation, disappointment, or anywhere in between. I worked with one family, for example, who placed a ninety-dollar ad in the Tulsa, Oklahoma, *Little Nickel* shortly before Christmas, a notoriously bad time to advertise; they got a stunning return on their investment. They connected almost immediately with a couple who wanted to relinquish their nine-month-old son, and the adoption proceeded smoothly. Only a few months after it was completed, the birth parents called the adoptive parents again, with the news that the birth mother was three months pregnant and wanted to know if the adoptive parents were interested in adopting the new baby as well.

They were.

Few families managed such a quick-and-easy adoption, but this type of advertising was how most of our families connected with birth parents in the early years of the agency, and it was generally the case that if a family placed an appealing ad, someone would respond and they would eventually become parents.

In later years, families began advertising on the Internet and investing $1,000 or more in creating a profile that could be easily found and seen by an enormous number of people. While this was much more efficient in terms of reaching a broader array of potential birth mothers, it came with a significant downside: not only did the greater exposure seldom lead to a faster or smoother or less expensive (or more ethical) adoption—it also led to a dramatic increase in the number of responses we received from scammers. (More about that later.)

After the initial flurry of activity in preparing a family for adoption and getting their ads in place, the excruciating wait for the phone to ring would follow. Families put the agency phone numbers in their ads so that we could take (and screen) the calls for them. In our first conversations with a prospective birth parent, Patti and I would explain who we were in relation to the family placing the ad, answer questions about adoption and about the family, and then take whatever next step was indicated.

We learned early on to identify ourselves to callers as "adoption specialists" rather than counselors because most callers didn't seem to see themselves as someone in need of counseling. We also learned to downplay the fact that we were an agency because many callers equated an agency adoption with a loss of control. Birth parents were reassured when we told them that legal custody of the child would go directly from them to the adoptive parents, and that they controlled the process—and the destiny of their child—throughout the pregnancy, birth, and eventual decision on whether to go ahead with the adoption.

After that first call, if the situation seemed promising, we would usually arrange for a conversation between the caller and the adoptive parents. I would always wait anxiously to hear from both parties after their first talk. Sometimes the conversations didn't go well, and sometimes concerns came up—an unwilling birth father, for example—that made an adoption seem unlikely. Other times, the call would seem to go well, but the caller would never call again. Remarkably often, though, things would go very well, and the birth and adoptive parents would both report back to me with delight and the desire to proceed with planning a possible adoption.

A surprising number of referrals and adoptions proved to be serendipitous. Placing ads in newspapers was only one way for prospective birth parents to become aware of Adoption Connections. They also learned about us from attorneys, medical professionals, other adoption agencies and counselors, school personnel, other adoptive parents, birth parents who had had a good experience with us, and still other sources. When prospective birth parents came to us through a referral rather than in response to an ad, we would talk to them about all the families with whom we were working at the time.

Our families also sometimes benefited from the ads that other families placed. When it was apparent to us that a caller responding to a particular family's ad was going to be a poor match with them, we would talk with her about not only that family but also about other, potentially more promising, families. One birth mother, for example, wanted her baby adopted by a family practicing a particular religion; another wanted adoptive parents of a different race from that of the family whose ad had prompted her call.

In such cases, we would secure the advertising family's permission to talk with the caller about other families. Patti once worked with a very blond adoptive couple who were adamant about wanting to adopt blond children. At first glance, this seemed unduly picky (and likely to require Patti to put in many extra hours trying to find them the right match), but it turned out to be a blessing; the ads the blond couple placed resulted in successful adoptions by two other families, with each adopting wonderful, non-blond children. Eventually, the blond couple was able to adopt several blond babies, and they were not only spared any guilt feelings over their preference for children who looked like them, but also took a great deal of pleasure in knowing that they had played a part in helping the other families find their children.

Some of our Adoption Connections families found children through sheer luck—being in the right place at the right time. In addition to being co-directors of Adoption Connections, Patti and I had private practices as counselors, and we often did home studies for families who were not signed up with our agency. It sometimes happened that one of these families had the precise quality that a birth mother responding to another family's ad wanted. For example, I worked with one young woman whose baby was going to be part Hawaiian native. She had looked at all our waiting families, but there was no match that felt just right to her. Coincidentally (mysteriously? marvelously?), I was in the middle of completing a home study for a family in which the wife was of Hawaiian native heritage. I hadn't had time to fully prepare the couple for an open adoption, but the birth mother was due soon, so we all decided to go ahead and set up a meeting. They loved each other, and everything went smoothly toward a happy adoption.

This sort of random good luck was surprisingly frequent; there were more than a few times when someone would call about a baby who had already been born, Patti and I would start contacting families . . . and fate might simply take the form of the first family to answer when we called.

Sometimes everything would happen in a rush. One morning, a hospital social worker on a nearby island in Puget Sound called to say that a baby had just been delivered and to ask if we could get there immediately, as the mother wanted to do an adoption. We jumped in the car with a handful of family profiles and went to meet with the birth mother, who was in her mid-thirties, had kept the pregnancy a secret from her family, and was determined to keep the adoption secret as well. She claimed that she didn't even want to look at the profiles we had brought but wanted us to pick the adoptive family for her. I explained that if that was the case, then we would go with the family who had been waiting the longest and asked if she wanted to see their profile. She agreed, looked it over, and declared them to be "fine." That gave us an opening to ask if she wanted to try for something more than "fine," and she cautiously accepted our pile of profiles. To our relief and delight, she looked carefully at them all, then settled on a couple she seemed genuinely enthusiastic about. Patti and I left the hospital late that night, just managed to catch the last ferry off the island, and arrived home tired but happy. Obviously, we were happy for the adoptive family, but we were also happy for the birth mother and tremendously grateful to have been able to provide some comfort and reassurance to a woman who was expecting neither.

More typically, we found ourselves working with birth mothers for many months before they made their decision. The process was slow and careful, as it should be, and we got to know both the birth mothers and the adoptive families well as we navigated the endless highs and lows characteristic of adoption.

Sometimes our successes took the form of a birth mother deciding that she would be able to raise her baby after all. One nineteen-year-old couple, on their way to college, were certain throughout the pregnancy that adoption was the right choice, but were struggling with the decision and continued to struggle after the baby was born. On Day Three, still insisting that they planned to go through with the adoption, they wanted to meet with me a final time before going to court. I asked them at our meeting to tell me how they envisioned their futures, thinking they might say something about the education and careers they hoped to have. Instead, they each talked about their desire to be together and settle in the community where they lived, to eventually buy a house with a little land where they could do a lot of gardening, and to have at least two children. After a long silence, I finally asked, "Then what are we doing?"

The couple did get married, getting a lot of support from his parents while they grew up a bit more and figured out how to handle things on their own. Some years later, I saw that lovely young mother walking down the street with a new baby in a carrier on her chest and her little first-born boy by her side, and it looked to me as though that hoped-for future was being realized.

We also dealt with monumentally bad outcomes. One prospective birth mother was a fourteen-year-old girl who was prevented from completing an adoption by the abusive, alcoholic mother of the birth father, a seventeen-year-old boy who was afraid to stand up for his own right to decide what should happen for his baby. The girl had no choices other than to become a parent at fourteen or to hand her baby over to a family she knew could not properly care for him. She ended up keeping her baby, and the birth father (in practice, the alcoholic mother of the birth father) got joint custody. This was a nightmare for that poor girl and a decisive end to her childhood and plans for the future. Her own mother had returned to work a few years earlier, to a job she loved, and the family had just been getting back on its feet financially after some hard times. Eventually, things improved, and, of course, everyone in the birth mother's family fell in love with the baby, but the girl and her parents never felt that raising him was the best thing for her or the baby. And they were extremely unhappy about the enforced contact with the boy's dysfunctional family and the role those people would always have in their lives and in the life of the child.

Society's image of a typical unwed mother is someone who is young, relatively uneducated, without sufficient financial resources, and without the support of the birth father and her parents. A charitable image casts her as an innocent victim. An uncharitable perspective sees her as hapless and irresponsible, perhaps even immoral. It would seem logical that factors such as youth and low income would correlate highly with a woman's decision to choose adoption. In fact, people make the decision to relinquish a child for uniquely personal reasons. Their stated reason might be something as straightforward as, "I'm too young" or "I can't afford to raise a child," but rarely is the situation that uncomplicated. After all, most young girls who become pregnant end up raising their babies within their extended families, and most pregnant women who can't afford a child end up relying on their families or some form of government assistance.

What makes prospective birth mothers look toward adoption rather than one of these other, far more common, courses of action? Our experiences at Adoption Connections taught us that birth mothers make the decision to relinquish out of genuine and unselfish love for their child and the conviction that adoption will provide the life for him or her that they do not feel able to provide.

The women we see at Adoption Connections have never fit a stereotype. They have ranged in age from thirteen to forty-three, with the most typical client being in her middle-to-late twenties. They almost always have at least a high school education or have attained the appropriate grade for their age. About one-third of the women have some college or have completed college, including some with graduate degrees. Their financial situations range from being homeless and destitute to having secure, well-paying jobs and an upper-middle-class lifestyle. Some women are completely on their own and have no outside source of emotional support. Others have the love, concern, and full participation of the birth father (who may even be their husband), and they have the support and understanding of family and friends.

The single quality that these birth mothers share is their belief, or perhaps recognition of the fact, that they are not able, at this time in their lives, to provide their child with the life they want him or her to have. Each birth mother's image of what that life will be like is uniquely personal, and she is the only one who can or should decide what she feels is best for her child and for herself.

We have worked with many hundreds of women who were considering adoption for their babies. Obviously, each one of those babies also had a father, but only a small percentage of these men chose to take an active role in planning for their baby's future. This is a sad comment on society's still closely held assumption that an unplanned pregnancy is to be handled by the woman. Most men in these situations hope to be compassionate and responsible, but too many of them seem to cope with the stress by distancing themselves, both from the birth mother and from their own emotions. Of course, there were wonderful exceptions, but it is sadly true that men who chose to be involved in the pregnancy and adoption were the exception.

Sometimes the couples we worked with made mutual and thoughtful decisions, but other times they had different ideas about the right course of action. It was particularly difficult for women who had gotten pregnant after a short (and now ended) relationship to come to terms with the idea that the father's legal rights to the child were equal to her own. If the woman wished to plan an adoption and the father did not, he could prevent it from happening, whether or not he intended to have a role in parenting the child.

There was also a small but distressing group of men who were some combination of immature, selfish, abusive, irresponsible, unloving, criminally involved, and so on, who, sadly, became fathers, too. It was a depressing reality of working with men like this that the less capable they were of actually being parents, the more likely they were to refuse to allow their children to be adopted. These men were not usually motivated by the desire to raise their child or to do what they thought was best for the child. They often had a specific desire to antagonize and control the birth mother (usually as punishment for leaving them), and they were not concerned about any of the legal or financial responsibilities of parenthood. These were men who didn't hold regular jobs, so they weren't worried about garnisheed wages. Many of them already didn't pay child support for their other children, so they weren't worried about being required to provide financially for this new baby. They often had abusive relationships with other women and children and were extremely likely to establish the same sorts of abusive relationships again. These guys were sad, they were dangerous, and they could compel a woman to raise the child. The alternative to parenting the child herself, which was to have the baby placed with the father, was unacceptably risky to virtually all women.

I remember how stunned I was the first time I discovered that a man who had been accused, but not yet convicted, of raping an underage girl (who became pregnant) had legal rights in regard to adoption. The girl wanted to plan an adoption, and she and her family wanted nothing to do with the man. He was not going to be given joint custody against her wishes if she chose to parent the child, but he was able to prevent her from relinquishing her parental rights by refusing to relinquish his own. She and her parents had no reasonable choice other than to raise the child.

Fortunately, situations this extreme were rare, but it was common for us to get calls that were equally distressing. These were from women who were in abusive relationships and wanted to plan an adoption in order to extricate the child from a dangerous environment. We would have to explain that, while we were extremely sympathetic, we could not help them plan an adoption without the father's consent. If he were to find out that his child had been placed for adoption without his knowledge, he would have grounds for overturning the adoption, even years later. A great deal of time was devoted to commiserating with these women and trying to explain the reasoning behind laws that seemed counter to common sense and detrimental to the baby.

Sometimes everything went smoothly from start to finish: a birth mother chose a family and went on to place her baby with them. More often, we would get calls from a number of potential birth mothers before a meaningful connection was made with a particular family. Patti and I also spent a great deal of time talking with girls and women who wanted information and counseling about adoption, then either decided against it or decided to work with an adoptive family we did not represent.

The workload at Adoption Connections was such that Patti and I would each take on no more than five or six families at a time (in addition to the families we saw in private practice). There was plenty of downtime when nothing urgent was happening, but even with such small numbers, there also seemed to be plenty of overlapping crises or dilemmas, such as babies being born in distant locations on the same day, with each situation requiring our presence. Most of our families were able to adopt within a year, although the range ran from immediately to just over two years. When we examined our statistics after the first two years of operation, we discovered to our surprise and amusement that the average wait for a baby was exactly nine months.

Patti and I spent many sleepless nights worrying about our clients and trying to control various aspects of a process that was largely out of our control. We agonized over couples trying to adopt but meeting with heartbreak. When one young woman, who seemed certain that she was going to place her baby, changed her mind after the birth—and after the hopeful adoptive family had joyously traveled to the Midwest at her request—I second-guessed myself for months. I asked the couple if they felt I should have advised them to wait until the baby was legally free for adoption before they traveled; incredibly, they did not. The wife explained that if they hadn't gone when the birth mother asked them to and she had then changed her mind about the adoption, they would have always wondered if things would have been different if they had been there. As it was, they knew that they had done everything possible to reassure her that they would be good parents. Unhappily, it took another year for them to successfully adopt, but, extremely happily, that child was everything they had been waiting and hoping for.

By far the most stressful aspect of running an adoption agency is dealing with the sheer weight of emotion from both birth and adoptive families. Almost all of our adoptive parents came to us after they had exhausted a great deal of physical, emotional, and financial resources in their effort to have a child by birth. They had been through varying degrees of heartbreak about this loss and were still grieving when they started the adoption process. Most people presented themselves as ready to move on, but their nerves were still raw, and it was a lot to ask of them to endure the frustrating and sometimes heartbreaking uncertainties of the adoption process. And of course, it was incredibly painful for the birth parents, who were facing the decision either to relinquish or to parent in less than optimal circumstances. They were often contending with other problems that made their lives difficult as well and that further contributed to their feeling that they would not be the best parents for their child. So a great deal of what Patti and I did for our clients was simply to be available to them when they wanted to talk about their frustrations or unhappiness. Sometimes that unhappiness was directed at us and at the constraints of adoption practice or adoption law; more often it was just a necessary outpouring of emotion.

Adoption is a difficult process, and almost every person we work with has gone through extreme highs and lows along the way to becoming parents—or to making the decision not to become the parent of this particular child. The payoff for adoptive parents is evident, but the process also can offer birth parents rich satisfactions and even happiness. These come from the knowledge that they have taken control of their situations and have made fully informed decisions about what is best for themselves and their babies. More concretely, this resolution comes from feeling that they have chosen just the right family for their babies—and from the ongoing reassurance that an open adoption allows.

22

Birth-Parent Counseling Etiquette

A LTHOUGH I SUPERVISED THE pregnancy counselors in the Options for Pregnancy program at WACAP, I hadn't really had a lot of direct interaction with birth parents during the years I held that job. My responsibilities were a step removed from actual counseling. I did, however, know people at most of the agencies in western Washington who were active in adoptions, and I was familiar with their approaches to counseling. Many of the agencies that handled infant adoption were church affiliated, and one had a particularly energetic, charismatic counselor. This woman, June, had dramatically increased the number of adoptions at her agency, and when she eventually left, its placement numbers dropped off dramatically.

The 1980s was an era when birth mothers who had relinquished their babies in the past were finally speaking out—sometimes shyly, sometimes angrily. They were often heard from at adoption conferences, which provided an excellent opportunity for them to tell their stories to the people who most needed to hear them. The women who spoke were of all ages; some of them told cautionary tales about the cruelties birth mothers had endured and the ongoing suffering inherent in closed adoptions, after which they weren't allowed to have information about their babies or even to seek reassurance about their child's continued well-being. Fortunately, there were also birth mothers from a newer generation at these conferences, and they served as evidence that changes had been made in the way adoptions were being handled. They talked about how the decision to relinquish their baby had been painful but completely their own, and they described various versions of openness in the relationships they had established with the adoptive family. Listening to these birth mothers was usually the highlight of any conference, and I—along with most of my fellow counselors—understood the importance of their message to us.

One especially memorable conference included a birth-parent panel made up of three young women who had been June's clients. The roomful of professionals and adoptive parents listened in rapt and respectful silence as these women told their stories. All of them expressed extreme gratitude to the counselor and to God for steering them in the right direction. All of them declared that babies needed two parents and that it would have been selfish for them to have kept their babies. All of them received hearty approval from the many people in the room who benefit in one way or another when birth parents make the decision to relinquish.

But I grew increasingly uncomfortable as one sad young woman told us about how the counselor had helped her to "stay strong" after her baby was born and as she was considering changing her mind about the planned adoption. She explained that even her own mother hadn't been "able to be there for me" and had tried to talk to her about keeping her newborn baby. The young woman told us about how her mother had been "weak" and that she had fortunately been able to rely on June, her counselor, who was there to help reaffirm her belief that God wanted her baby to be adopted.

There were few dry eyes in the house at that point except for my own, which were narrowing in anger.

It got worse when a couple in the audience, who appeared to be in their mid-twenties, stood up at the end of the panel discussion and introduced themselves as former clients of June. As they fervently praised her for giving them the strength to relinquish their baby a number of years earlier, they both were in tears and clearly actively grieving the loss of their child. I suspected that this couple, still together and still in such pain, had received the same sort of affirmation from June that adoption had been the only acceptable choice.

I came away from that conference feeling profoundly troubled, and dubious about the motives behind June's "counseling."

Later, I shared my concerns with the Options counselor I supervised, who worked in the same county as June. She told me she had had a similarly unsettling experience at a support-group meeting sponsored by June's agency. Birth parents had started off lavishly praising June, but the meeting had veered off script when several of them started to express regret about their decisions. It deteriorated to the point where people were saying that they felt they had been led to believe that they would be hurting their child if they decided against adoption. The Options counselor said that the depth of pain and anger in these birth parents was so extreme that she actually felt concerned about June and how she would respond. Never fear, though; the charismatic counselor simply chose not to respond. She just sat there, seemingly untroubled—because, clearly, she believed that she was doing God's work and that He heartily approved.

It is, of course, normal for birth parents to grieve after they have relinquished a child. Even birth parents who are rock solid in their adoption decisions and completely at peace in their belief that they have done what is best for their baby still suffer from the loss. As with any type of grief, birth parents vary in how they express themselves and receive comfort, and there is a wide range of normal with respect to how long and how intensely people grieve.

But birth parents who feel pressured into their decision to relinquish have an extremely difficult time recovering. Having been denied the opportunity to make such an important decision for themselves, they have tremendous difficulty accepting responsibility for it and moving on with their lives. They have been robbed of a vital source of comfort—that of knowing that they made the decision to relinquish of their own free will and in the best interests of their child.

When other people intervene in a directive way, they strip the birth mother of the power to make her own decision. Rather than being able to gain emotional maturity from this experience, a birth mother pressured to relinquish is often left with ongoing feelings of confusion, anger, regret, sadness, and disbelief. Even more insidiously, birth mothers sometimes cope with these feelings by clinging to denial, insisting that they are fine and don't need help from anyone—an approach that can lead to long-term depression, psychosomatic ailments, substance abuse, and other coping mechanisms that continue to affect their quality of life.

A birth mother once showed me the literature she had been given by June's agency when she sought information about their services, replete with heavy-handed messages such as, "For God so loved the world that he gave His only begotten Son." The implication in that statement—that a birth parent could be God-like in his or her sacrifice—was obviously much closer to coercion than counseling. Several years later, I happened to meet the woman who had been hired to replace June when she left her agency. This woman hadn't lasted long in her job, and when she told me her story, it was obvious why. "One of my first assignments," she said, "was to drive out to some little town to meet with a pregnant teenager." June had already met with the girl several times, and an adoption was under way. "I'll never forget walking into the restaurant where we were supposed to meet. I saw her sitting in a booth with her boyfriend; they were holding hands. I sat down with them, and the more we talked, the less sense it made to me that they would consider adoption. They were a close couple, both of their families were willing—anxious, even—to provide support for them, and they were extremely distraught at the idea of relinquishing their baby. They seemed to be not only a loving young couple but a really capable one as well. I thought they'd probably do well with a year or two of assistance from their families, as quite a few young couples in this situation do. I felt like saying, 'You know what? Don't do this!'"

It was not long afterward that this woman left her job, having concluded that the agency wanted her to continue her predecessor's policy of counseling all birth mothers in the same coercive way, insisting that their baby deserved an older, married couple as parents and that there really was no acceptable alternative to adoption.

Our approach to counseling was entirely different at Adoption Connections, where we encouraged all our clients to consider every possible choice available, especially parenting. Every woman who called the agency spoke with either Patti or me, sometimes daily and for months-long stretches. We dealt with whatever issues arose and sometimes found ourselves counseling them about concerns such as abusive relationships or financial problems that had little (or possibly everything) to do with an adoption decision. It was a steep learning curve and, as with child welfare, the situations people were in were often sad and frustrating, but they were always compelling.

It didn't take long for us to come to the realization that we didn't and couldn't necessarily know what was best for our clients and shouldn't sit in judgment of their decisions. Even with clients we got to know especially well, we were not in a position to determine what the right course of action would be for them, nor was it ethical for us to do so. We were careful to avoid even the appearance of coercion or bias about what a birth mother "should" do in regard to her decision to relinquish. This was equally true whether she was someone who we felt would be a completely capable parent or someone whom Child Protective Services would prevent from taking her baby home from the hospital.

Our emphasis on counseling for all options sometimes seemed confusing to adoptive parents. After all, we were working for and being paid by them and, ethical considerations aside, if our job was to help them adopt a child, why wasn't it also our job to encourage birth parents to relinquish?

Some adoptive parents initially fear the involvement of a counselor, believing that if everyone can just avoid bringing up the tough issues throughout the pregnancy, and also avoid having the birth parents bond with the baby right after the birth, then everything will be fine. The goal seems to be to accomplish the adoption before the birth parents have had a chance to reconsider. Not only is that unethical, but it often backfires—as it should.

Waiting adoptive parents can feel that they want a baby almost at any cost. However, no adoptive parent would really want to be involved in a situation in which the birth mother regretted having relinquished the child. If, as a hopeful parent, you doubt the truth of that statement, imagine a situation in which your child was one day faced with a birth mother who was filled with sadness, bitterness, and regret, and who felt that she had been pressured into the adoption. This scenario is among an adoptive parent's (and a counselor's) worst nightmares.

All of these considerations informed our counseling philosophy at Adoption Connections: namely, that everyone benefits when birth parents address the reality of their situation early on. If birth parents are going to change their minds about adoption, we want them to do so as soon as possible, both so that they can start preparing for parenthood and so that the family hoping to adopt can avoid deeper emotional and financial investment and loss.

Especially in the early years of Adoption Connections, many callers said at the outset that they felt committed to relinquishing and were simply looking for the right adoptive family. They insisted that they didn't need counseling around this issue—they just needed assistance with coordinating an adoption. Nevertheless, we made it clear, both to them and to the adoptive parents, that we felt it was important to also talk with all birth parents about the idea of parenting their child. We felt it was necessary to at least acknowledge the possibility that the birth parents might change their minds about adoption at some point, and we wanted them to thoroughly explore their motivation for an adoption and to thoroughly understand their alternatives. We were intent on avoiding the scenario in which the birth mother single-mindedly insists that there will be an adoption, never allows for any other possibility, and rejects any sort of discussion about this issue.

Indeed, birth parents who are adamant about adoption are the most likely to change their minds after the birth. This is because many of them have essentially been in denial throughout the pregnancy, not allowing themselves to fully comprehend how much they will love their child and how incredibly painful the loss of the child will be. Once the baby is born, they may find themselves overwhelmed by the unexpected emotion and interpret the love they feel for their baby as a sign that they should change their minds about the adoption. And, in all probability, they should—but they also should have allowed themselves to get the counseling that would have helped them recognize their true feelings before the birth.

I am periodically asked to meet with a prospective birth parent who is "definitely" planning an adoption. The request often comes from a family who is planning a private adoption and working with an attorney who has referred them to me. This adoptive family has become aware of a friend-of-a-friend's daughter's boyfriend's sister, who is pregnant and has chosen them as the adoptive parents for her baby. They assure me that this girl is headed for college and says she doesn't even like children, so there's no way she'll change her mind, and everyone involved agrees with this assessment. My services are usually called upon late in the pregnancy to help create the post-placement contact agreement, which will spell out the details of their ongoing contact.

Often, what I discover when I meet this girl is that, while her parents and the baby's father are assuming she'll do the sensible thing and relinquish, she is secretly hoping that they'll all do the sensible thing once they see the baby and realize that she and they can't possibly give it up. And she's almost always right—the other people almost always do change their minds when confronted with both the baby and the mother's desire to parent, and there is no adoption. If this girl had been allowed or had allowed herself to get some counseling and honestly explore the option of parenting, everyone would likely have foreseen this outcome—and been able to plan for it—much earlier in the pregnancy.

Fortunately, our emphasis on counseling at Adoption Connections greatly reduced the incidence of eleventh-hour changes of heart. This is not to say that we eliminated them entirely. But because we focused on counseling, it was more common for a birth mother to change her mind during the pregnancy, after a counseling session or a meeting with an attorney, or after some other concrete step in the process. Adoptive parents sometimes struggled to understand that such a change of heart wasn't caused by the counselor or attorney but was simply a matter of the birth parents facing the reality of the pregnancy earlier rather than later.

It is crucial for adoptive parents to understand that, just as unbiased counseling does not cause a birth mother to change her mind, women who choose to relinquish do not do so out of any failure to bond with their babies. It is not the case that if a birth mother is given time to bond with her baby, she won't be able to follow through with the adoption. On the contrary, the exact opposite is more likely to be true: birth mothers are able to relinquish precisely because of the strength of their love and their commitment to giving their child a life they feel unable to provide. Most of the birth mothers we worked with relinquished their babies for the same basic reason: they did not feel that, at that time in their lives, they were able to be the type of parent they wanted their child to have. They all loved their babies and bonded with them during the pregnancy. Their decisions to relinquish were reinforced by that bond.

It is certainly less complicated and less painful for us all to believe that good women and good mothers would never consider relinquishing their parental rights. Imagining the loss of a child is so unthinkable that it is easier for us to assume that women who would consider adoption simply must not care as much about their children as the rest of us do. It is easy to believe, from the vantage point of a stable and comfortable life, that there is no circumstance in which you would willingly give up your child.

But in reality, there are circumstances in which loving parents make incredibly painful and selfless decisions because they believe these decisions are in the child's best interests. The majority of the women I've worked with chose adoption because they truly believed that their children would be better off in an adoptive home. It is through their love for their children that these women find the strength to endure their own grief over the loss of the child.

It should go without saying that the decision to relinquish is as difficult and painful a decision as a person can make, and also that a woman facing this decision deserves unbiased counseling. Sadly, many birth parents planning adoptions get no counseling at all, let alone the unbiased, professional counseling they deserve. There are strong forces working against this type of counseling for birth parents, and there don't appear to be any counterbalancing forces at work to promote the involvement of a counselor, other than in the most minimal ways.

A few years after becoming co-director of Adoption Connections, I sent a letter to the many Crisis Pregnancy Centers (CPCs) in Washington State, introducing myself and my agency. I held out a shred of hope that they would read what I had to say about unbiased counseling and respecting the wishes and values of each client, but I was soon disabused of that notion. I got exactly one response—a phone call from a woman in eastern Washington who wanted to know only one thing: "Do you believe that marriage is between a man and a woman?" "That is the definition of traditional marriage," I told her, and added that most of the birth mothers we counseled were looking for couples in a traditional marriage. She then asked if we would ever place a baby in anything other than a traditional family, and I responded that the choice of the adoptive family was not the agency's to make. I told her that our job was to help birth parents make whatever decisions and plans they felt were right for their baby. This was greeted by an audible "tsk, tsk" so I added that good counselors would never presume to tell their clients what they should or shouldn't do. The woman said a crisp goodbye and hung up.

I wasn't really surprised that a Crisis Pregnancy Center counselor wasn't interested in unbiased counseling; I guess I wasn't even surprised that she would be so blatant about it.

Obviously, Crisis Pregnancy Centers aren't going to provide unbiased counseling. Their primary purpose is to prevent abortions, and everyone is entitled to promote their own beliefs on that subject. What is objectionable is the way they lead women in crisis to believe that they can come to Crisis Pregnancy Centers for decision-making counseling that covers a full range of options. Instead, CPCs provide a reasonably appropriate service for clients who already share their views about abortion, and hard-sell anti-abortion rhetoric for those who don't. But that is not how they advertise themselves.

They promote a misleading image: that of a garden-variety pregnancy/adoption counseling service to which you can turn for help with an unplanned pregnancy.

Typically, the first decision someone with such a pregnancy makes is whether to have an abortion. Also typically, because the pregnancy was unplanned and often not even acknowledged in the early stages, the decision about abortion is extremely time sensitive. Despite the wishes of the CPCs, many, probably most, women with unplanned pregnancies consider abortion as an option and believe they have the right to make that decision for themselves, without the interference or condemnation of others. Because the CPC ads clearly state that they provide counseling and assistance, with no mention of an anti-abortion agenda, women have no way of knowing what they will encounter when they contact a CPC counselor. Expecting counseling, they will instead be assaulted with proselytizing, at best, and underhanded coercion, at worst.

A good birth-parent counselor, by contrast, helps her clients make their own decisions. Rather than persuade or pressure her clients to adopt a particular stance on abortion or single parenthood or on what the religion or sexual orientation of an adoptive family "should" be, or on other such topics, she lets birth parents work through their own feelings about these things, with the counselor being careful not to signal suggestion or judgment.

This does not mean that a counselor must remain passive in a situation where a clearly incapable birth parent makes the decision to parent. In fact, the opposite is true: counselors are legally required to make a referral to Child Protective Services if they feel a child is endangered. In such situations, I believe it is ethical, reasonable, and helpful to talk with the birth parent about alternatives to having the state put the baby into foster care. But even in these situations, it is unethical for a counselor to pressure a birth parent to relinquish. While other forces may compel her to do so, that is not the role of the counselor.

23

Two Open Adoptions

O UR SOCIETY OFTEN VIEWS BIRTH parents and adoptive parents as natural enemies, fighting over a prize they can't both have. My experience has taught me that this perception couldn't be more distorted. What I've almost always seen, in the adoptions I've been privileged to be a part of, are people who come together out of a shared need for each other and with the shared goal of providing a wonderful life for a child they all love. But birth parents and adoptive parents are like everyone else in the world; they're all different. Some are people who will develop a valued relationship with each other, even outside the realm of planning an adoption. Others are people who will have a special bond because of the child, but little else in common. In some extreme situations, the circumstances may be such that an ongoing relationship isn't desirable or even possible. Happily, almost all of the birth- and adoptive-parent relationships that I have been directly involved with fall into one of the first two categories.

Adoptive parents who recognize and freely acknowledge the significance of the birth mother's gift to their family will, in turn, give her the gift of their understanding. The birth mother's contribution can be acknowledged by talking with the child about how it took love and courage for her to be able to plan an adoption for her child. It can also be acknowledged in simpler, day-to-day ways such as telling the child, "Your birth mom has beautiful brown eyes [or a wonderful sense of humor, or loved music, or whatever the case may be], just like you." A few comments like these go a long way toward helping a child avoid the impression that there is something negative or unmentionable about birth parents or adoption (or the child). When adoptive parents demonstrate comfortable, nonjudgmental attitudes toward birth parents, it has a profound effect on the child's self-esteem and sense of well-being.

One spring day, a college student who had just discovered that she was seven months pregnant called me. Emma had gotten my phone number from a friend whose mother had placed a child through our agency several years earlier. She was calling from North Carolina, where she was in her junior year at a small private college. She sounded stressed, but also polite and articulate, and we weren't long into the conversation before it was clear that she was highly intelligent, responsible, and thoughtful. She had been dating a fellow student, and they had gone their separate ways months before she knew she was pregnant, but they remained friends. Both were good students on athletic scholarships.

An unplanned pregnancy was so far out of the realm of possibility for Emma that she had managed to avoid "knowing" until the end of her seventh month. This seems incredible, but denial can be overpowering, and when coupled with strong stomach muscles and a forgiving wardrobe, it is indeed possible to hide a pregnancy. I've known a number of young women who managed to hide their pregnancies from everyone—including themselves—until they delivered a baby.

The more I talked with Emma, the more I liked her. She told me that she had definitely decided on adoption because she felt she wasn't in a good position to give the baby the home she wanted her to have. She did not see herself resuming her relationship with Garrett, the birth father, although he had offered, and she didn't want her baby to be raised by a single parent. Emma had obviously done a lot of thinking before she called me and had tried to educate herself about adoption.

At first, Emma had assumed that she would work with an adoption agency in the state where she lived but had been terrified when agencies there told her that she would not be able to select an adoptive family prior to birth because her baby was going to be biracial. It seems they needed to know what the baby would look like before finding an "appropriate" family. I was skeptical when she told me that this was the policy there, but it turned out to be true—and was a real eye-opener for me about the still-present regional differences in this country regarding race.

Emma's first and most pressing question for me was whether she would be able to go ahead and choose her baby's adoptive family. Happily, I was able to reassure her that she could, and that she was going to have a lot of families to choose from. I told her that I would spend some time contacting prospective families and would send her a package of profiles within a few days.

Calling families about Emma was a pleasure; I had to restrain myself from going on and on about how great I thought she was, even though I didn't know much about her beyond her basic biographical information and the fact that I thoroughly enjoyed talking with her.

When I asked Emma what she thought she wanted regarding ongoing contact with the adoptive family, she was fairly vague, insisting that she didn't want to make demands—she just wanted to find the best family. Since the portfolios I was sending her were all from families in Washington, it seemed that frequent, ongoing, in-person contact was unlikely. I sent her five family profiles, and after talking with most of them, Emma settled on one couple. She expressed relief to have found an adoptive family, they were excited, and we jumped into preparations for a long-distance adoption because the baby was due in not too many weeks.

Emma and I talked almost every day, problems arose and were resolved (i.e., how to tell her mother, the birth father's second thoughts about adoption, problems with medical care and insurance coverage, etc.), and time went by until the day I got a call from the prospective adoptive mother saying that they didn't want to proceed. I don't remember the exact reason they gave, but I suspect the real reason was discomfort with the idea of becoming a mixed-race family. I remember feeling a combination of relief and dread after their call. I was relieved because I had begun to have my own doubts about them, probably in response to the uncertainty they were feeling. But I dreaded having to tell Emma. Her reaction, however, made me feel incredibly dense but also incredibly relieved. She told me she had also been feeling that maybe they weren't the right family and had been wondering what to do and how to tell me.

This time around, I was able to answer questions from prospective adoptive families much more thoroughly because I had gotten to know Emma so much better. I also told them that her ideas about ongoing contact had evolved. She still wasn't sure exactly what would be best, but she imagined a perfect scenario in which someday she would be sitting in the audience, possibly anonymously, watching her daughter graduate from high school or college.

Most of the families were hesitant about this idea, but one woman, deeply moved, took a long pause before finally managing to say, with a lump in her throat, "It's just like in that movie *Stella Dallas!*" (in which a birth mother stands, unidentified, in the crowd watching her daughter's society wedding). I knew then, without any doubt, that she was going to be this baby's mother.

Emma and the new adoptive family, James and Melissa, got along famously. Within a few weeks of having chosen each other, everyone was together at the hospital welcoming Haley, an exquisitely beautiful and enormously beloved child. Emma, as most birth mothers do, struggled with her decision after Haley was born, but ultimately decided on adoption and was tremendously comforted by the belief that she had found the perfect family for her baby. Garrett cooperated with the adoption because it was what Emma wanted, but he opted to stay in the background at that time.

James and Melissa brought Haley home to Washington and joyously began their lives as parents. They maintained close contact with Emma, primarily through phone calls, and sent her many pictures. They also invited her to come for a visit, and Emma spent time with them during her Christmas break that year, when Haley was six months old. During this visit, I got to meet Emma at last, and she proved to be even more delightful in person than she had been in all those phone calls. She, Melissa, Haley, and I went out to lunch together one afternoon, and Emma handled herself like a skilled ambassador for adoption. She and Melissa unhesitatingly answered people's questions about Haley with complete poise and candor, and their obvious comfort with the situation and with each other was lovely to behold. The staff in the restaurant—and probably some of the patrons as well—got an amazing inside glimpse of how wonderful open adoption can be. Emma and James went on to provide a more formalized version of adoption education by taking part in a number of conferences together over the years, where they spoke about their open-adoption experiences. Emma did a superb job of dispelling scary stereotypes about birth mothers.

James and Melissa established a truly open relationship with Emma, and they all grew close. The adults took pleasure in getting to know one another better and in their mutual delight in Haley. There have been many shared activities—with and without Haley—many good times, and many good conversations over the years. The degree of openness in their relationship and the frequency of their visits was not something that any of them requested, anticipated, or even necessarily wanted. It developed naturally because they discovered that they genuinely liked and trusted one another and enjoyed the time they spent together. It may have worked so well because they were all heavily invested in having it work, but it wasn't long before they discovered that they were good friends in addition to their more formalized relationships as Haley's adoptive parents and birth parent.

After finishing college, Emma went on to get a master's degree in counseling. Her graduate studies included work on adoption, and she educated not only her fellow students but the faculty, most of whom had serious misperceptions about birth parents and adoption. By virtue of her experience and intelligence, Emma is uniquely qualified to be a spokesperson for birth mothers, and she has enthusiastically taken on that responsibility. She has been working as a counselor for many years now, and her combination of intelligence, wisdom, experience, and empathy make her extremely good at her job. Haley, who is now twelve, and Emma keep in touch through occasional texts and email and, although in-person visits have become a little less frequent over time, they still usually see each other a couple times a year, and everyone looks forward to and enjoys these get-togethers.

When Haley was a toddler, James and Melissa were able to meet Garrett on a trip to the East Coast. They stayed in touch through Facebook, and some years later, when Garrett was getting married, James and Melissa sent a gift. They received a thank you card that included a note from his wife saying that she would love to meet them someday. Garrett is a park ranger, his wife is a teacher, and they now have a young daughter.

James and Melissa have answered Haley's questions about why Emma and Garrett decided not to raise her by explaining that the timing was just not right for them to become parents. They were both in school, didn't have jobs, hadn't planned to stay together, and felt they couldn't give a baby the life they wanted her to have. There are undoubtedly more conversations to come on this subject, some of them with Emma and Garrett. Haley has full access to information about her birth family and the circumstances of her adoption, and full permission and encouragement to talk with any of her family members about anything that interests or concerns her. She also has ample evidence that the adults in her life love and care about one another and that they all believe that adoption was the right choice for her.

This degree of openness, which works so well for this family, is not the norm. It is not generally expected or even appropriate for everyone. But lest you dismiss their success as a fluke, consider James and Melissa's second adoption. When Haley was just about one year old, a young couple in Seattle called to talk with me about adoption. I met with them at the boy's mother's home, where they were staying. They were both extremely polite and pleasant. The birth mother, Josie, was African American, and the birth father, Jarod, was Caucasian; the baby was due soon, and they wanted an adoptive family that would reflect their child's mixed-race heritage. I showed them some family profiles in which the parents were of different races. I also took them James and Melissa's (and Haley's) profile—Caucasian parents and a mixed-race child—and the couple chose them.

Because James and Melissa had had such a positive experience with Haley's adoption, they didn't hesitate to agree to a completely open adoption with the new birth parents. Prior to the baby's birth, both birth and adoptive parents made and signed a post-placement-contact agreement stipulating that there would be abundant ongoing contact. James and Melissa were to send pictures once a month, phone calls were welcome, and visits (including visits with extended family members) were expected. All of that seemed completely natural to James and Melissa, even though this time the birth parents were across town instead of across the country.

Everything was in place for an adoption but, as often happens in rushed situations where counseling has been minimal, when the baby became a reality rather than an abstraction, the birth parents reconsidered—in this case, for several weeks. Then they called to say that they were ready to move forward and baby Charlotte joined her new adoptive family.

It all seemed fated and perfect—until, several weeks later, after a visit with Josie and Jarod at James and Melissa's home. Almost immediately after the young couple left, Josie's grandmother called James and Melissa to ask if Josie had spoken with them about getting the baby back. She was very polite about it and James was equally polite in responding that nothing had been said and that "the matter is settled." And then he called me and I called Josie. She explained to me that her mother and grandmother felt that she had made a mistake in agreeing to the adoption and that her grandmother was particularly upset because she "didn't believe in adoption" and didn't believe her granddaughter hadn't been coerced.

It wasn't clear what Josie actually thought about all of this. She freely acknowledged that she had not been coerced into an adoption, and was gracious in accepting the fact that she could not simply change her mind and reclaim her baby after relinquishing her parental rights. She may actually have had a change of heart and was considering raising her child after all, or she may have been placating her mother and grandmother by simply exploring the idea of undoing the adoption. Josie did not make any further attempts to urge James and Melissa to return Charlotte to her but, obviously, the relationships between the families became strained after that phone call. It would have been easy for James and Melissa to respond fearfully but that is not what they chose to do.

Everyone was scheduled to get together again just a week later for Haley's first birthday party celebration. It was a big event with lots of people, including Jarod and Josie and their mothers, but the grandmother stayed away. It turned out to be a happy and uneventful day Charlotte and Haley were admired, compliments were given all around, and there was laughter, warmth, and talk about future get-togethers. There were also serious and poignant moments, but there was no talk about regret or undoing the adoption.

Things went so well for these two families that by November, when Charlotte was five months old, James and Melissa and their daughters were invited to celebrate Thanksgiving with Jared's extended family. The following year they were invited to share Thanksgiving dinner with Josie's extended family, including the grandmother, and James was even called upon to carve the turkey. The day was a huge success, and celebrating Thanksgiving together became a tradition for the next five years. As they did with Haley, James and Melissa have nurtured Charlotte's relationships with her birth family, and she too knows how well loved she is by them all.

Josie and Jarod have gone on to successful careers and other relationships. Jarod and his mother stay in touch with James and Melissa and are invited to such family events as Charlotte's birthdays and choir concerts. Contact with Josie is much more frequent; she regularly comes to Charlotte's soccer and basketball games, where Charlotte introduces Josie as her birth mother. Josie also comes to occasional "movie nights," which include spending the night at James and Melissa's home. Charlotte, who is now eleven, has overnight visits at Josie's three or four times a year and Josie has stayed with the girls while James and Melissa were out of town on occasion. She even accompanied them on a three day vacation, including a whale watching excursion, several years ago.

One year James and Melissa hosted a Christmas party that included many members of Charlotte's extended birth family. Even Josie's grandmother was there. In talking with her, James and Melissa learned that she had been adopted herself and that it had been a very unhappy situation.

Happily, the grandmother had come to accept the fact that Charlotte's adoption experience was entirely different from her own. James and Melissa were grateful for the opportunity to see the situation from her perspective, and to know that her earlier objections had been resolved. They were also grateful to be able to take pictures of the four generations of women together, including Charlotte, Josie, Josie's mother, and Josie's grandmother—pictures that became particularly precious when the grandmother died just a few months later.

Haley and Charlotte and all the people in their families serve as examples of the enormous benefits of open adoption. James, Emma, and Josie have done formal presentations, sometime all together, and are enormously informative and reassuring to their audiences, which are usually made up of prospective adoptive families. More significantly, the way they all simply live their lives serves to educate others. When Josie stands on the sidelines of a game with James and Melissa, cheering Charlotte on, the four of them do a beautiful job of letting the rest of the world know what they already know about how well openness can work for everyone.

24

Choosing an Adoptive Family

ADOPTIVE PARENTS, UNDERSTANDABLY, always want to know the secret formula that will lead a birth mother to choose them. You would think that the formula is obvious: birth mothers want families in which the parents are good people who are able and eager to provide a happy and stable life for a child.

But how do you convey that message to a birth mother? There is no universal agreement about the definitions of "good people," "happy and stable life," or "able and eager." One birth mother may feel that anyone with an income and a roof over their heads can provide for her child, while another might be determined to find an upper-middle-class Mormon family with a stay-at-home mom. And the prospective adoptive parents' eagerness might be seen by one birth mother as pushy and neurotic but by another as marvelously endearing evidence that they will be properly devoted to her child.

The process by which birth mothers select an adoptive family is fascinating and mysterious. As part of my work, I help couples create a profile of themselves, typically in book or website form, that is sent out to prospective birth mothers searching for an adoptive family. The profiles usually consist of a two- or three-page letter and at least twenty-five photos intended to give the reader a good idea of what it would be like for a child to be part of that family. The letter usually covers basic biographical information, says something about why the family wants to adopt, and describes their views about child-rearing and openness. The intent is to provide appealing information without boasting or aggressive salesmanship. The photos are a collection of mostly casual shots depicting the couple involved in the various activities of their lives; the hope is to show how much fun it would be for everyone if a child was with them.

Most prospective adoptive parents are eager for guidance in creating their profiles, and I am happy to provide them with opinions I have developed over the years. But the most important thing I've learned is that you can never know what will make a particular profile stand out to a particular birth mother. As with beauty, adoptive-family appeal is in the eye of the beholder; birth mothers pick their babies' families for completely unique and personal reasons that can't be predicted or second-guessed. All the years of watching birth mothers scrutinize family profiles have taught me that it is almost never an adoptive family's good looks, the size of their house, or the extravagance of their vacations that grabs a birth parent's attention. Instead, it seems to be something less tangible: the birth mother's sense of connection and familiarity with a family—and there is no end to the surprising ways that that feeling can come about.

When I meet with a birth mother who wants to look at profiles, I usually show her five or six at a time. Often she will have given me some initial parameters, such as wanting a stay-at-home mom or a couple who don't already have children. I bring her profiles of families who meet her description, but I also throw in a few who don't because, more often than not, women change their minds about their parameters when they see a family that appeals to them for unexpected reasons.

People enjoy finding common ground, and it is this sense of connection that birth mothers cite when they tell me why they chose a particular family. One young woman told me that she picked her adoptive family because they had a black Lab named Smee (Captain Hook's sidekick in *Peter Pan*) and she had had a black lab named Smee when she was a child. Obviously, that wasn't the only reason she thought they would be good parents, but the coincidence made a family with other appealing qualities feel especially familiar and comfortable to her. Another birth mother picked a couple because they had included a picture of their Aunt Bootsie, and she had a favorite aunt named Bootsie. It seemed like fate to her that her child might be able to have the same treasured relationship with an aunt. (Given the rarity of the name Bootsie, it seemed pretty fated to me, too.) Yet another birth mother explained that what had tipped the scales in favor of a particular family for her was a picture of the prospective adoptive grandmother with a plate of chocolate chip cookies. She told me that chocolate chip was her favorite kind of cookie, and she loved the idea of her child having a cookie-baking grandmother. Liking, and baking, chocolate chip cookies wouldn't normally single someone out but, in the eyes of that birth mother, it did.

Sometimes the connections between birth parents and adoptive parents are easily recognized, and sometimes they are mysterious. One birth father was delighted to see a profile in which the prospective adoptive father talked about his interest in a particular type of cartooning. Although he never would have thought to specify that he wanted his baby to be raised by a dad who liked cartooning, their mutual interest was a catalyst for a deeper connection between the two men. Another birth father, who was from Guatemala, chose an adoptive family in which the father had spent time working in Guatemala during his college years. It wouldn't seem surprising that the birth father was attracted by this except that there was no mention in the profile of the adoptive dad's experience in Guatemala. I have never again worked with either a birth father from Guatemala or an adoptive father who worked in Guatemala so, yes, that adoption also seemed fated.

One of the most poignant requests I've heard was from a young woman who first listed some of the more typical qualities birth mothers ask for in an adoptive family: things like a stay-at-home mom, no other children, and an involved extended family. Then she said, in a wistful voice, "This will sound funny, but what I'd really like is to find an adoptive mom who is into things like manicures." It did sound funny, and I chuckled, but I also reassured her that I would look for someone like that. I pulled out a stack of family profiles, most of which, as expected, didn't reveal any information about manicures. But there was one startling exception with a professional cover shot featuring the woman's beautifully manicured hand draped over her husband's shoulder. The hand was front and center in the picture, looking almost like an ad for a nail salon. Manicures might seem like a frivolous quality to look for in an adoptive mom but, as I got to know the birth mom better, I discovered what was behind her unusual request. She wanted to save her child the complicated combination of emotions, including love, worry, shame and sadness, that she had experienced growing up in chaos with a mother who was a hoarder. She wanted her own child to live in a well-ordered home with a mother she could be proud of, and she felt that a woman who took care of her fingernails would also take care of other aspects of her appearance and her home. That birth mother did pick the woman with the manicure, strong sense of self-esteem, and very tidy house to be her baby's mother.

The lesson I have learned from birth mothers and have tried to pass on to adoptive families is that it is impossible and pointless to try to design a profile that will appeal to the broadest possible range of birth mothers. I have learned from long experience that something completely unexpected is likely to catch the right person's attention. So I recommend that families include all sorts of detail in the captions of their pictures, and that they never pass up an opportunity to provide the name of a dog or an aunt or their favorite kind of cookie. Other than that, I urge them just to be honest and create the profile that represents exactly who they are. There is no single best approach and only a few things to avoid including in their pictures, such as evidence of lots of drinking at social events, crotch shots (believe it or not, I have had to tell people to remove them), and elaborate collages of tiny pictures that make it difficult to actually see the people in the photographs or what they are doing.

While I am very opinionated about what I think makes a good profile, I also have been very wrong on occasion. I remember one family who designed their profile to be from the perspective of their cat. I told them that I wasn't sure it was a good idea, but maybe they could try it for a while, then revise it if need be. (Secretly, I thought that it was a horrible idea and that they were limiting themselves to cat-lady birth mothers.) Much to my amazement—and delight—they were chosen immediately by a lovely girl who thought cats were fine, but—more importantly—really liked the family's sense of humor.

Speaking of a sense of humor, I feel safe in saying that what birth mothers hope to learn from a profile is that it would be fun to be part of the profiled family. This is not to say that a profile should strive to be overtly funny; rather, it should show that the people in this family know how to enjoy life and each other. My favorite example is from a family that was nowhere near the typical demographic for adoptive parents of an infant. The parents had married at a young age, had two children together, then divorced. The woman then remarried, had two more children, and divorced again. The four children shown in the profile ranged in age from high school to their mid-twenties, and there was even a grandchild in the family. The couple had reunited about five years earlier and had recently suffered the loss of a baby at birth, due to gestational diabetes. They were delightful people, but certainly didn't meet the average birth mother's parameters for the perfect family. Yet they were immediately chosen by a birth mother.

For more than twenty years, I have been using their story as a lesson for other profile creators. The picture that caught the birth mother's eye showed the prospective adoptive dad being pelted by Jell-O in a backyard food fight with his older sons. No matter how one feels about food fights, it was evident that this dad was having a great time, that he could take a joke, that no one was going to get in trouble for throwing Jell-O . . . and that it would be fun to be part of this family.

Contrast this family with the attractive, obviously wealthy, young couple who created an elaborate silver-plated picture album (it weighed a ton) filled with professional shots of the two of them posed stiffly in various locations around their spectacular home and yard. They did not look like people who knew how to have a good time, and it took several years for a birth mother to choose them. Their opulent lifestyle did not make up for the fact that their home looked like a place where people could never relax. I've also had birth mothers reject families whose profiles were full of spectacular pictures of vacations and exciting social events because it didn't seem credible to them that people who had a life like that would be content to give it all up in order to become soccer moms and dads.

In the final analysis, there will always be an element of mystery (or fate or God's will or whatever term you choose) in the way that birth mothers and adoptive parents find each other. I have witnessed and been delighted by the apparently fated nature of these connections on countless occasions. This feeling may be primarily a reflection of the fact that everyone wants so much to believe that this birth mother was destined to find this family because this particular child was destined to become theirs. There may be logical and not at all romantic or mysterious explanations for why a family and birth mother find each other, just as there are explanations for how a particular sperm and egg come together to make a baby, but the mystery in the latter case lies in why—not how—that particular egg and that particular sperm came together. We can certainly explain *how* these things happen, but *why* they happen the way they do for any particular baby, whether adopted or not, remains wonderfully in the realm of the unexplained.

25

Money Matters

When Adoption Connections started, it was rare for birth parents to start a phone conversation by asking about financial assistance. Now it is the norm, and many callers are quick to move on if they aren't promised money. This change is not due to increased financial need; rather, it is a reflection of the fact that most people in this high-demand market for babies no longer seem to want to examine the ethics of providing payment to women in exchange for their babies. Birth parents who benefit financially have little incentive to question the practice, and adoption professionals and hopeful adoptive parents can't help but feel that they had better go along with it if they expect to compete in today's adoption market.

It's not that women considering adoption for their babies did not receive financial assistance in the past. But the general rule of thumb held that all expenses covered by adoptive parents had to be adoption related and—in Washington, at least—court approved. For example, if a woman had a job that became difficult for her during pregnancy, she could request help with basic living expenses during the months when she was unable to work. Judges were sympathetic in these situations, and requests for assistance were typically granted as long as proper procedure was followed. Other pregnancy-related expenses, such as maternity clothing, transportation costs, and any uncovered medical or counseling fees (both before and after delivery) were routinely approved by the courts.

These financial arrangements were almost always short-lived and for specific purposes. People on all sides—birth parents, adoptive parents, and legal professionals—took great pains to avoid behavior that gave the appearance of baby selling or baby buying. Black and gray markets existed in the adoption world (and no doubt always will), but legitimate adoption professionals could usually steer clear of them. That certainly seemed to be the case in Washington State, where there was strong incentive to avoid any exchange of money that could be considered coercive or possibly even grounds for later overturning an adoption. Other states had different policies regarding adoption finances, and ideas about what was ethical varied widely. Sometimes these ideas were most directly influenced by where a person lived; more likely, they were influenced by a person's stake in the adoption. Previously held views on the ethics of baby buying, held by both birth and adoptive parents, were subject to modification to suit one's changing needs and perspectives.

The Internet has played a huge role in altering the finances of adoption. When families began posting their information online, birth parents suddenly had instant access to the elaborate profiles they created, including numerous pictures and even video. Instead of choosing between the handful of families who advertised in the local newspaper, birth parents now had hundreds of families to choose from. Quite suddenly, adoptive families found themselves competing with one another on a massive scale, with the primary way of distinguishing themselves in a crowded market being financial. Increasingly, profiles began to directly address living expenses for birth mothers but without anyone having a clear understanding of either the purpose for or amounts of money being promised. It pretty quickly became clear that there were many prospective families who would pay whatever they had to pay and do whatever they had to do in order to become parents.

Despite what we would all like to believe, baby buying has probably always been going on in this country. My first direct experience with it was in working with Jena, a struggling, pregnant, twenty-three-year-old mother who called me one day in 1994. She was in another state, where she had seen an ad in her local newspaper, placed by a family I was counseling. I spent a great deal of time over the next month in long telephone conversations with Jena, and I came to regard her as a responsible, competent, caring mother to her three-year-old son. This new pregnancy had resulted from a short-lived relationship; the father did not want to be involved, and Jena felt she could not handle two young children on her own. She was managing to be the sort of mother she felt her son deserved but had decided she would be hard-pressed to do the same for a second child.

Jena was happy with the adoptive family she had chosen—the couple with whom I was working—and everything was proceeding smoothly toward adoption until she met with the attorney in her state to whom I had referred her. I hadn't worked with this man before, but he had come highly recommended.

The day after Jena met with him, she called me in tears. She said the attorney had deeply insulted her by offering her money to switch to one of the adoptive families he represented. He had explained that he knew families who would pay $40,000 (an extremely large sum at that time) for her baby because Jena was pretty and blond. She told me that she was tremendously upset by the suggestion that she would take money, and she felt I should know that the attorney my adoptive family was paying for was actually working against their best interests. I told her I was extremely sorry to have put her in such a situation and offered to find her a different attorney. We spoke many more times over the next couple of weeks, but she never took me up on that offer.

Then she again called in tears, this time to say that she had agonized over the decision but felt that, for her little boy's sake, she just could not turn down the money. She had looked at the attorney's families' profiles, and they all seemed like nice people. Of course, while I was sad for the family I was helping, I could not in good conscience criticize Jena. The money would make an enormous difference to her and her child. The attorney's families all had court-approved home studies, and I had no reason to think they wouldn't be good parents. But I also understood that despite the financial security she would gain for a while, Jena now would always have to live with the thought that she had sold her baby to the highest bidder. I didn't say that to her, however. I just wished her well. After all, she was not the one to blame for this lamentable situation; she was simply trying to take care of her child. But I felt that she would pay a high price emotionally, as would the child to be adopted, should he or she ever learn about the financial arrangements between the birth and adoptive parents.

The attorney was triumphant in his conquest and told me that Jena apparently wasn't as ethical as she thought she was. He was utterly unconcerned about his own ethics and assured me that that was just the way they did things in his state. I hate to think about how he treated Jena. Obviously, the adoptive family I was working with was devastated. Even if they'd wanted to or could have matched the other family's offer, they lived in a state where such transactions were illegal.

I never heard from Jena again. I did do a lot of venting over the next few weeks, however, and Erin, who was in the ninth grade, got an earful about baby buying. To my surprise, she wrote a story about the situation for her English class. It was a beautiful, heartbreaking short story, as if a junior Flannery O'Connor had gotten hold of my case notes. The teacher gave her a good grade for her writing but said the story "lacked verisimilitude." I just shook my head at this, knowing that the story did seem pretty unbelievable. Several months later, at a parent/teacher conference, I had the opportunity to tell him that the story was factual, but I could tell he didn't believe me. He's far from alone in clinging to the idea that babies are not bought and sold in this country.

Baby buying and selling usually come disguised, allowing everyone involved to convince themselves that it isn't really happening. For most of my career, it was relatively rare for birth parents, even those who were struggling financially, to ask for any significant financial help with living expenses. In fact, a lot of them were pleasantly surprised to find that the adoptive parents were supposed to cover all of the medical and adoption-related expenses.

Laws, regulations, and accepted practices regarding adoption expenses vary widely from state to state. Washington has clear laws about which expenses can be legitimately covered by adoptive parents. Many other states are less clear, leaving room for finagling, and in some states there seem to be no rules at all. I consider myself fortunate to have been able to conduct most of my business according to the laws of Washington. When either the birth or adoptive parents propose something that Washington law prohibits, I can give them an easily understood reason why I recommend against it and choose not to be involved. But had I been a counselor in the state where Jena lived, I might well have helped broker an adoption that from my Washington perspective would look like blatant baby buying. In the other state, it would have looked as though I was getting the best for both my birth-mother client (her small share of the $40,000, most of which went to the attorney, of course) and my adoptive-parent clients (a child to adopt whose birth mother is pretty and blond).

There have been plenty of improvements in adoption over the course of my career, but not when it comes to the expense of an adoption. This is due in part to the laws of supply and demand, there being far more families wanting to adopt than infants available for adoption. But I think an even greater factor is the lack of regulation in adoption: the lack of clear, consistent—and consistently enforced—federal and state laws. Both birth and adoptive parents can reasonably plead ignorance and confusion about the rules regarding adoption finances and related aspects of the adoption process. I often feel ignorant and confused myself because proper procedure seems to vary, sometimes not only from state to state but even from judge to judge. It can be very difficult for people to fully understand both the ethics and the laws pertaining to adoption, and it is especially confusing when money changes hands.

And finally, the moral erosion of standards that were long ago put in place to make adoption something nobler than baby selling has given rise to a particularly insidious figure: the adoption scammer. But that troubling subject deserves a chapter of its own.

26

Scammers

ONE NIGHT EARLY IN THE LIFE of Adoption Connections, a man who identified himself as Dale called. He told me that he and his girlfriend Jackie, who was due to deliver any day, had seen a newspaper ad placed by one of our families. He explained that he and Jackie had come from Louisiana to Portland, Oregon, in order to meet an adoptive family they had selected for their baby, but that something had gone very wrong, and now Dale and Jackie were stuck in the Portland bus station. They were penniless, no longer wanted to work with the Portland family, and were interested in Jeff and Hilary, the couple who had placed the ad. Dale said that Jackie was close to delivery and that they had no resources and nowhere to turn for help. They were committed to placing this baby for adoption and thought they had made all the necessary plans but suddenly found themselves in these desperate circumstances.

I called Jeff and Hilary and told them what I had learned about Dale and Jackie. After talking with their attorney to get approval for the expense, they decided to pay for two bus tickets to Seattle and a few days' motel bill so they could meet with the couple and decide what to do next. There was a flurry of phone calls to get all these arrangements made, and by the next day, we believed that Dale and Jackie were settled in at a Seattle motel. Everything seemed reasonable until Dale said that Jackie didn't want to meet with the family, so he would be coming to the breakfast meeting they had arranged by himself. Jeff, who is a psychologist, and Hilary, a designer, were an intelligent and sophisticated couple; intellectually, they knew they should proceed with caution. All of us were suspicious about Jackie's no-show, but Hilary felt strongly that there must be a reasonable explanation, and she didn't want to risk alienating Dale with our mistrust. Jeff and Hilary had what they considered to be a reasonable, if weird, meeting with Dale, and then we just waited to see what would happen next. Since Dale said the baby was due any minute, it seemed that the wait couldn't be long. Jeff and I were skeptical but hopeful that Jackie would appear soon, while Hilary had thrown caution to the wind and was wholeheartedly focused on the baby she felt would soon be hers.

I had more conversations with Dale over the next few days, and at one point he mentioned that he and Jackie had traveled from Louisiana by shrimp boat. That seemed like a suspiciously complex story, but I decided that it wasn't impossible; there was certainly plenty I didn't know about shrimp boats, navigation, and the Panama Canal. I was feeling increasingly uneasy about Dale, though, and wanted to insist on seeing Jackie before any more court-approved nights in the motel were provided, but Hilary still didn't want to confront him.

A few more days passed. Dale then called me to say that he had taken Jackie to the hospital for what turned out to be a false alarm. I called the hospital social worker to see if there was any record of Jackie having been there. There wasn't, but even that couldn't persuade Hilary to let go of her hopes. So we waited some more and paid for some more nights at the motel. After another few days, Dale called to say that he and Jackie were at the hospital again. This time, the social worker was there at the same time and was able to confirm that there was no one who could possibly be Jackie in labor and delivery at that time, nor had there been in the previous hours.

By now it was undeniably clear that Dale was lying, either about Jackie having been at the hospital, about her pregnancy, or about her very existence. But even in the face of all this evidence, Hilary still held out hope. Only when Dale abruptly disappeared did she begin to let go of the idea that somehow things would work out, and there would be a baby for her to adopt.

The experience was devastating for Jeff and Hilary. They decided to put the adoption on hold for a while and eventually told me that they were going to divorce. I don't know what their reasons were for divorcing, but the scam certainly took its toll on them. The only satisfaction came eight months later, when Hilary called to tell me that she had just seen Dale on *America's Most Wanted*. He had apparently been pulling similar scams up and down the West Coast and had finally been arrested. Satisfying as it was to find that Dale had been stopped, it proved small comfort for Jeff and Hilary.

Needless to say, this was a real learning experience for me, and my anxiety about scammers was on high alert. So when a man who called himself Darrel called three months after Dale had disappeared, with the same accent, I almost hung up on him. I was on the verge of telling him that I knew he was a scammer . . . but something held me back. Patti and I kept talking with him over the next week and eventually connected him with one of our families; the effort ended a month later in a happy adoption. It was an excellent lesson on the benefits of following through on every "lead" even in the most suspicious of circumstances.

You would think that adoption scammers would be easy to detect, but a combination of factors (and emotions) makes it extremely difficult to avoid the pain and heartbreak that couples inevitably suffer when they are manipulated in this especially cruel way. Scammers can be stunningly skilled at parrying attempts to ferret them out. I have asked for proof of pregnancy, only to have scammers provide fake medical records. I routinely ask for a "release of information" in order to talk with the "birth mother's" doctor, but lots of legitimate birth mothers either haven't yet gotten medical care or feel uncomfortable providing the family with access to their medical records so early in the relationship, so a refusal to provide the information isn't necessarily evidence of dishonesty. I routinely ask that callers speak directly with the family's attorney, but many honest birth mothers feel reluctant to take this step until they have gotten to know the family better.

I have found that the most reliable method of detecting a scam is simply to put in the time necessary to get to know the woman. I listen a lot, gather information, and eventually we reach a point where we can go no further until she takes some sort of concrete action. A scammer at that point will invariably say that she miscarried, or she will simply stop calling and stop responding to calls or email messages. But even callers who are not scammers may, for some other reason, decide to break off contact, and we can never know for sure if they were actually pregnant or if they were really considering adoption for the baby.

The majority of adoption scammers come in two varieties: the financial scammer and the emotional scammer. In Washington State, it is relatively easy to recognize and weed out the financial scammers because state law requires court approval for any payments by adoptive parents to birth mothers for anything unrelated to medical or legal expenses. So before any money can change hands, the birth mother has to communicate with the family's attorney—something scammers generally try to avoid. Many other states have much more lenient laws, so Washington families are at a disadvantage when it comes to competing for birth mothers, but at a distinct advantage when it comes to avoiding financial scams. For the most part, families living in Washington respect these legal restrictions because disregarding them puts the entire adoption at risk. Giving money to a birth mother without court approval can be interpreted as coercion—which can be grounds for overturning an adoption.

Financial scammers often call with an urgent request for financial assistance, so it is always best to take things slowly and allow time to get better acquainted with the caller and the situation. Callers who are in such a crisis that they cannot tolerate any delay or understand why the family can't immediately send them money are unlikely prospects for completing an adoption. In any event, the decision to place a child for adoption should not be made in the midst of a financial crisis, nor should it be based solely on the inability to provide financially for a child. Pregnant women in the United States have options other than surrendering their babies in hard times, and they should be steered toward them if it appears that their sole motivation for relinquishing is financial stress.

Emotional scammers—those scamming for other than financial reasons—are different, nearly always being motivated by the desire for power and attention. Some also have significant mental-health problems. I spent a lot of time talking to emotional scammers in the early years of Adoption Connections; in an effort never to overlook possible connections for my adoptive families. I would take calls twenty-four hours a day, and every few months I would find myself sitting on the edge of the tub in our downstairs bathroom, which was the most soundproof location in our silent house, and listening to someone's tale of woe in the middle of the night. It took nearly a year for me to finally realize that accepting collect calls from men in prisons wasn't a good use of my time. Collect calls from women in prisons, on the other hand, sometimes did end up leading to successful adoptions.

The typical emotional scammer starts out sounding like any other caller. But the pattern of their calls and the way they disclose information—or avoid disclosing it—can be quite distinct. Many scammers call at inappropriate hours; they tend to call frequently, often multiple times a day, and talk for long periods of time; their stories are invariably dramatic and heart-wrenching. Many want immediate contact with the adoptive mom, usually by phone, and typically they tell her in their first conversation that they have already chosen her and are absolutely committed to their decision to relinquish. The caller's excitement and reassurances make the adoptive family feel happy and hopeful. I then have the unpleasant task of reminding them that there are some red flags about the caller.

I know the warning signs of a scam all too well, and I air my concerns to the adoptive family, although none of us feels certain enough about a suspicious situation to walk away immediately. So we cautiously play it out. We set up "steps" for the woman to take, such as asking her to send back forms, call the family's attorney, give us her doctor's name, sign a release of information, and so on. Of course, even legitimate callers sometimes fail to follow through with these steps, so they are not foolproof. I have, however, gotten much better at detecting scammers, and Patti and I have our "red flag" list for prospective adoptive parents to consider. It includes the following warning signs.

1. The birth mother says she is expecting twins.
2. She says she has done some modeling.
3. She claims that she or the birth father "come from money."
4. She tells you that the birth father has recently died—typically as the result of a dramatic illness, accident, or crime.
5. She says she was a victim of ritualistic sexual abuse.
6. She wants to tell the adoptive mother that she has chosen her even before talking with her or asking for more information about the family.
7. She expresses little interest in finding out more about the family, beyond the information in their ad or online profile.
8. She repeatedly insists that she is sure about her adoption decision.
9. She calls multiple times a day and talks for long periods of time.
10. She gets confused about details and has no explanation for discrepancies in the information she provides.
11. She is either highly emotional or has a flat affect.
12. If the communication is by email, she has a somewhat inappropriate email name, such as "hotvixen."
13. She brings up the subject of scamming, reassures the family that she is "real" and/or wants reassurance from them that they are not being dishonest with her in some manner.

(Before going on, I should add that I have worked with wonderful, completely truthful women who raised one or more of each of these red flags.)

Emotional scams usually play themselves out in a few days or weeks. While the Internet has made scamming much more widespread, it has also made it easier to identify scammers, many of whom aren't savvy about protecting their identities. Fortunately, adoptive parents and professionals have gotten smart about sharing information with each other, and they are highly motivated to stop scammers. But even though most scams are short-lived and unsuccessful, they still take a heavy emotional toll, and some are lengthy, costly, and devastating to the adoptive parents. At best, scammers just waste everyone's time. At worst, they break people's hearts and spirits.

Being scammed feels horrible. It is especially painful to have something as precious as your search for a child be tainted by cruelty and dysfunction. Couples who have struggled with infertility hardly need reminding that life is not fair, and being targeted by scammers after all they've been through feels like an extra low blow. Couples struggling with infertility have lost control over their expectations about parenthood, and scams intensify this loss exponentially. They evoke feelings of sadness, anger, frustration, helplessness, hopelessness, and rage.

The first time I dealt with an emotional scammer, I was determined to track her down and exact revenge. She had given me her address so that I could mail her some family profiles, and I called the police in the small town where she lived. They went out to talk with her; but when they later described the encounter to me, I mostly felt pity for her. The policewoman I spoke with told me that the woman seemed genuinely sorry and scared but was probably incapable of understanding the damage she did with these scam calls. I was still furious about all the grief she had caused my clients, but I realized that this woman didn't do it out of a desire to hurt them or waste our time. Rather, she just wanted to connect with someone and feel important. She wanted to talk with people who would ask her questions about her life and her feelings. She wanted to hear an adoptive mom tell her how much she admired her for trying to do the best for her baby by planning an adoption. She had found a source of eager listeners, and it was gratifying to talk with them. There likely were no other people in her life who gave her so much positive attention— chances are that no one was paying much attention to her at all, in fact. This doesn't excuse her of course, but I do think that understanding the extent of sadness and dysfunction in the lives of some of these women helps take a little of the hurt out of being emotionally scammed.

27

Trevor and Amanda

I N ADDITION TO MY WORK with Adoption Connections, I have a private practice and work with families who are planning to adopt independently rather than through an agency. This means that they will search for a prospective birth mother on their own, generally through newspaper advertisements, adoption websites, and personal networking. Once a couple forges a connection with a prospective birth mother, they hire an attorney to handle the adoption's legal matters. My role in these adoptions is often limited to preparing the home study and submitting a post-placement report to the court after the baby is in the home and before the adoption is finalized. But a number of adoptive families ask for more advice or help in the course of their independent adoption.

Several years ago, a couple whose home study I had done called me, excited. They had just connected, through a friend of a friend, with a young woman who had a two-month-old baby boy and was looking for the right adoptive parents for him. This young woman had thought about adoption during the pregnancy but never got as far as making specific plans. Now that she had actually experienced parenthood, she realized that she didn't feel capable of being the mother she wanted her son to have.

The couple decided to travel to the small town to meet with the young woman and learn more about the situation. When they arrived at her home, they found both birth parents, the grandmother, and various other extended-family members, all of whom were in favor of adoption for the baby. Everyone got along famously at the visit, and within a week, the birth parents had chosen this couple to adopt their son. They arranged for a semi-open adoption and agreed to exchange pictures and letters and to stay in contact over the years. The legal process went smoothly, and the child was placed in his adoptive home in approximately two weeks. Other than the fact that I felt the birth parents should have had some counseling, this adoption was a good example of how direct and uncomplicated the process can be. The birth and adoptive parents were happy, and the baby got to his permanent home without unnecessary delay, thereby lessening the trauma of the move for him.

But efficient endings in situations like that are uncommon. Little more than a month later, the same couple received a call from their son's birth grandmother. She wanted to tell them that meeting them had eased her anxieties about adoption—so much so that she also wanted to tell them about another relative of hers who was considering adoption for her baby, and wondered if they knew of any other potential adoptive parents. The family referred her to me.

The second baby was seven months old and had been in foster care for all but the first two weeks of her life. After a series of calls, I found myself talking with this child's paternal grandmother, who told me that her son Trevor and his girlfriend Amanda had lost custody of the baby to the state, and she thought it unlikely that they would get her back. She had heard about the first adoption and started thinking about how Trevor and Amanda would like to be able to pick their baby's adoptive family and get letters and pictures over the years instead of just having her disappear into the foster care system without knowing anything about where she was or how she was doing.

I explained to the grandmother that I did know about prospective families and would be happy to send her some information about them. However, because the baby was in state custody, even if Trevor and Amanda decided that they wanted to pursue an adoption, the process would be very different from the first adoption, and everyone would have to be extremely patient.

Trevor, Amanda, and the grandmother studied the family profiles I sent them and asked to meet with one of the couples. The following weekend, John and Kelly and their five-year-old daughter Olivia—who had been adopted as an infant—traveled across the state to meet the birth family, and the visit went extremely well. That evening, both families called me to say that they were interested in moving ahead with an adoption.

While the two families relayed much of the same information to me about their visit, their reactions were markedly different. The birth father and grandmother expressed excitement and amazement at their good fortune in finding such a great family. By contrast, the adoptive mother—usually the person whose emotions are off the charts at this point—was subdued. While Kelly definitely felt that the visit had been a success and was excited about the possibility of adopting this baby, she had been terribly sobered by meeting the birth family. The birth mother, Amanda, had been particularly taken with Olivia and had spent quite a while playing with her; and when the visit was over, she declared that she could tell that John and Kelly were good parents because Olivia was "so clean." This was especially poignant in light of the fact that Trevor and Amanda's baby had been put into foster care at two weeks old in part because she had serious lesions caused by having gone many days without a diaper change.

As I knew from past experience, it can be difficult at best, and more often impossible, to extricate a child from the state foster care system and free him or her for adoption in a timely manner. But in this case, we had birth parents who wanted to relinquish their child to a particular family that was willing and eager to adopt her. We also had an adoption counselor from a licensed adoption agency, a nationally respected adoption attorney, and a number of child welfare professionals from the county where the birth family lived—all working to advance an adoption. Everyone agreed that the birth parents (who turned out to be part of a large extended family with a number of children in foster care) were highly unlikely to make the improvements necessary for them to regain custody of their baby. So their caseworker had been planning to "move to termination" of their parental rights at some point in the future. Her resolve had grown stronger, she told me, after Trevor had been observed masturbating in full view of everyone during a recent supervised office visit with his baby.

Besieged by memories of children who languished for years in foster care, I was anxious to move the adoption forward as quickly as possible. Here was a seven-month-old baby who had already lived in three different foster homes; she needed permanence and stability. She had already suffered from early neglect, repeated disruptions in placement, and the disadvantage of having been born to parents who could not provide for her. I felt there was no time to waste and I knew that if DSHS handled the adoption, it wouldn't proceed quickly.

I hoped that Trevor's and Amanda's enthusiasm about John and Kelly and the fact that they now wanted to voluntarily relinquish their parental rights would seem like a positive development to the state caseworker. But she was unfamiliar with private adoption and was understandably cautious. John and Kelly's attorney—a past president of the American Academy of Adoption At-torneys—and I did our best to educate the caseworker's office about private adoption, to allay their suspicions, and to encourage them to feel the sense of urgency we felt about getting this child to her adoptive parents as quickly as possible. Even so, the placement took more than two months to accomplish, instead of the two weeks the other adoption had taken—much too long a time in the life of a seven-month-old and the family waiting for her. But I know from my own experience in working for DSHS in Michigan that the process must have seemed like a nerve-wracking whirlwind to the caseworker, who didn't understand that our approach was every bit as legal and ethical as an adoption handled by the state.

I had had a much more discouraging experience several years earlier when I tried to work with the foster care system in another state on behalf of a family from Washington. They were an exceptional family and, a number of years earlier, had adopted a child with developmental delays caused by a rare medical condition, who was now thriving in their home. The adoptive mother, in particular, was a tremendous advocate for all of her children, and she left no stone unturned in finding the best resources for her son with special needs. One day, she called to tell me that she had seen a registry of waiting children from another state that included a little boy with very similar special needs to those of her own child and to ask if I would investigate the situation for her.

I called the child's caseworker, discovered that they were indeed looking for an adoptive home for him, and told her that I would like to send her information about this particular family to consider along with other applicants. We had a long conversation in which she agreed that they seemed like a good family for this child since they were not only experienced parents but were already knowledgeable about how to care for a child with his particular needs. So, I sent her their home study, and then we waited. I had warned the family that it would probably be a slow and frustrating process to work within the state system, but I had not anticipated how thoroughly infuriating and ultimately defeating things would become.

The first sign of trouble came about a month after my initial conversation with the caseworker, when she informed me that although my prospective adoptive family was obviously well qualified to parent this child, they could not be considered until every family that lived in her state had been eliminated as a possibility. My clients were saddened by this news and wondered why it had never been mentioned before, but felt they still had a chance since the caseworker had let them know that there weren't likely to be many families as well qualified to parent this child as they were. Several more months went by, with me periodically calling to check on the status of things with the caseworker and, more frequently, receiving calls from the adoptive mom who needed to express her amazement and annoyance at the situation. Finally, in the fourth month, my family was informed that they were out of the running because the child couldn't be placed out of state. An appropriate in-state family hadn't been found yet, but they would just have to keep looking.

My first reaction to this news was anger on behalf of my family. Why had they been so misinformed and allowed to spend four months thinking about this child and imagining him as their own when that had apparently never even been a possibility? Then I got angry on behalf of the three-year-old boy who could and should have had the opportunity to become part of a family that was uniquely qualified to care for him but instead was going to remain in foster care even longer because of some arbitrary restriction on the pool of people who were eligible to become his parents.

Although I was given no further information about exactly why this state didn't like to send kids out of state, it seemed likely that their reasoning for this policy had nothing to do with the best interests of the child. Instead, I suspect it was about funding or possibly avoiding placement statistics that would make that state look bad. When the caseworker finally met with her "higher-ups" to discuss an out-of-state placement, they must have informed her that it couldn't happen, at least not without a much longer effort to find an in-state family. The whole thing was a sad waste of time and emotion for my family. But the one who really suffered was the child who was under the "care" of a child welfare system that could somehow justify putting the urgency of his need for a family second to its own need to adhere to policy.

I don't blame that caseworker for not understanding that she couldn't place this child out of state even when there was no family ready to adopt him in state. Policies like that are beyond understanding.

Things went better for Trevor and Amanda's baby. Several months after the placement, the adoptive family and I visited with the birth family. They had asked that we meet at a local shopping mall and said they were planning to bring along some relatives. I had learned a bit more about the extended family from the DSHS worker during the intervening months and was concerned that these extra family members who wanted to be at the visit might be the ones who were frequently in and out of jail. John and Kelly were nervous as well, but wanted to go ahead as planned and not put any limitations on how many people could be at the visit.

As it turned out, my fears were unfounded. There were a few extra people there in addition to Trevor and Amanda, the grandmother, and some small cousins, but everyone was wonderfully gracious. They treated John and Kelly and their girls like family celebrities. There was a great deal of oohing and ah-hing over how darling the baby was, how much she'd grown, what a great big sister Olivia was, and how grateful everyone was to John and Kelly. For their part, John and Kelly thanked Trevor, Amanda, and the grandmother repeatedly, assuring them that they would do everything in their power to give this child a wonderful life.

The only awkward moment came when Amanda cheerfully announced that she had just discovered that she was pregnant again.

Six months later, Trevor called, this time from a small town in Oregon. He told me that he and Amanda had moved there hoping for a fresh start and hoping to avoid the Washington caseworker in their hometown when the new baby was born. But he was worried. He believed that she had already alerted the authorities in Oregon because a Child Protective Services worker had come to their home that morning. He wanted me to tell him what to do to keep the authorities away, and I told him the best thing they could do would be to take good care of the baby. Trevor seemed to feel that that was good advice and a workable plan, and the call ended with each of us wishing the other well. I haven't heard from him again.

V
CHANGES

28

A Battle for Gay Adoption

"Don't ask, don't tell" was a well-established (if unstated) policy in the adoption world long before the phrase became widely known with respect to members of the military during the Clinton administration. The "don't ask" part of working with gay or lesbian clients in the 1980s and early 1990s was tremendously easy because the concept of gay and lesbian adoptive parenthood was almost completely unacknowledged by society during the early years of my work with adoptive families. As incredible as it sounds now, there weren't even all that many individuals who were comfortably "out" to their own families or in their professional lives. Most adoption agencies, many of which were religiously affiliated, either had strict policies against working with gay and lesbian clients or considered the idea so far off the radar that no policy was necessary. Most private agencies didn't even accept applications from single parents, thereby imagining that they were eliminating the problem of sexual orientation altogether. When agencies did work with single parents, female applicants, often with "roommates," were under no suspicion. Single men, almost never with "roommates," were effectively considered guilty (of unspecified moral failings) until proven innocent. They were routinely asked to provide evidence of psychological screening far beyond the normal home study requirements, and were viewed with caution if not outright suspicion.

The "don't tell" side of the coin was especially problematic—and in some ways exceeded even the daunting ethical and psychological ramifications essentially ordering soldiers to live a lie during their military service. In order to be approved for adoptive parenthood, gay or lesbian applicants had to misrepresent themselves throughout the home study process—a demeaning, frustrating, infuriating, depressing, and logistically difficult exercise. During a time when they should have been focusing on the busy, joyful anticipation of parenthood, they were forced to create guarded relationships not only with the professionals guiding them through the adoption process but with society in general. There was no way for them to anticipate where outrage might come from, and no predicting how an adoption agency that officially didn't know about the applicant's sexual orientation would respond if it was revealed after the child's placement. This was an era in which gay and lesbian biological parents sometimes lost primary custody of their children after a divorce simply because of their sexual orientation; and if a biological parent could not feel secure in his or her parenthood, adoptive parents certainly could not.

The situation was further complicated by the fact that the adoptive parent who didn't mention his or her sexual orientation during the home study interview was being less than forthcoming—grounds for invalidating the home study as a reliable assessment of the applicant's suitability for adoption. If dishonesty could be proven after an adoption had been completed, an agency could claim breach of contract and ask that it be overturned. Mercifully, this didn't seem to happen often, in part because these families avoided working with clearly homophobic agencies.

But, more significantly, adoption professionals working with gay and lesbian applicants, having gotten to know them firsthand, ended up advocating for them regardless of whether they recognized or acknowledged the adoptive parent's sexual orientation. Even in those unenlightened times, many gay and lesbian parents successfully adopted, and in the process, slowly but surely raised the consciousness of adoption professionals. Social workers who completed post-placement reports observed the successes for both parents and children, and they turned (sometimes much to their own amazement) into champions of gay adoption. But they were generally very quiet champions, as much of mainstream society still regarded gay and lesbian adoptive parenthood as problematic, if not taboo.

Because gay and lesbian parents were adopting as single parents, they typically could not expect to adopt healthy infants, who were in short supply even for two-parent families. Instead, many pursued parenthood through the state, so their children often came from the foster care system. These kids were typically considered hard to place due to age, special needs, or other complications, and there was only a small pool of available prospective adoptive parents who were willing and able to take on the challenges they posed. The number of able and willing parents was considerably smaller than the number of kids needing homes—hence the state's willingness to welcome single-parent applicants. Rather than adhere to an across-the-board preference for two-parent families, caseworkers for some of the children in state care actually requested single parents, typically when a child's history of abuse made bonding with an opposite-sex parent problematic. For these and other reasons, including changes in state antidiscrimination laws, the Washington State Department of Social and Health Services found itself on the forefront of what was coming to be called "gay adoption."

It was in this context that I was contacted by a gay couple, Joe and Alex, who were trying to do an in-country adoption. They were actively involved in a local adoption support group for same-sex parents and were well informed about their options, including the possibility of adopting a child from the state foster care system. They had learned of a four-year-old boy in state custody whose birth mother had had considerable difficulty parenting and had decided to relinquish her rights and allow the little boy to be adopted.

Happily for Joe and Alex, the Department of Social and Health Services (DSHS) was open to the possibility of placing this child, who had some special needs, with a same-sex couple. While there already were numerous gay and lesbian adoptive parents by this time, this degree of openness from a state agency about such a placement was not at all the norm. Official policies and unofficial practices varied widely from state to state (and, no doubt, even from caseworker to caseworker), but it is safe to say that there were many average citizens in the mid-1990s who would have been surprised to hear that the state sanctioned gay and lesbian adoptive parenthood. Even strong supporters of these families were a bit surprised that the state was taking this stance.

Predictably, there was a group of citizens who were not only surprised but outraged when they discovered what DSHS was doing. And their leader was a ferocious character named Lon Mabon who, in 1986, had founded a group called the Oregon Citizen Alliance (OCA), a conservative Christian political activist organization. Originally focused on ousting the Democratic U.S. senator from Oregon at the time, the group continued to be involved in Oregon politics through the next decade. A primary goal was to repeal the governor's order banning discrimination based on sexual orientation, an effort that was approved by the voters, 52.7 percent to 47.3 percent, in 1988. In 1992, the OCA attempted to go even further to prevent what it termed "special rights" for homosexuals by adding a provision that the state "recognized homosexuality, pedophilia, sadism and masochism as abnormal, wrong, unnatural and perverse."[1] This time, not only did the voters defeat the measure, 56 percent

---

1. Nicola, George T. "Oregon's Other Gay Record: A Recent History of Anti-Gay Ballot Initiatives from Around the State." *Street Roots News.* May 6, 2014. http://news.streetroots.org.

to 44 percent, but also the Oregon Court of Appeals declared the earlier vote, known as Measure 8, unconstitutional.

So Lon Mabon was upset in 1993, and when he learned of a pending adoption by a gay couple in Washington, he launched an all-out media war focused on turning the birth mother into an undeserving victim of Washington State.

The birth mother was a young woman who had a long, troubling history of problems with drinking and petty crime and was well-known to juvenile authorities years before she showed up on the national talk-show circuit at age twenty-two. She had given birth to her son when she was eighteen, and he had spent most of his life in foster homes. When the child was three, the birth mother decided to relinquish her parental rights. By that time, she had gotten married, and she and her husband had a five-month-old daughter. It is not clear why the birth mother felt capable of raising her daughter and incapable of raising her son; it may have been because of his special needs.

After the birth mother relinquished her parental rights, the DSHS caseworker began searching for a suitable adoptive home for the now four-year-old child. There were a number of applicants, including Joe and Alex, who eventually rose to the top of the list. The caseworker arranged for them to begin visiting with the little boy, and the three of them began forming a bond.

Everything was going well until someone who was upset about the idea of DSHS placing a child with a gay couple alerted the Rutherford Foundation, a conservative religious-rights group based in Charlottesville, Virginia. Outrage ensued, the media circus began, and Joe and Alex found their happy preparations for parenthood abruptly put on hold. They were both private people and hardly the type to seek the spotlight for any reason, let alone one so controversial and personal. It would have been much simpler, practically and legally, for them to decide not to get further involved in such a high-risk and now high-profile adoption. Joe and Alex had the option of telling the caseworker to withdraw their application so they could move on to adopt a child who didn't come with these complications. But they chose not to walk away from the situation because they had already dared to believe that this child might become their own. For many adoptive parents, simply hearing the coming child's name or seeing his or her picture for the first time begins the attachment process.

Telling Joe and Alex to forget about this child at this point would have been like telling expectant biological parents to forget about this particular pregnancy and move on to the next.

Joe and Alex were about to find out how hard—and how weird—it is to take on the religious right. The Rutherford Foundation, with Lon Mabon as its spokesman, decided that the birth mother could be the perfect poster child for the national campaign they were waging against the LGBTQ community. In 1993, Washington was one of only six states that allowed same-sex parents to adopt, and the religious right was working aggressively to get the state's laws changed. The birth mother's situation as presented by the Rutherford media team—a now-reformed, formerly troubled young woman whose baby was stolen from her by the state and turned over to gay men—evoked sympathy, even outrage, and proved predictably irresistible to daytime television programmers.

Mabon's team put her through a thorough makeover, with a new wardrobe, new hairdo, and new makeup—all of which aged her dramatically, somehow managing to make her look more like Dana Carvey's famous *Saturday Night Live* Church Lady character than the young woman she actually was. The birth mother may not have looked anything like her actual self, but she was right out of central casting for the role of Wronged Mother. The role called for her to act devastated at the prospect of her son being snatched from her to be raised by gay men, and she dutifully told the various talk-show hosts and audiences that she wanted to have her son back in order to spare him this awful fate.

Her story was designed to be horrifying to the homophobic in the classic "born again" tradition. It had the added virtue to its promoters of being unsettling, as well, to a broader audience of people susceptible to government-overreach stories. Watching her on these shows was no doubt incredibly frustrating to the DSHS caseworker, who was constrained from talking about the birth mother's history, and it was terrifying to Joe and Alex.

The drama surrounding the boy's placement grew over the summer, and the parties found themselves back in court. The birth mother testified that DSHS had promised that her son would be placed with a mother and a father, and that placement with a gay couple was "my worst nightmare come true." Her attorney claimed that she "was not fully competent and did not fully understand the consequences" of relinquishment, and had only done so "through duress and fraud."[2] The birth mother also claimed that she had straightened out her life, gotten married, had another child, whom she was raising, and now wanted to rear her son as well. The attorney for DSHS argued that her parental rights had been relinquished a year earlier and that the child had been in several different foster homes since that time, while the birth mother had made no effort to reverse her decision. She no longer had legal standing in this matter, and her efforts to regain custody were "the same

---

2. Norton, Dee. "Possible Gay Couple's Adoption Bid Halted." September 11, 1993. http://community.seattletimes.news source.com.

as if someone came in off the street and started voicing their opinion about the welfare of this child."[3]

As for the issue of placement with a gay couple, the regional administrator for DSHS testified that state antidiscrimination law forbade DSHS from considering sexual orientation in selecting adoptive parents and that "the issue is parenting skills." Joe and Alex had been thoroughly investigated, and it was determined that they were a good match for the child. Nevertheless, the birth mother's attorney was briefly successful in obtaining a temporary restraining order against DSHS, and the placement was delayed. DSHS immediately appealed to the County Superior Court, and the temporary restraining order was dissolved, allowing them to proceed with the adoptive placement. Joe and Alex had been meeting with the child since summer, and he moved into their home within a few days of the September ruling. But that certainly didn't end the battle.

The parties were back in court in October, when the birth mother's request to have the child returned to foster care was denied, but the maneuvering wasn't over yet. In November, the birth mother and her husband filed their own petition for adoption and, incredibly, they found a Whatcom County judge who issued an order later that month for the boy to spend up to sixty days with them to see how well he did in their home. DSHS appealed this decision, arguing that it should be allowed to present arguments against that placement. In December, the same judge declared the DSHS desire to present evidence about the birth mother's unsuitability as a parent "old news" and denied the agency a new hearing. DSHS then appealed to a higher court and eventually the earlier order for a sixty-day placement with the birth mother was blocked, with the appellate judge noting that "this blanket attempt to circumvent the legitimate exercise of the department's custodial authority is utterly devoid of merit" and "contrary to established principles in the law of adoption."[4]

During the months of legal maneuvering, a number of "irregularities" having nothing to do with gay adoption came to light, raising questions about the wisdom of restoring the birth mother's parental rights. Most alarming was the husband's filing of a separation petition accusing the birth mother of threatening to kill him, herself, and their two-year-old daughter. Her attorney dismissed the couple's problems with the statement, "If these things

---

3. "Mother Files to Ban Adoption by Gay Couple." *New York Times.* September 20, 1993. http://nttimes.com.

4. Klass, Tim. "Mother Loses Bid for Return of Son, 3—Court Rejects Case Tied to Adoption by Gay Couple." April 12, 1994. http://seattletimes.nwsource.com.

were said, I don't think for a minute she was serious."[5] All the same, the birth mother, who was pregnant again, remained apart from her husband as they both continued to claim that they wanted to adopt the boy.

By April, the birth mother's life had become so obviously unstable that her husband was given custody of their daughter, and a judge ordered that custody of the new baby be given to the father immediately after it was born. Earlier that month, while pregnant, the birth mother had been hospitalized after taking an overdose in an apparent suicide attempt. By now, it had become impossible for anyone to argue that she should be allowed to adopt her son, but the religious right soldiered on without her in their war against gay adoption. Her attorney noted that he was handling the case without charge, although he did concede that the Rutherford Foundation had paid some of his expenses.

The media reported extensively—and often breathlessly—on this story. People automatically took sides, depending on their views about gay adoption. No one was interested in the actual legal issues, which primarily concerned the legal intricacies around relinquishment of parental rights. It was clear that the battle was about gay rights and that the fight had never really been between Joe and Alex and the birth mother. Rather, it was a war waged by the religious right against liberal thinking and the LGBTQ community. The child was a very small but effective pawn in their game.

While all the upheaval swirled around them, Joe and Alex quietly busied themselves at the job of becoming parents. The boy, traumatized by all the upheaval in his life, was a challenging child. Joe and Alex realized as they got to know and love their son that they had to do everything they could to prevent him from being hurt by all the negative publicity directed at their family. Not only did they not want him to become collateral damage in the anti-gay war being waged by the religious right—they felt well prepared to help him with that issue as he grew up—but they were concerned about protecting him from negative portraits of his birth mother as well.

When the legal issues were finally settled, Lon Mabon went away, and Joe and Alex were free to finalize their son's adoption and get on with their lives without the scrutiny of the media. They decided to reach out to the birth mother in an effort to give them all the opportunity to get to know each other and hopefully dispel some of the bad feeling between them. Joe and Alex wanted to put her fears about them to rest and reassure her that they would give her son a wonderful home. They also hoped to reach some sort of agreement with her about ongoing contact, since they believed it would be in the child's best interests to maintain relationships with various members of his

5. Broom, Jack. "Troubled Couple Fight to Get Back Son." February 17, 1994. http:community.seattletimes.nwsource.com.

birth family. A meeting was set up at which all three adults got along well, and the birth mother reassured Joe and Alex that now that she had met them, she felt just fine about the fact that they were a same-sex couple.

For some reason, the media wasn't interested in this part of the story. There were no more talk-show appearances, and no one asked the birth mother to explain why her feelings had changed or how it was that she could have been so thoroughly manipulated by Lon Mabon.

After my involvement with Joe and Alex, I became known as someone who was "gay friendly," and attorneys began referring their gay and lesbian clients to me. Most of the time these people were either gay couples who were starting the search for an infant or lesbian couples in which one partner was adopting her partner's baby. Often the two women had planned for the baby together, usually with the assistance of a sperm bank and sometimes with the assistance and ongoing involvement of a male friend or a relative of the partner who wasn't giving birth. The gay couples would need a full home study for an infant adoption, whereas the women needed a home study for what is called a "second parent" adoption.

For obvious reasons, it is harder for gay couples to become the parents of an infant than it is for lesbian couples. Traditional surrogacy, in which a woman (sometimes a relative or friend, sometimes someone they have hired as a surrogate) gives birth to a child that is genetically hers, has long been an option for gay couples. One of the men in the couple is usually the genetic father, through artificial insemination, and some couples opt to use a mixture of sperm from both of them so that they will have an equal chance of being the child's genetic father.

Gay couples may also choose to do what is called a "gestational surrogacy," in which the surrogate mother carries a baby who is the genetic child of an egg donor (maybe a relative or friend or someone the couple has contracted with). Surrogate arrangements can be extremely complicated, both logistically and emotionally, as well as risky and very expensive. I've known a number of men whose happy families have been created through surrogacy, but it isn't usually an easy process.

During most of my career, adoption facilitators were the primary source of babies for the gay couples I knew. The facilitators they worked with were usually in California; they were expensive, and the babies usually arrived fairly quickly. This was because the men were willing to take risks that heterosexual couples typically didn't want to take, such as working with women who had a history of substance abuse, criminal involvement, and other worrisome lifestyle choices. It may have been that gay couples tended to be more openhearted and empathetic, possibly because they knew what it felt like to be marginalized. More likely, they just felt they couldn't afford to be picky.

Despite the "outrageous sex columnist" style that made some conservative readers reject its advice, Dan Savage's *The Kid*, written in 1999, is an accurate, encouraging, and tender portrayal of what it was like for a gay couple to go through the open-adoption process at that time. It is also both hilarious and frightening, depending on your comfort level with people who are different from you in one way or another. Savage eloquently explains how he and his partner found common ground with other adoptive parents in an era when gay adoption was supposedly frowned upon by most of society. They also found common ground with their son's birth parents at a time when most adoptive families wouldn't have agreed to an open relationship with a couple of "gutter punks," as the birth parents described themselves. Dan and his partner worked with an agency called Open Adoption and Family Services, with offices in Seattle and Portland, which quickly became the go-to agency for same-sex couples who wanted to adopt an infant, and it seemed to me that things began to improve for same-sex couples slowly but steadily.

I so clearly remember the time when my initial phone conversations with same-sex clients would start out tensely. Even though they had almost always been referred to me by people who knew that I was happy to work with gay and lesbian couples, the callers still seemed to feel the need to approach with caution.

As the years passed, same-sex couples became more confident about being welcomed and supported by adoption professionals (sometimes the same people who had previously been conservative in their views on the subject), and eventually there were plenty of adoption counselors around Seattle who were eager to work with these families. Many adoption professionals these days routinely ask birth mothers if they are open to a same-sex couple, and many birth mothers say that they are, or at least that they are willing to hear about them or look at their profiles. Some birth mothers specifically seek out gay adoptive parents because they like the notion of being able to remain the only mother the child will have. This isn't exactly a healthy or realistic expectation, though, and birth mothers who are motivated by the idea of co-parenting with a couple of men are likely to be unrealistic about other aspects of an adoption as well. The "Three Men and a Baby" (and a woman who flits in and out of their lives) fantasy is just that . . . a fantasy.

In December 2012, when same-sex marriage became legal in Washington State, everything changed for the lesbian couples. If they were legally married, and one of them gave birth to a child, the partner/spouse was automatically also considered to be a legal parent, just as it is with heterosexual couples, even when the husband isn't the biological father. I remember a night spent at the Seattle offices of the ACLU (where my daughter Caitlin now works) making last minute get-out-the-vote calls about legalizing same-sex marriage and the elation/amazement everyone felt the next day when it actually passed. The 2015 Supreme Court decision legalizing same-sex marriage throughout the nation further cemented the rights of these families.

As a result, I have lost most of my lesbian clients, although some still go through the adoption process in order to ensure their legal rights in states other than Washington. Gay partners, even when they are legally married, still need to adopt children who are born through surrogate arrangements; however, as these arrangements become more common, for both same-sex and heterosexual couples, the laws will eventually catch up with that reality, and I will lose those clients as well. Normally I would not feel good about such a significant decrease in business, but in this case, I will be delighted, just as I am delighted to have had the opportunity to get to know so many same-sex couples over the years as they changed and improved upon society's under-standing of what it means to be a family.

29

Baby Brokers

I USED TO BE FAIRLY CONFIDENT in my ability to recognize and avoid unethical people and practices. I worked only with licensed agencies and with
counselors and attorneys who had good reputations, and I didn't work with
birth or adoptive parents who wanted anything ethically questionable. I was
always guided, as are most adoption professionals, by the knowledge that
carelessness on my part could lead to tragedy for a birth parent or an adoptive
family, in the form of a lamented decision or an overturned adoption. The
possibility of these things happening because of a mistake on my part kept
me on a very cautious path. The rules were clearer in those days, and I knew
how to remain on the legal, ethical, and helpful side of things. But now I find
it increasingly difficult to determine which people and situations are likely to
become ethically problematic.

Part of the problem is the proliferation of "adoption facilitation services,"
which are allowed to function much like child-placing agencies but typically
lack the rigorous state oversight that is required of licensed agencies. The efforts of facilitators are largely focused on connecting adoptive families with
pregnant women who are considering adoption, generally through extensive
advertising. Before I go on, I want to point out that adoption facilitators run
the gamut from being dedicated, hardworking, and professional to uninformed, unethical, and a nightmare for both the birth and adoptive parents to
work with. In fairness to facilitators, I also want to say that there are licensed
agencies that manage to be ethical nightmares as well, despite strict oversight
and regulation.

The initial idea, and enthusiasm, for adoption facilitators grew in response to the skyrocketing costs of agency adoption. The idea was that the facilitator, for a much, much lower fee than an agency would charge, would take over what was considered by many families the most time-consuming and scariest part of an adoption—finding the birth mother. Once facilitators had done their initial research about advertising, their knowledge could be broadly applied, and they could be far more efficient than individual families in placing ads. Even more importantly, facilitators would screen the calls generated by their ads and presumably protect families from stressful, demanding, or even dangerous callers. After successfully connecting a birth mother and a family, the facilitator could hand things off to an attorney, who would complete the adoption. It was actually a good business model and very similar to that of Adoption Connections, except for one huge difference. There was no requirement that facilitators have training or experience as counselors, and there was no requirement for knowledgeable supervision by someone who did have the necessary training or experience. I can't explain why this lack of attention to credentials and oversight seemed like a good idea to anyone, except that it did save some families money . . . for a while. And then it all backfired in a big way.

The ads placed by adoption facilitators in the early days of their existence almost always offered to pay a pregnant woman's "living expenses." This was a real departure from traditional adoption agencies, who advertised their agency services, not their individual families. The agency might offer a birth mother assistance in the form of services (including concrete things like housing, maternity clothes, and medical care), but rarely was there talk about money changing hands. This was considered unethical. As a result, while the adoption professionals were preserving their ethical stance, the adoption facilitators were busily turning into baby brokers. Many facilitators enjoyed enormous successes in regard to the number of babies placed in adoptive homes and the length of time adoptive families had to wait until placement. Although there were some well-publicized problems, the speed of the placements easily overcame the objections. Families wanting a quick and relatively inexpensive adoption were, of course, drawn to facilitators. As businesses do when they are successful, facilitators began to raise their rates and, in an effort to attract more pregnant women than other facilitators did, also began to increase the amount of "living expenses" for birth mothers. In no time, the race to the top (in regard to cost of adoptions) and the bottom (in regard to ethics) was on . . . and, as far as I can see, there's no end in sight.

I know quite a few families who have successfully adopted through facilitators, and I still refer people to the facilitators I feel operate ethically. But I am increasingly insecure about my ability to make this judgment call, and increasingly reluctant to suggest that families get involved with this type of adoption. I also know quite a few families who have had to unhappily extricate themselves from unsuitable "matches" arranged by facilitators. Being "matched" used to mean that a pregnant woman had chosen an adoptive family after careful consideration. Now, it often means simply that this is the family from whom the woman has chosen to take money.

My sample is skewed, given that I most often hear from families who have not been successful in working with a facilitator (since the happy ones have no reason to call), but their anger and disappointment are hard to ignore. Sometimes people are angry for good reasons, sometimes they are angry about situations beyond the facilitator's control, and sometimes they are angry about things that were simply beyond anyone's ability to control.

Like other adoption professionals, I am contacted regularly by facilitators seeking adoptive parents for birth mothers with problematic situations, such as ongoing substance abuse or mental health issues. These women are often asking for, and perhaps in dire need of, substantial living expenses. Facilitators in these situations are not looking only for a good family for a baby, but also for a family who is willing to take on medical risks and possibly long-term developmental and psychological risks and . . . a family willing and able to pay about $35,000. My question is, "Why does the facilitator have any sort of financial control over this child's future?" This country is full of wonderful waiting families, many of them already licensed by the state or home study certified by another agency, who would love to adopt that child but who simply don't have the $35,000 to do so. In these situations, the facilitator is able to essentially put a price tag on this baby. And they are being given this power by the birth mother, who is likely to be unaware of the fact that the facilitator's "assistance" is actually serving to limit her choices and her baby's options.

If the situations the facilitators called me about were not problematic, they would not be calling me. Facilitators also contact families directly, presumably after searching websites where hopeful adoptive parents post their profiles. Families I have worked with are often excited rather than wary when they get this sort of call, but fortunately, they usually call me before sending money off to the facilitator. Then we have a depressing conversation in which I usually end up, as gently as possible, dampening their hopes. But every once in a while, maybe as often as one call in twenty, there is something potentially encouraging about the situation, and the family decides to pursue it further. I can think of only a few times in my entire career when this sort of unsolicited call actually resulted in an adoption. More typically, it results in a loss of money, time, and peace of mind for the potential adoptive family.

It's not uncommon to get calls from facilitators about birth mothers who have relinquished previously—maybe even several times. I consider this to be a huge red flag, although the facilitator generally presents it as a positive sign since it indicates that the woman knows what to expect and is more likely to follow through with an adoption. But from the perspective of a counselor, it raises serious questions about why someone who had suffered through a relinquishment wouldn't do everything possible to prevent having to repeat the experience. The possibilities (none of them good) include exceptionally bad luck, an inability to successfully/willingly use birth control, complicated psychological issues, and/or a financially motivated pregnancy.

That last possibility is a particularly telling and troubling reflection of the current state of in-country infant adoptions. The ratio of high demand to low supply of babies allows facilitators to find adoptive families willing not only to take on a variety of potentially serious problems but also to pay heavily for the privilege. A typical expense scenario in 2016 involves approximately $16,000 for the facilitator's fee, $15,000 for the estimated attorney's fee (which can go much, much higher depending on the legal complexity of the situation), and from $3,000 to $20,000 for "birth mother expenses." When you include additional expenses such as any medical fees not covered by insurance, a trip or two for the adoptive parents to wherever the birth mother lives, and an approximately weeklong stay away from home when the baby is born, the cost can start at well over $35,000 and go into the $50,000-plus range.

Furthermore, if the adoption falls through, the would-be adoptive parents are not reimbursed for anything they have spent on legal fees, birth-mother expenses, or travel costs. Typically, a portion of the fees they have paid specifically for the facilitator's services can be applied to a new adoption effort through the same facilitator, but their money is not returned if the family chooses to go elsewhere to search for their child. Even families who have had a bad experience and lost faith in the facilitator are reluctant to forgo such a significant amount of money and are likely to try again, with ever-decreasing faith in the process. These are some of the unhappy people I hear from, and I definitely feel their pain.

I recently received a call from an out-of-state adoption facilitator asking if I knew of any families who were interested in a baby who was going to be of Hispanic/Caucasian heritage. I had never worked with this caller before, but I had heard her name and didn't have any negative associations aside from my normal skepticism about some facilitators. After talking with her, I decided to call a family I had worked with who now had a two-year-old son of Hispanic/Caucasian heritage and was about to start the adoption process again. I told them I was unfamiliar with this facilitator but that, if they were interested, they might call her and find out more.

The family eagerly called the facilitator and found out that the twenty-nine-year-old prospective birth mother was raising two children, ages twelve and five, and that she had given birth to four other children, all of whom had been adopted. She had gotten pregnant again only a few months after the last baby was born, and this new baby would be her fifth relinquishment. This baby's father was the father of two of the babies who had been adopted; he also had five other children, none of whom he was parenting. The family was told that the woman used meth "sometimes" and that she was asking for about $2,500 a month in living expenses, for a minimum of seven months. The facilitator spoke enthusiastically about the woman's beauty, assuring the family that she "looks just like Julia Roberts." She then emailed them a picture of a woman who looked nothing like Julia Roberts—even if Julia had been playing a meth addict who'd been pregnant for seven out of the past twelve years. The whole situation took on a weird "Emperor's New Clothes" feel, as though the facilitator felt that if she just kept insisting that everything was great, the family would ignore the massive amount of evidence to the contrary.

Rather than going along with the facilitator, the family asked some questions, the most important being, "Is this woman getting any counseling?" Instead of reassuring them that part of her service (for which she charged $16,000) was to provide for counseling (hopefully with someone qualified to provide it), the facilitator took offense, supposedly on behalf of the birth mother (let's call her Julia). She asserted that Julia did not want counseling (no doubt true) and that it wouldn't be ethical to force someone who didn't want it to take part in counseling. She acknowledged that Julia's pregnancy likely was financially motivated, but felt that this was Julia's choice and shouldn't be questioned or criticized. The facilitator also informed the family that many of the birth mothers she worked with were financially motivated and that that was just the reality of adoption today. The family told her they didn't think her services were "a good fit" for them, then contacted me to vent about the sorry state of infant adoptions these days.

Although I am thoroughly dismayed by this sort of story and by this type of adoption facilitation—which should simply be called "baby brokering"—this facilitator was telling the truth. There are indeed women who are motivated to become pregnant and relinquish their babies simply because there are other people who are willing to pay them for doing so. I'm talking about situations in which women deliberately, and sometimes repeatedly, get pregnant in order to receive money (usually in the form of "living expenses") in exchange for their babies. Adoption facilitators reap financial benefits with each successive pregnancy; since facilitators charge a flat fee for their services, their hourly earnings skyrocket whenever they work repeatedly with the same birth mother. It is not that time-consuming to shepherd someone through a second, third, fourth or—heaven forbid—fifth relinquishment, especially when all they want from you is a monthly check.

The practice of paying finder's fees to people for locating adoptable babies used to be a common (and highly problematic) practice in some of the other countries whose children were sent to the United States for adoption. The idea was that the "finders" would be social workers, medical professionals, ministers, and others who act ethically and have the children's best interests at heart. Instead, they often turned out to be people (sometimes even social workers, medical professionals, ministers, etc.) who were primarily motivated by the opportunity to earn per-child fees that could be as high as the average yearly income in their country. Horrifying stories about the kidnapping of babies and the coercion of birth mothers led to investigations that unearthed a history of corruption in Guatemala, Cambodia, Vietnam, Romania, and other countries. In 2008, the Hague Adoption Convention instituted reform and regulation aimed at eliminating rampant abuses in international adoption and, although many of the problems it hoped to solve have proved intractable, there is widespread agreement that the practice of paying people large sums in exchange for locating adoptable children is a powerful corrupting influence and should be prohibited.

In international adoption these days, it is generally considered unethical to pay finder's fees to people who connect babies and/or birth parents with adoption agencies, attorneys, or other individuals who arrange adoptions. But in the United States, we seem to have no effective regulation of such practices. Some facilitators do provide counseling for birth and adoptive parents, as well as other services consistent with those offered by a licensed agency, but many do not, nor are they required to do so. Some simply act as brokers between birth and adoptive parents; they attract birth mothers primarily by making promises of financial support.

There are negative consequences for both birth and adoptive parents in the way the exchange of money can erode their confidence in, and respect for, one another. In the current adoption climate, where money rules, it is hard for adoptive parents not to question the motives of prospective birth parents. The financial rewards for "considering adoption" are high, and women who are less than ethical and/or under financial stress can be tempted to say that they are "considering adoption" whether or not they actually have any thought of doing so. Even women who are completely honest about their intentions are affected by the cloud of suspicion created by false "birth parents," and it is undeniably true that if these women weren't claiming to consider adoption, no one would be paying their living expenses. For their part, the adoptive parents are put in the position of trying to ignore or justify the fact that they have found themselves in a position that feels perilously close to (or exactly like) paying a woman for her baby.

There are also negative consequences for babies who have been adopted in these circumstances and who will one day grow up and discover that they were produced for money. This information is likely to be difficult for them, to say the least, and potentially will damage their relationships with both their birth and adoptive parents.

One would expect adoptive parents to object most vehemently to current practice, forced as they often are into what amounts to bidding wars for babies. Clearly, they are unhappy that the cost of infant adoption has skyrocketed to the point where anyone who is not solidly upper-middle-class is likely to be priced out of the market. Many people have had to give up on their dream of having a baby because of the cost of adoption. We won't hear from most of them because they have had to turn their hearts and their attention elsewhere and do their best to accept the fact that adoption of an infant is not a financially realistic possibility for them.

We also won't hear much from the people who have managed to adopt an infant. While most will be unhappy about the high cost of their adoptions, and while many will be unhappy about other aspects of the process, they probably won't be too outspoken. They are now happy and busy being parents and have concluded that their child was well worth whatever it took to get him or her into their lives. They may hope to adopt a second child as well and don't want to jeopardize their chances by complaining about a system they will be relying upon again.

Furthermore, few families who have successfully adopted want to be whistleblowers who put other families' adoptions in jeopardy. Even families who have suffered egregiously during their own adoption process tend to forgive, forget, and move on once they have their child. And the attorneys, who may well share my concerns about ethics, have little incentive to change their lucrative relationships with adoption facilitators. I'm sure most attorneys do their very best to keep their clients as far from trouble as possible and keeping one's clients out of trouble in such an inherently troubled system can require a lot of billable hours of hard work. The attorneys are not themselves unethical—quite the opposite—but they do benefit financially from working with adoption facilitators and thus have little direct incentive to put a stop to this barely disguised baby brokering.

So who's going to blow the whistle? Surely we can all agree that babies should not be sold and that birth parents should not be given money in exchange for their children, either as an incentive to relinquish or as a reward for doing so. Pregnant women who need financial assistance should be guided to services and sources of support that are not influenced by or dependent upon the possibility of adoption. They should not receive payment in exchange for "considering adoption" or for pretending to do so.

But my wishes are for an ideal world. In the real world, we are dealing with pregnant women who are living lives of poverty and dysfunction and babies who are suffering even before they are born. And sometimes the process of adoption facilitation, imperfect as it is, makes things better for both of them, as well as for the adoptive parents. I did quite a few home studies over the years for gay couples, many of whom then worked with an adoption facilitator in order to find a birth mother. I remember one extremely appealing couple who were quickly chosen by a woman in California who had a long history of substance abuse and identified herself as a prostitute. This baby was going to be her seventh child; she did not know who the father was or what race the baby was going to be. When the couple first met her, she was serving a jail sentence that was supposed to last until well after the baby was born. That all sounds pretty bad, but the good news was that the woman had been in jail since month two of her pregnancy, had not used drugs during that time, and would be getting reasonably good medical care and nutrition throughout the remaining three months until delivery. The couple was not naïve about possible problems, but they decided to go ahead with this adoption.

About a month into what was supposed to be a predictable third trimester, the court system threw them a huge loop by suddenly deciding to release the woman. At this point, the men made the decision to fly down to California, rent a condo, and spend the next two months taking care of (monitoring? controlling?) the birth mother so that she wouldn't be tempted to go back to her old lifestyle and endanger herself and the baby. After everything was set up at the condo, one of the men flew home and went back to work (to return every other weekend) while the other devoted himself to pampering the birth mother. He made delicious meals and together they went shopping for both mom and baby, watched movies, went to the spa and to medical appointments, and—most importantly—did a lot of talking. Obviously, it wasn't all fun times for the whole two months, but that man's dedication to the well-being (both physical and psychological) of his future child was indeed impressive. And it paid off, primarily in the adoption of a healthy and beautiful baby girl and also in a close and caring relationship with her birth mother.

But these situations are enormously complex, and I wasn't too surprised when the birth mother called the men about six months after the birth of the baby girl to ask if they wanted to adopt her next child. They adopted that child, but when she called again the next year, they made the painful decision not to adopt their almost two-year-old daughter's and not yet one-year-old son's half sibling.

I'm certain that the birth mother found another adoptive couple to work with. Presumably the baby is now part of a happy family, so this isn't exactly a sad story, but it certainly has its troubling aspects. Did the men's solicitous behavior and financial support encourage the woman to keep getting pregnant? Probably. Would she have gotten pregnant again without their involvement? Probably. Did the birth mother and the two babies benefit from the men's involvement during the pregnancies? Definitely. Is it a good thing to encourage women who can't, or won't care for their babies to get pregnant? Definitely not. Is it a good thing these three babies were born? Definitely yes. It's complicated, to say the least.

30

The Ethics of International Adoption

THE IDEA THAT MONEY CAN buy children is openly accepted in international adoption, where parents typically pay high fees in order to adopt. Although we try not to focus on such blunt descriptions, the fact is that money changes hands in adoption, and there is almost always significant financial disparity between birth and adoptive parents as well as between the countries that place the children and the countries that receive them (with Korea's more recent economic successes making it something of an exception). This financial disparity has contributed to an increasing discomfort with the ethics of international adoption, and there are very vocal factions (adult adoptees among them) calling for its elimination on geopolitical grounds.

These objections are based largely on the image of Western (white) society using its wealth and power to rob poorer countries of their children, and on the ill-gotten gains by the individuals and governments who orchestrate these adoptions. Those who call for a halt to international adoption believe that it commodifies children and deprives them of their heritage and culture. They make a complex and compelling intellectual argument about the immoral imbalance of power between the children's home countries and the adopting parents' home countries.

But while this argument has validity on a societal scale, it has little timely relevance for any one particular child. It is neither realistic nor ethically acceptable to expect children in need of a home to atone for the world's political and financial inequities by spending their childhood without a family. The sad truth is that international adoption arose out of a need to find homes for children and recognition that these children had little chance of being adopted within their own countries.

Historically, most people in the United States had a generally favorable view of international adoption when it came to the country's attention on a large scale in the mid-1950s after the Korean War. The well-publicized plight of children orphaned by war moved many Americans to sympathy and moved some of them to take action by adopting a child. Less well publicized was the fact that many of these "orphans" were the children of American servicemen whose Korean mothers were effectively abandoned and forced to relinquish their babies rather than raise them in a society that rejected their mixed-race heritage. For a combination of social, political, and financial reasons, Korean adoption thrived, and over the past sixty years approximately two hundred thousand children were placed with families outside of Korea, three-quarters of them in the United States.

For the most part, children in need of families inspire affection in American society, and the families who adopt them receive approval. This was never more evident to me than when I worked with a family who wanted to adopt a Korean baby in 1983. The family consisted of a mom, dad, and grade-school-aged son and daughter. I had done their home study a year earlier, and the family was eagerly awaiting their referral. When I received the packet of information for them, it contained quite a surprise: instead of pictures and information about one baby, as they had been expecting, it was a referral for twin baby girls. At first, the prospective parents were ecstatic, but their excitement quickly turned to concern about financial reality. They were a young couple with a stable income but a tight budget, and it had not been easy to save the money needed for an international adoption. After a great deal of agonizing, they finally were forced to acknowledge that they didn't have enough to cover not only the unexpected fee for the second baby but the extra costs of raising twins. The agency allowed them a week to make their decision, and the couple struggled unsuccessfully to come up with the money. But on the night before they were to tell the agency that they could not move forward, something incredible happened.

The family's son, while too young to be fully involved in discussions with his parents about family finances, nevertheless understood that they were upset and that he was in danger of losing the chance to have twin baby sisters because of a lack of money. He shared his worry with his teacher one day at school. The teacher verified the story with the mother, then did something brilliant. She realized that the final episode of *M.A.S.H.* (a wildly popular television show that takes place in Korea during the Korean War) was going to be airing on television that night, that much of the nation would be watching, and that public attention and sentiment would be focused on Korea in a way it probably hadn't been since the war itself.

This teacher contacted the television station that would be running the local news right after "M.A.S.H" and told them about the family's situation. It was the top story that night, with pictures of the babies appearing on screen almost as soon as the "M.A.S.H." theme song had ended. I remember watching the interview in amazement, enormously happy because it seemed obvious that this family would now be able to adopt these babies. By the next morning, they had received enough donations to pay for the adoptions, buy the extra baby equipment they would need, and start college funds for their new daughters.

That was a simpler time. Today, international adoption's critics demonize it as being an economically motivated endeavor preying on desperate birth parents and creating irresistible financial incentives for people to engage in unethical procurement of children. There have been a number of exposés over the years about countries where corrupt attorneys, adoption agencies, and government officials paid "finder's fees" to individuals who would engage in unethical methods of locating babies who could be adopted. No doubt there were many more instances of abuse that were undiscovered and unreported. Tragically, there are situations in which the birth parents hadn't actually consented to an adoption or, if they had, didn't really understand what legal adoption meant. There were also accusations of out-and-out kidnapping for the purpose of adoption. Of course, there have always been regulations against this sort of procurement of children, but when there are powerful-enough financial incentives, people find a way to work around the regulations—sometimes quasi-legally, sometimes through overt corruption. And it can be almost impossible for adoptive parents to recognize when they are in danger of involving themselves in this sort of unethical situation and to fully understand the consequences for the birth parents, themselves, and the children.

Much of the media-reported criticism of international adoption these days singles out celebrity parents. It makes sense that female celebrities, who are often focused on career rather than marriage and children during the years in which they would be most likely to have children biologically, would turn to adoption as a method to bring children into their lives. Adoption also makes sense for them because celebrities have the ample funds needed for an international adoption or two (or more).

The most public "villain" in international adoption for a few years was Madonna, the singer. The outcry over her efforts to adopt a baby boy and then a little girl from Malawi was long and loud, and the media coverage was so outraged and convoluted that I doubt anyone ever really reported the story completely accurately (making it hard to piece together now). The basics of the baby boy's story were that he had been brought to an orphanage by his father after his mother died. Madonna and her then husband hoped to adopt him and were initially told they could do so. It appears that they went through all the appropriate steps to accomplish this, but prior to the placement, a group called The Human Rights Consultative Committee in Malawi objected. Their reasons included unhappiness about the ethics of international adoption, a belief that Madonna had used her wealth and position to circumvent Malawian adoption law and policy, and the conviction that the particular child's father did not want his son to be adopted.

There were numerous dramatic and heart-wrenching stories in tabloids, in mainstream papers, online, and on television news depicting Madonna as a prima donna who had, purposely or naïvely, assumed she would receive special treatment and could bend the rules to suit her desires. The fact that various officials, including the president of the country, made it possible for Madonna to adopt this child without asking her to live in Malawi for the required eighteen months before adopting makes one wonder why it was Madonna who was singled out for condemnation. But it seems both understandable and questionable that an exception to normal policy would be made for someone such as Madonna, who had donated a great deal of money to be used for charitable purposes in the country.

The more poignant stories about the irregularity of Madonna's adoption of this child surfaced when someone interviewed his birth father and reported that the man said he had not understood that his son could be adopted and didn't want him to be adopted by Madonna. This of course spurred a real media frenzy, but when the man was interviewed again a short time later, he said that he supported Madonna's efforts to adopt his son and that he was concerned that all the criticism she had received from the media might discourage not only her but also other families who wanted to adopt Malawian children.

The father acknowledged that he had been responsible for some of the confusion when he told the Associated Press that authorities had not made it clear to him that he was giving up his son "for good" when he had earlier agreed to the adoption. But he clarified that what he meant to say was that he "wasn't selling my son. I said I wouldn't . . . sell my son for anything but I had agreed with Madonna before a judge so my comments were taken out of context and I hope Madonna is not angry."[1] I remember all the horrified reporting about the father's first statement and very little about the second

---

1. Tenthani, Raphael. The Associated Press. October 26, 2006. http://washington post.com.

statement, which was made a short time later. The adoption was ultimately approved by the Malawian courts, but in the eyes of the world Madonna was possibly a baby snatcher who had left a bereft and powerless widower in Malawi mourning the loss of his child.

The story gets much more complicated. It turns out that the charity Madonna was funding (called Raising Malawi), which had been doing a great deal of good for many children, was not being managed well in Malawi. Stories about the extreme misuse of funds (for things like luxury cars and country club memberships) came to Madonna's attention, and the Malawian director of her foundation, who happened to be the sister of the country's president, was relieved of her duties. While all of this was happening, Madonna was in the process of adopting a second child, a little girl she had met prior to her son's adoption.

Perhaps it was a complete coincidence, but it was at this time that the president, Joyce Banda, reversed her previously high opinion of Madonna and began to characterize her as someone who demanded VIP treatment, bullied state officials, and lied about the accomplishments of Raising Malawi. The president issued a statement saying that "among the many things that Madonna needs to learn as a matter of urgency is the decency of telling the truth. . . . For her to tell the whole world that she is building schools in Malawi when she has actually only contributed to the construction of classrooms is not compatible with manners of someone who thinks she deserves to be revered with state grandeur."[2] To which Madonna's publicist responded, "Madonna is the largest individual philanthropist in Malawi. We will continue to fund programs that support the children of Malawi." When a new president took office in May 2014, Madonna received his endorsement and support, and his press secretary issued a statement saying, "We welcome Madonna as a guest of the government and people of Malawi. . . . The president appreciates the charity work she is doing for Malawi."

But Madonna's troubles were not over, even though she was allowed to adopt the second child, now three years old, who had also been orphaned by her mother's death. This child, Mercy, had been living in the orphanage when Madonna first saw her as a baby in 2006 and stayed there until an uncle signed the adoption papers in 2009. The difficulty this time seemed to stem from the enormous cultural differences between this child's birth and adoptive families and their understanding of the meaning of adoption. Madonna promised to bring both of the children she had adopted back to Malawi every few years, and she did, but some members of Mercy's birth family felt especially unhappy about their lack of access to the child during these visits.

---

2. "Malawi Labels Madonna a 'Bully' after Recent Visit." April 11, 2013. BBC News. http://bbc.com.

As her birth grandfather poignantly and accurately explained in a December 2014 interview with Peter Jegwa for *The Daily Mail*, "White foreigners who decide to take our children away from Africa have no understanding of our culture. They don't realize that in our African families each one has a responsibility to the others. If a half-brother or half-sister does well, they share their fortunes with all of the others. A child like my granddaughter Mercy, if she succeeds in her career, she is expected to share that success with all of us. That is how our extended family system works." He went on to say that he now understood that what Madonna meant when she said she would bring Mercy back to Malawi every few years was simply that they would come to the country, stay in an expensive lodge, and ignore her blood relatives. "That cannot be the right way to do things," he added. "No foreigner has the right to interfere in our culture like this." The grandfather now apparently felt that the family had made a mistake in allowing the adoption because, "What is the point of us wanting Mercy to get a good education and a good life if in the end she does not help her relatives?" An uncle added that Mercy had lots of cousins who wanted to see her but didn't understand her life of luxury. "They wonder why this famous rich woman should allow them to live in poverty while their cousin is living big. This is not good for Mercy herself. What will she think when she discovers her people are wallowing in poverty?"[3]

What is it that we Westerners expect Mercy to think? Do we expect her to think she should share her wealth and advantages with her birth relatives? And, if so, to what extent? How much of her money should she give them, and which relatives (half siblings, cousins, aunts, uncles, second cousins, third cousins) qualify? Do we expect Mercy to devote her life not only to helping her birth relatives but also to the plight of all Malawian orphans? Are she and her brother expected to take over their mother's charity work in Malawi? On a more fundamental level, do we admire the image of extended-family financial responsibility and solidarity that the grandfather characterized as "African" and feel that Mercy and other adopted children of African heritage should embrace it as their own? Do we expect this of all internationally adopted children? Are they not as free as other people to choose the direction of their lives? Would it be selfish or irresponsible for them to choose to be poets or stay-at-home moms instead of pursuing more financially rewarding careers in order to be able to send more money to their birth families?

I feel that Mercy's grandfather's statement about no foreigner having the right to interfere in another country's culture speaks eloquently to the problems in international adoption, but not in the way he intended.

---

3. Jegwa, Peter. "Madonna Betrayed Us over Our Daughter Mercy." December 1, 2014. Daily Mail. com. http:dailymail.co.uk.

The separation from one's birth culture is an inherent part of international adoption: No matter how many times Madonna takes her children to Malawi, their primary home is not there, and, just like all children, they have become part of the culture in which they are being raised. In Western culture, one of our strongest beliefs is in the right to self-determination. Viewed from a Western perspective, we want Mercy to have the freedom to live her life in whatever manner suits her needs and desires. We do not believe that American children should always be financially responsible for their extended families or that wealth must always be shared equally. We do admire people who have charitable instincts, but we don't criticize (or even especially notice) those who don't. As Americans, we consider ourselves to be responsible and independent, and we admire these traits. But from an African perspective, we must look selfish and hardhearted. And the expressed desire to agree to "adoptions" only as a means to provide for and educate a family member who can then return to the country to help support their relatives sounds too much like indentured servitude to the average American.

Of course we have a hard time understanding each other, but there are no villains—just very different perspectives and realities.

This difference was illustrated to my family in a seemingly small and easily explained manner during our trip to Korea when Jocelyn was thirteen and we met with her foster mother, Shin Hae Soon. Shin Hae Soon had been a foster parent for Holt Children's Services for seventeen years and was presumably a proponent of international adoption for the children who had been in her care. After the first ten minutes of smiling and crying at each other, the visit suddenly turned serious and a little tense when Shin Hae Soon asked the translator to ask us why Jocelyn's skin was so much darker than the rest of the family's. We explained that Jocelyn spent many hours outdoors playing soccer, and Shin Hae Soon nodded as though she understood. But she was really asking if Jocelyn, unlike her sisters, was forced to work outdoors, as if she were a servant in the fields. The question was not unusual, and our explanation, quick and truthful as it was, didn't really address the root of Shin Hae Soon's underlying concerns about the possibility that we might not really be the good parents we appeared to be. More significantly, it didn't address the fact that even a foster parent who worked for an adoption agency apparently still had doubts about the possibility of adoptive parents using their children as laborers.

I recently saw an article written for CNN by Srey Powers, a young woman who had been adopted from Cambodia as a six-year-old. Srey was an eighteen-year-old star soccer player in 2013 when she and her mother traveled to Cambodia, found the village where she had lived and had a wonderful and highly emotional reunion with her grandmother. This grandmother had raised Srey for either three or four years ("dates and details of my past were obscured by my grandmother's hardships") and had ultimately decided that adoption would be best for her. Nevertheless, when the woman saw her granddaughter fourteen years later, she asked for forgiveness. Dropping to her knees in tears, the grandmother said, through the translator, "Forgive me for giving you away." Then added, "But I would do it again . . . you are a beautiful woman." The grandmother then described what life had been like for the family and what Srey had been like as a child. Everything was going well until the grandmother suddenly turned to the adoptive mother and harshly asked why Srey's skin was so tan. The translator explained that "in her life, a dark tan suggests hard work on the land rather than long hours of practice on the soccer field." Srey and her mother did everything possible to reassure the grandmother that "I was a girl with many opportunities in America, that I would be educated and would prosper."[4]

I wonder if a few hours together could really overcome long-held beliefs and fears. I certainly hope so, for the grandmother's sake.

There are other concerns that no amount of reassurance can properly address. I remember Jocelyn's pleasure at meeting a girl who had been adopted from Colombia and how it quickly turned to horror when she heard more of the story. This girl and her twin sister had been placed with their American adoptive parents as babies, and although they grew up knowing they had been adopted, they had been given only very basic information about where they had lived prior to the adoption. As teenagers, they had undertaken to find out more about their history and eventually their efforts led to a return trip to Colombia and a meeting with their birth mother.

Their adoptive parents must have been supportive, at least enough to have allowed and funded the trip. But instead of the happy and reassuring visit they all hoped for, the sister's worlds were rocked by what their birth mother told them. She said that she had never consented to the adoption and that she had mourned them ever since the day they had been taken from her. I don't know if the birth mother meant to give them this idea, but the girls came to the conclusion that their adoptive parents must have been complicit in their "kidnapping" and were therefore responsible for the birth mother's suffering. Needless to say, all family members were in crisis.

I encountered a similar situation recently in which a young woman who had been adopted from Vietnam as a child sought out her birth mother. She too was told that her birth mother had never consented to the adoption. In fact, the birth mother said she had been tricked into it by someone who had taken the girl to an orphanage without her knowledge. The birth mother

---

4. Powers, Srey. Special to CNN. September 18, 2013. http://cnn.com.

said that she went after her child immediately, but it was too late because her daughter had already been sent out of the country. The young woman had a good relationship with her adoptive parents and didn't question their ethics in adopting from Vietnam, although she did question the ethics of Vietnamese adoption overall. The biggest difficulty for her now came from the fact that along with the tremendous empathy she felt for her birth mother, came a little doubt about the story she told. The young woman had been about five years old when she was adopted and she had frightening and chaotic memories of her early childhood. She also had memories of being in a children's home for what seemed to be a very long time, possibly even several years. It is certainly possible that, despite some inconsistencies, the birth mother was helpless to reclaim her child and, as it was with the Cambodian grandmother, the details of the past were obscured by hardship.

These are heartbreaking stories, and enormous harm has been done to all of the people involved. The birth mothers' losses are obvious and irrevocable. The adoptive parents' relationships with their children have been jeopardized, and the children have been thrust into emotionally painful and confusing positions. But it's highly likely that neither the birth nor adoptive parents were uncaring or untruthful; children who have been adopted in these circumstances shouldn't have to decide whom to believe or have to declare allegiance to one side or the other. Unraveling their histories may prove to be impossible, and it is unrealistic and unfair to expect either birth or adoptive parents to account (or atone) for everything that happened.

As it was with the birth father of Madonna's Malawian son, the birth mothers from Colombia and Vietnam denied that they had wanted their children to be adopted. But when the question to the birth father was rephrased to ask if he had agreed to the adoption, he acknowledged that he had and that he felt unhappy about people questioning him and interfering in his decision. I wonder, if the questions were rephrased to these two birth mothers whether their answers might be more nuanced.

I think it's safe to say that virtually all birth mothers would answer the question "Did you want your child to be adopted?" with an emphatic and honest "No." Of course they didn't want to find themselves and their children in this situation. But if you ask birth mothers the question, "Did you want your child to have a life you weren't able to give her?" the answer might then be different.

It is undeniable that there are kidnappings and other abuses in international adoptions and that some adoptees are destined to hear tragic stories when they contact their birth parents. There are also birth mothers in both domestic adoption and international adoption who deny agreeing to an adoption because they are afraid their children won't understand and will feel unloved. It seems less risky and more sympathetic to tell a story about being victimized by individuals than to try to explain all the complicated and painful circumstances, including victimization through poverty and hardship, that led up to the relinquishment. Clarifying these situations in international adoption is greatly complicated by the fact that people are usually speaking either with extremely limited mutual language or through an interpreter. Conversations that are already extremely delicate in nature are further burdened by the logistics of communication, and there are numerous opportunities for misunderstanding.

There is general consensus that children are best raised in the country and culture of their birth. Even among families created by international adoption, there is widely held agreement that, in an ideal world, their child would not have needed to be adopted and would be living happily with his or her birth family. But is living happily with one's birth family really an available alternative for the majority of children who are adopted internationally? People would probably also agree that, in an ideal world, children who need to be adopted would find families in their country of origin, thereby retaining their cultural heritage. But is that a realistic expectation? Historically, very few families in "the placing countries" (China, Korea, India, Ethiopia, Guatemala, etc.) adopt, usually for reasons based on cultural beliefs and personal economics.

The lack of emphasis on in-country adoption in the placing countries has also been influenced by the fact that out-of-country adoption brings in far more money, providing little incentive for local adoption agencies to use their limited time and resources to encourage domestic adoptions. If that makes them seem like cold-hearted businesses, focused only on profits, please consider to what use those profits are put. In all but the corrupt agencies, that money is used to provide for the children in their care.

International adoption brings money from wealthy countries into poorer countries, and this in itself is certainly not a bad thing. When the adoptions are carefully regulated by reputable agencies, a portion of the adoption fee is used to provide care for children who are in need but who for one reason or another are not going to be adopted. These may be children who are older or have special needs, or they may be children whose parents cannot provide for them but do not want to relinquish their parental rights. These parents hope that their children can be cared for and educated in a children's home or some similar facility, then be returned to the family when they are older and better able to take care of themselves.

Most reputable adoption agencies attach a required "donation" to their international adoption fee that is earmarked for the care of such children, and adoptive parents are generally happy to have their money used for this purpose. It is hard to understand the reasoning of someone who dismisses this gesture as no more than a display of wealth and power. It is even harder to understand what the critics of international adoption feel should be done instead for these children.

We can hope that in the future, there will be another source of funds to support children in need, and there will be more domestic adoptions in the placing countries. Korea has been working hard to increase its own domestic adoptions since the 1990s, with limited success. Someday, in-country adoption in these countries may be more widespread, but that is not the case today.

The arguments against international adoption, in their assumption that children should always stay in their countries of origin, remind me of my long-ago conversation with Charles (the social services director) and his insistence on always working to reunite the family. Both are laudable goals, worth pursuing, but sometimes, for some people, they are simply not attainable.

It is a fact of international adoption that children leave their country of origin in order to come to a wealthier country. It is also true that, if life was fair, birth parents would never feel they needed to relinquish their children because of poverty, war, natural disaster, and other hardships. But life isn't fair, and many people the world over do relinquish their children for those reasons.

Birth parents in other countries also relinquish children for the same reasons that children are relinquished in wealthier countries: cultural disapproval of single parenthood, physical or mental health concerns, substance abuse, or feeling that adoption serves the child's best interests. Birth parents in other countries who relinquish for these reasons deserve the same consideration and respect for their decisions that we are finally learning to give birth mothers in the United States. There are also situations in which birth parents in other countries are abusive or absent by choice. Assuming that every adoption in other countries is caused by conditions beyond the birth parents' control or desire is simplistic reasoning.

People in both the placing and receiving countries who actually work with the children understand that we need to do our best for each of them. They also understand that even when everyone works their hardest and every possible safeguard is in place, some adoptions don't work out for the best. Sometimes children end up in bad homes with adoptive parents who are abusive, troubled, or unloving. Sometimes they end up with parents who are none of those things but are still somehow just fundamentally the wrong parents for that particular child. When this happens, it is tragic—just as it is when this sort of dysfunction happens in biological families. These problems are not unique to adoptive families; they are just more noticeable and more remarked upon than they are in birth families.

But what about all the happy adoptive families? The vast majority of families created through international adoption fall into this category, and they cannot be expected to be overly concerned with the "political correctness" of their relationships. Adult adoptees from this sort of family are busy going about their lives, as are most people, focusing on their family, friends, jobs, and other interests. While having been adopted is important to them, as is their racial and cultural heritage, it does not dominate their lives.

There is presently an outspoken group of Korean adult adoptees who object vehemently to having been separated from their birth families and sent away from Korea as children. Their unhappiness deserves careful attention, but it is interesting to note that many of the particularly outspoken and poignant members of this group had been adopted not as babies but as toddlers or young children. They were undoubtedly traumatized by the losses they experienced; some of them were old enough when they were adopted to remember the families they lost. There are also people in this group who reported growing up in unhappy adoptive families or in racist communities. Others have reported that their parents had been loving but essentially clueless regarding their children's need to learn about and identify with their cultural heritage. While their parents were not unkind, and their families were not unhappy, the children felt isolated both racially and emotionally. It is not surprising that people from these sorts of families would conclude that international adoption causes harm. But most international adoptees have had different experiences and have reached different conclusions about the ethics of allowing children to be raised by parents who do not share their race or culture.

Once again, I am reminded of Charles's maxim to "always work to reunite the family." In theory, I never disagreed with him, nor do I disagree with those who oppose international adoption in theory. In an ideal world, children would never need to leave their birth families or their birth countries, and that ideal world is one we should all be working to attain. But the real world is full of children who need to be safe and loved right now, and they should not be asked to put their lives on hold while we wait for a perfect world.

31

The Ethics of Foster Care

YEARS AGO, ON A LOVELY June evening after ten-year-old Jocelyn's first piano recital, I was happily listening to the teacher's little speech of congratulations to both students and parents when something struck me as amiss. She told the children they had worked hard and done well, and she told the parents essentially the same thing. It was all very pleasant. Then she talked about the "Mozart effect," often cited by people who maintain that children who study music also do better in school, and she pointed out that all of her piano students excelled academically. It was an atmosphere replete with the kind of self-congratulation and self-satisfaction that accomplished children can bring out in their parents (and to which I am highly susceptible), but this time something felt wrong.

As I listened to the piano teacher, it occurred to me that her students, and my daughters, talented and hardworking and wonderful as they are, are "children money can buy." Their successes in music or academics or athletics or whatever are certainly not unearned, but I think it is important to understand that they have not been earned on an even playing field. These children have been given a huge assist in the form of music lessons, accelerated classes, special coaching, and so on *ad infinitum*. Even more significantly, they have been given the message that they are destined for success, not only at the immediate goal but at life.

Certainly there is a downside to all of this in the form of pressure, but it is definitely preferable to the type of pressure faced by children from the foster care world. Children without a stable home life need to work hard all day every day just to maintain their equilibrium in that tremendously insecure world—a more difficult endeavor than practicing piano and playing your recital piece well or stressing out about which college you'll get into. And society rarely recognizes or congratulates them on their efforts.

I am distressed by the tendency to attach moral virtue to the abilities and accomplishments of children of privilege, as though their successes result simply from the combination of good genes and hard work. While it is certainly appropriate to value the child's efforts and his or her particular skill or achievement, it is nonsense to attribute it to moral superiority. What about the moral superiority of the child who goes to his fast-food job every day, even though he despises it, because his family needs the money? This child gets virtually nothing in the way of acknowledgment from society. Instead, he gets poverty-level wages, which make it clear that neither the job nor the person who holds it is valued.

The young person our society admires is the one who, because he can afford not to work, is able to spend a gap year before college volunteering somewhere or on an extended trip. We're even more admiring of the child whose family has spent countless hours and dollars on turning him into some version of an Olympic hopeful. We completely ignore the fact that the world is full of equally goodhearted, talented, hardworking, and deserving kids who will simply never have these sorts of opportunities to excel or even to discover what their special gifts might be. The adults in their lives just aren't in a position to nurture and fund their talents and dreams.

Raising children with advantages is expensive for families, but raising them without advantages is far more expensive to society. Even without considering the hardships to the children themselves, the social costs to society of raising children poorly (poverty, crime, substance abuse, teen pregnancy, joblessness, etc.), are obvious.

Consider the cost of doing a good job of supporting a child in foster care compared with the cost of maintaining an adult in the prison system, not to mention the cost of the legal system that put him there or the cost to society of his criminal actions or untreated emotional problems. Prisons are full of people who were once in the foster care system, and—unlike in foster care—the state doesn't stop paying for their care when they reach the age of maturity.

We ought to be motivated to improve the lives of children in foster care simply by the self-serving desire to save money down the road when we don't need to confine them in jails or institutions later in life. We ought to think about the various benefits to society when crime and mental illness are reduced. Doesn't it seem a good idea to spend a bit extra on a child (perhaps even for things like piano lessons or athletic coaching, but certainly for things like therapy, tutoring, and adequate support for foster families) in the hope that it might improve his prospects for the future? Giving these kids the sort of assists from which more privileged kids routinely benefit might boost their confidence in ways that would have all sorts of beneficial repercussions.

Of course, I know that piano lessons aren't likely to turn a traumatized kid in foster care into what I have described as a "child money can buy." That's not the goal, anyway. I'm not concerned about them becoming musicians or athletes or acquiring some other specific skill. I'm concerned about nurturing their spirits.

What I want money to be able to buy for the children in foster care is a share of the security and self-esteem that other children enjoy. I want it to buy some of the social, emotional, and practical skills that will help these kids succeed in the world, both as children and as adults. It's not too much for them to hope for or to expect, it's not too much for society to provide, and the benefits to everyone would be far-reaching.

All of these financial arguments aside, surely it also makes sense to improve the lives of children in foster care simply because it is the kind and right thing to do. Every year, approximately twenty-three thousand children "age out" of the foster care system and find themselves suddenly living as adults, without a family or any other sort of safety net. They have no one to rely on in hard times and no one with whom to share the good times. They have no place to stay for a month or two if they lose their jobs and no place to go for Christmas. Few eighteen-year-olds have the self-sufficiency to make it in the world on their own, and children whose families have been so dysfunctional as to warrant their removal from the home are obviously already at an enormously increased disadvantage. A heartbreakingly high number of these kids end up homeless, in jail, with an unplanned pregnancy . . . or dead.

I look back at the children I knew in the foster care system with tremendous remorse for all I couldn't do for them. I wasn't derelict in my duties, but the scope and certainly the goal of those duties (to reunite the family, remember) was often beyond me. In fact, I think we should acknowledge that the scope and goal of the entire foster care system is often beyond all of us and come up with a more realistic approach. My experiences were a long time ago, and I'm sure there have been numerous overhauls and improvements in the system since my days as a foster care worker in Michigan. I'm certain that there are many, many good people currently devoting their energies, their expertise, and their hearts to the plight of children in foster care.

So I want to believe that things have gotten much better for these kids in the past forty years, but I keep hearing stories that force me to acknowledge that the situation remains grim. The media bring us increasingly frequent accounts of children who somehow fall between the cracks but finally come to everyone's attention by being horribly abused or killed, usually by a parent or stepparent. Typically in these cases, the family was already known to the child welfare system, and there was an abundance of warning that the child was at risk.

It horrifies us each time we hear these all-too-familiar stories about how the parent had a long history of problems, perhaps with substance abuse and impulse control. We might hear about how the child had been in a foster home and was doing well despite having been born drug affected and suffering abuse and neglect during his first year of life. And we might hear that after a couple of years spent with loving foster parents, the now three-year-old had recently been returned home to his mother because she had gone through rehab and had tested clean for three months. The mother had completed her part of the bargain, and the caseworker and the judge were giving her a second (or third or fourth) chance. They understood that the odds that she had permanently ended her dependence on drugs, changed her abusive behavior, and would now be a "good enough" parent were not great, but they wanted to at least give her the opportunity to prove them wrong.

Quite probably, they had no other legal option but to return the child to her care. They were working to reunite the family and, too frequently, with the best of intentions, they were also setting this woman and her child up for tragic failure. In this particular case, the child died shortly after being returned to his mother's care, leaving the foster family that had loved and nurtured him for most of his life bereft. And leaving most people saying, "How can this sort of thing happen?" and assuming that someone, somewhere, was at fault, and that this sort of tragedy is an anomaly.

Each time we hear one of these stories, we react with shock and disbelief. It makes sense to react with sadness, horror, anger, and frustration, but how is it that we can keep being so surprised? We act as though we just can't imagine that these things happen, despite a steady dose of evidence to the contrary.

It seems that, between horror stories, we just blot these children from our memories. I understand that, just like caseworkers who need to keep an emotional distance from the situations they confront, we all need to distance ourselves from life's tragedies. It would be neither healthy nor helpful to dwell on the sadness and anger we all feel when a child is harmed. But it certainly isn't healthy or helpful to stick our heads in the sand and act as though we just don't know what's happening or that we couldn't possibly do anything about it. We have the ability and the responsibility to voice our opinions about child welfare to our lawmakers, just as we do about other matters of public concern. I suspect that our inaction is due in large part to the fact that we have accepted the problems in the child welfare system as unfixable and in part because, for some reason, these children just aren't all that high on our list of priorities.

Let's go all the way back to the beginning of my career and look again at my supervisor Charles's question about promising to always work to reunite the family. After a career spent primarily on creating new adoptive families rather than trying to rebuild broken birth families, it is obvious to me that there were plenty of circumstances in which I did not work to keep biological families intact. One of my main goals in working with birth and adoptive parents was to avoid exerting influence over their decisions. Instead, I wanted to help them decide for themselves on the course of action that was right for them. I certainly didn't want to have pressured someone into either a relinquishment or an adoption they would later regret. I figured out a long time ago that if I took any credit when things went well for my adoption clients, I also needed to be prepared to take the blame when things went wrong. I didn't want to be held responsible for such important decisions in people's lives, whether they turned out to be very good decisions or very bad ones.

But it wasn't that way with my foster care clients. With them, it was my job to make decisions about their lives. No, I did not promise to always work to reunite the family. Sometimes I worked tremendously hard not to reunite a family, and I believe that some of my foster care clients, both children and parents, could have benefited enormously if there had been a more nuanced goal for them. The clients who would have benefited most were the ones who were angry about losing custody but didn't take any action to regain it. They were the ones who wouldn't show up for visits or for court hearings, wouldn't attend anger management or counseling sessions, wouldn't do any of the things specified in their service plan, but would still profess to be unhappy about the separation from their kids. They too were clearly not working to reunite the family. Much of the time, they didn't even seem to be particularly interested in their children, yet the stalemate between them and DSHS would drag on for years, sometimes for an entire childhood of years.

It was difficult to avoid the impression that that status quo was actually somehow working for the parents whose kids lingered in foster care while they failed to take action to regain custody. These parents didn't really have to change their behavior, nor did they have to permanently lose custody of their children. Occasionally they had to put up with some social worker or lawyer bothering them, but most of the time they were free to go about their business. It wasn't that they were necessarily such bad people, it was just that their children weren't safe with them. Chances were excellent that these parents weren't simply willfully lazy, self-absorbed, or unloving, but that they had been victims themselves of other people's (parents') bad behavior, or perhaps just of circumstance. But whatever the explanation, they were not safe parents, they weren't taking steps to become safe parents, and I was not going to recommend that their children be returned to their care.

I think these people needed realistic advocacy and mandated counseling that included an honest and timely recognition of their limitations as parents and the possibilities for improvement. Instead, they got a few minutes every three months or so of legal representation and an ongoing adversarial relationship with DSHS. I know I had clients who did not want to raise their children (other than in an idealistic sense) and/or felt incapable of doing so, but who kept battling with DSHS because they could not admit this even to themselves. It was far more comfortable for them to see themselves as victims, to believe that DSHS had taken their children away without cause, and to focus their anger on having been treated unjustly.

That's how it was with Michelle, the young mother who was mentally ill and whose impulsive actions and poor decisions, such as taking her baby out in winter weather wearing only a diaper, repeatedly endangered the child. Michelle could not realistically have been expected to understand her own limitations, but she could have been treated in a more caring and respectful manner if the system hadn't been so adversarial and if the outcome hadn't had to be all or nothing for her.

In order to terminate her parental rights, I had to create a case against Michelle, and she had to sit in a courtroom and listen to all her failings. Although it was evident that Michelle wasn't able to act as a responsible parent to her young child, maybe she could have had another sort of role in her daughter's life. What if, instead of simply terminating her parental rights and ending all contact between Michelle and baby Ayla, we had encouraged Michelle to be involved in Ayla's future? What if Michelle had been able to meet Ayla's foster parents and to see for herself how kind and loving they were? What if we had been able to arrange for letters and pictures to be sent regularly, both while Ayla was in foster care and after she was adopted? What if we'd been able to arrange for ongoing visitation in a supervised setting?

This sort of involvement wouldn't be safe or realistic in all situations, but it might have worked for Michelle and Ayla. Michelle wasn't a dangerous person, at least at that time; she was just dangerous as a parent. Maybe I'm being unrealistic in thinking that Michelle could ever have cooperated in an open adoption. Maybe her volatility would have made it impossible. But I wish we could have given her, and other clients like her, the opportunity to find out.

In later years, when I worked with clients like Trevor and Amanda on an adoption for their baby, it seemed so obvious to me that it would be mutually beneficial for the foster care and adoption systems to work together, as happened in their case. It also seemed obvious that parents who were facing the termination of their parental rights by the state ought to be given the opportunity to explore their options to voluntarily relinquish, instead, thereby having input into the decisions made about their children.

Trevor and Amanda were on schedule to lose their daughter and to be put through the same sort of excruciating experience that Michelle endured.

They escaped that fate simply because someone they knew had done a private adoption and suggested that they explore that option themselves. In other words, it was a complete fluke that Trevor and Amanda did not find themselves embroiled in a courtroom battle with DSHS in the lengthy and painful process of having their parental rights terminated. Instead, they initiated a private adoption and were, at least at that time, happy about the outcome. Even more importantly, after having been placed in three different homes during her first nine-and-a-half months of life, their daughter was safely removed from the state system that would have greatly prolonged her stay in foster care and was legally adopted by the family her parents chose for her.

After working so successfully with DSHS on Trevor and Amanda's adoption, I allowed myself to imagine that the DSHS caseworkers in their town would have a change of heart about private adoptions. Maybe they would even come to see that the process of freeing a baby for adoption (which they were already planning to do in this case) didn't always have to be a ponderous, demeaning, and expensive undertaking. My own relationship with the baby's caseworker evolved over the months we worked together, and her outright suspicion and negativity about private adoption abated a bit. But even after the adoption had been accomplished and everyone was happy, the caseworker still seemed to not quite be able to believe that the attorney and I hadn't done something illegal or irregular. She was a nice person who was no doubt doing her job, but she embodied the glass-half-empty attitude that afflicts so many people who work in large bureaucracies. Trying to work with her took me back to the days of trying to get $400 for Darcy's rent so that her children could be returned to her care. So often, the sensible course of action (spending $400 in order to get three children out of foster care that was going to cost much more than that every month, in Darcy's case) is resisted simply because someone, somewhere, has deemed it against policy, and no one wants to take the responsibility or the time to think about it further.

There is too often a pervasive "can't get there from here" attitude in working with DSHS that is both extremely discouraging and extremely confusing. Why didn't Trevor and Amanda's caseworker recognize that we were all working together toward the same goal? Why didn't she understand that Trevor and Amanda were saving the state a great deal of time and money by doing a private adoption and thereby avoiding an expensive legal action and the ongoing need for foster care? Why didn't she see that my involvement was helpful to her personally, in regard to both her time and the decrease in drama and unhappiness in her dealings with Trevor and Amanda? Why didn't she educate (and thereby reassure) herself about the legality of private adoption and about the attorney's and my credentials at some point in the process? Most importantly, why didn't she feel the sense of urgency that the rest of us felt about getting that baby into her permanent home? And, finally, why didn't she, and the staff in that DSHS office, learn from the experience they had that was such a success for the baby, her birth parents, the adoptive family, and the taxpayers? As I've said, it was both discouraging and confusing.

I know the response to this criticism will be that no one outside of DSHS could possibly understand all the constraints the agency must work with, and I accept that that is certainly true. However, while I know I don't understand all the issues that DSHS workers contend with these days, I am extremely sympathetic to the position they find themselves in when dealing with an elaborate system of rules and policies that seem to prevent them from doing what they feel is right for their clients. I feel sure that most of them care about their clients every bit as much as I did when I worked for DSHS and that they understand that the current system often fails them and therefore fails us all.

Most of my experiences with DSHS are ancient history now. But, sadly, I recently encountered new evidence that things haven't changed a great deal— at least in their most important aspect—since that time.

The most important aspect, of course, is in the damage done to the children who find themselves in the child welfare system. I was recently contacted by a woman who wanted to adopt a fourteen-year-old girl for whom she and her husband had been providing respite care for the past five years. It seemed that respite care was needed in this situation because the girl and her adoptive mother didn't get along. A little further questioning revealed that they didn't get along to such a degree that Child Protective Services had been involved. But let's go back to the beginning of Lily's story.

Lily came into foster care as an extremely skinny little three-year-old, with knobby knees and a head that had been shaved in preference to tackling her lice-infested mat of long blond hair. Along with an eight-year-old brother and a six-month-old sister, she had been taken away from her birth parents, who were meth addicts. CPS was contacted by the woman who had grown weary of babysitting for the children after their parents failed to return for them.

The first tragic mistake DSHS made was to place the children in separate foster homes. I'm willing to believe that the eight-year-old boy may have had behavioral issues that made finding the right placement for him difficult, and it may even have been unsafe for him to be placed with his sisters. But I cannot imagine that it was impossible to find a foster home that would take three-year-old and six-month-old sisters, if not immediately then at least within a few months. Lily must have been traumatized by finding herself separated from everyone she knew and loved at an age when she couldn't possibly understand what was happening to her.

Nevertheless, Lily did well in her foster family and, according to the foster parents, they were told that it was extremely unlikely that the birth parents would be able to regain custody. This family had entered the foster/adopt program with the stated goal of adopting a child. They thought they had made their feelings clear, about taking only foster children who would eventually be available for adoption (as much as anyone could know), to the social worker who called them about Lily. The foster parents, their young son, and Lily all got busy with the process of adapting and bonding to one another. Lily's adjustment to her new life is chronicled in a beautiful photo album/scrapbook that her foster mother made for her. In the early pictures, her shaved head appears in stark contrast to her beautiful clothes and the happy events the photographs are recording. Here's Lily at a party, here's Lily with her Easter basket, here's Lily with a new stuffed animal. Each page is decorated with lots of little embellishments and a description of what is happening. As you thumb through the pages, Lily's hair begins to grow, and eventually it starts to seem less incongruous that this child could actually be part of a normal, happy family.

The happiness of the family—and of Lily—was being sorely tested at this point, however. The social workers were doing their best to reunite the family, and Lily and her little sister, Abby, were being taken to their birth parents' home for weekly visitation. Then, when the social worker thought things had gone well enough during daytime visits, the parents were allowed to have the girls for weekends. It would take Lily several days each week to calm down after these visits and she began to "act out" in various ways, but the foster parents were still hopeful that they would eventually be able to adopt Lily if the state didn't return her to her parents' care.

And the state didn't, but it also didn't move to terminate the parents' rights, so the situation dragged on until Lily was six years old. Finally, the social worker let the foster family know that, although they weren't planning to return Lily to her parents, they were planning to place her with one of her grandmothers. Heartbroken, the foster parents decided that there was no point in prolonging the inevitable. They told the social worker that if they weren't even going to be considered as adoptive parents, after three years of what seemed to them to be a successful placement, the state should go ahead and move Lily to the new home.

Lily was moved, but not to her grandmother's home. Instead, she was placed in a new foster home and then, not many months later, into a third foster home. Lily remembers virtually nothing from that year of her life, although she does have happy memories of earlier times spent with her first foster family.

In retrospect, it appears that when Lily was seven years old, DSHS finally decided that it was time for her to be adopted. By this time, someone had apparently noticed the grave error made in separating the sisters, and their top priority suddenly became placing the two children in the same home. DSHS approached Abby's foster mother, Roberta, about adopting Lily as well. When Roberta said she did not want to adopt Lily, she was told that if she didn't, Abby would be taken away from her because the girls needed to be together. It took almost a year of persuasion, during which Lily was in the two other foster homes; Roberta finally, reluctantly agreed to adopt Lily. When Lily was almost eight years old, she went to live with a woman who did not want her, who made these feelings clear, and who went on to mistreat Lily in various ways for the next six years.

Not surprisingly, Lily's adoptive placement was a disaster from the start. In addition to Abby, there were two teenagers in the family, a boy and a girl, and there was a father, but the mother was dominant and everyone else deferred to her. Roberta told extended family members that Lily was severely disturbed, that she had problems with impulse control, was too talkative, was a thief, and was a fire starter. Lily was taken to a doctor who, based on the mother's report, put her on high doses of three different medications that were supposed to calm her down, get her to sleep at night, and improve her mood. She was also taken to a counselor who, according to Roberta, recommended that Lily sleep on the floor of a closet for two years after she was caught cutting her sheets with scissors. An older cousin recalls that the extended family questioned both the medications and the closet-bed, but felt unable to intervene. Roberta's sisters tried to talk with her about her approach to Lily, but any efforts to involve themselves in the situation were firmly rejected. When the family tried to reach out to Lily, it only angered Roberta, and it became clear to other relatives that when they did nice things for Lily or showed her any attention or sympathy, it made Roberta so angry that she would find a way to retaliate, always against Lily.

The situation reached a crisis point less than a year later when, as Roberta told her cousin, "The family voted and we decided that we didn't want Lily to be with us anymore." They contacted CPS and, much to their surprise, discovered that adoptive families aren't allowed to return children they no longer want (even in situations in which they never wanted the child in the first place and were effectively forced to adopt by DSHS).

I understand why families should not be allowed to overturn adoptions upon request, but I do not understand why, at that point, someone from DSHS didn't recognize the danger they had put Lily in and take decisive action to help her. There were repeated referrals to CPS, and caseworkers did meet with the staff at the school Lily attended after a teacher reported that Lily had extensive bruising around her neck, which she said had been caused by Roberta. There were a number of people at the school who were very much aware of the problems in the home because Roberta spoke freely to them about what a trial Lily was to her. It was after one of the meetings with CPS workers at school that Jan, the woman who called me about adopting Lily, stepped forward to offer respite care to the family. Everyone thought it was a good idea, and DSHS apparently thought it was so good that the situation required no further investigation from them.

So, when Lily was in the third grade, she began spending weekends with Jan and Mark. Jan was an administrative assistant at Lily's school and, although she didn't really know Lily at the time, she wanted to help her. Jan had also worked as a behavioral interventionist at the school and was skilled at working with children with behavior problems. She and Mark were prepared for the behavior that Lily's mother had described and were surprised to find that Lily was generally quite cooperative and well behaved when she was with them. There was one incident of "fire starting" when Lily burned a candle in her room without permission, but Jan and Mark saw that as an expression of wanting to burn a candle rather than of wanting to burn the house down. They had a long talk about why candles were dangerous, and there was no further "fire starting." Jan and Mark had two adult sons and well-formulated ideas about child rearing, which worked well with Lily. Of course, as time went by, they became more and more attached to her and more and more concerned about what was happening to Lily when she went back home.

Jan and Mark were also aware that they had no control over the situation in Lily's home. Their ability to make life better for her by providing respite care was granted by Roberta, who could cut off their interaction with Lily at any point. It was clear to Jan and Mark that Lily was the one in need of respite, but they were careful not to suggest that to Roberta. In Roberta's mind, Jan and Mark's desire was to give her a break from the hardship of parenting Lily. Jan and Mark were walking a fine line in trying to advocate for Lily and avoid alienating Roberta, and they never lost sight of the fact that if they lost favor with Roberta, she might refuse to let them see Lily any longer.

So began many years of heroic effort, especially on Jan's part, to be compassionate, supportive, and diplomatic toward Roberta and to somehow stave off her own feelings of rage and horror at the way Lily was being treated, all in an effort to continue to be allowed to help Lily.

It's amazing how much power a disturbed person can wield in an otherwise healthy family. Looking back at Lily's story raises the obvious questions: How could so many people have overlooked her suffering? How could Roberta, whom many family members recognized as having serious mental health problems, have maintained such absolute control not only over Lily but also over other people's interactions and relationships with her? Why didn't other family members realize how bad the situation must be when they felt afraid to defend Lily or to question any of Roberta's disciplinary measures?

Roberta talked openly and frequently about the severity of Lily's problems and about how unhappy and burdened she was as Lily's mother. This sort of talk would take place at family gatherings, with Roberta making no attempt to modify her complaints in Lily's presence. Meanwhile, she doted on Abby, and the disparity in the treatment of the two girls was evident to everyone. The father and older siblings were passive in response, and Lily's role as family scapegoat was firmly established.

There was one person in the family, however, who took note of what was going on—an older cousin who, in her early twenties, actually began making a written record of things she thought weren't right. But she too noticed that if she did something nice for Lily, Roberta would find a way to even the score by punishing Lily. The cousin concluded that Roberta was jealous of anyone else's attention to Lily and was enormously threatened by the idea that other people's sympathies might be with Lily rather than herself. So the family took a hands-off approach in an effort not to further enflame Roberta's anger. Lily was heavily medicated during the week and staying with Jan and Mark on most weekends, so things seemed calmer for a few years.

But of course, things were really only getting steadily worse and reached a crisis with Roberta's first suicide attempt. She agreed to see a counselor for a short time but quickly concluded that counseling wasn't helpful to her. I don't know anything about the specifics of her diagnosis, but there was a second suicide attempt less than two years later. By this time, everyone was walking on eggshells around Roberta, afraid to cross her in any way. The only good thing to come out of this was Roberta allowing Lily to stay with Jan and Mark for months at a time, and it quickly became evident that Lily thrived when she was in their care. During one extended stay, her grades went from D's and F's to A's and B's, and the change in her behavior and demeanor was pronounced. But, inevitably, Roberta would call for Lily's return, and Jan and Mark had to send her back home.

One day, when Lily was in the seventh grade, she called her older cousin to say that Roberta had kicked her in anger and she needed her cousin's help to get away from the house. The cousin contacted CPS, but when they investigated, Lily, who was thoroughly frightened, had changed her story. She told the investigating social worker that "nothing happened" and later told her cousin that Roberta said that if she did "something stupid, you'll never see Abby again." Roberta's summary of the situation was that Lily "kicked me to the curb and threw me out with the trash." But, happily, she allowed Lily

to go to Jan and Mark's and seemed to be entertaining the possibility of letting them adopt her. Roberta changed her mind about the adoption a short
time later, though, possibly after realizing that she would be sacrificing the
monthly stipend she received from Adoption Support Services.

But it wasn't too long before Roberta allowed Lily to return to Jan and
Mark's home and, after another seven months had passed, she said she
would agree to relinquish her parental rights and let them adopt Lily. Jan and
Mark were ecstatic but still not confident that Roberta wouldn't change her
mind. They had seen how much (mysterious) power she wielded over other
people—including social workers, and even including Lily.

Lily has just turned fourteen; there is ample evidence that she was emotionally and physically abused in her adoptive home, and there are many
witnesses to this abuse, all of whom feel it has been damaging and probably
unsafe for Lily to be with Roberta. But until very recently, Roberta was able to
retain control and frighten everyone sufficiently to prevent them from taking
any action that might upset her, presumably because such action could cause
either another suicide attempt or retaliatory behavior against Lily. When I
met with Lily and Jan and Mark, Roberta was living with her husband, her
two adult children, and eleven-year-old Abby in a house with rooms so overstuffed that people could move about only by a series of pathways through
the clutter.

Within a few days of my first conversation with Jan, she had returned
almost all of the forms and other information required for this type of adoption. People usually take at least a few weeks to gather all of this information,
but Jan and Mark clearly wanted to strike while Roberta was feeling agreeable.
I knew only the most rudimentary facts about the situation when I went out
to meet with them and with Lily a few days later. Almost immediately after
we started talking, my customary interview format was discarded by the need
to express varying degrees of confusion, astonishment, anger, and horror at
what they were telling me.

This book started out with a story about a social worker for the Department
of Social and Health Services who was unfairly blamed for a child's suffering,
and it is now ending with a story about negligence on the part of other DSHS
social workers that led to years and years of suffering for another child. The
latter story took place in full view of numerous people who cared about this
child, including extended family, school staff, her doctor, and her counselor,
and yet none of these people felt they had the ability to change the situation
for eight interminably long years.

Lily is an extremely appealing girl who seems a few years younger than she
actually is, in part because she is small and slim, and in part because she is shy
and quiet upon first meeting you. She has a pretty face and thick brown hair

shaped by a stylish layered cut. She sat quietly through several hours while Jan and Mark told the story from their perspective. Lily politely answered questions I directed to her, but she was not forthcoming until much later when she was showing me around the house. When we reached her bedroom, I asked Lily if she had any questions for me, and she said, "Yes, would you like to see my photo album?" She then brought out the album that had been so lovingly made for her by the first foster mother, and we went over each picture with care. There was three-year-old Lily in her fancy new dresses with her little shaved head. She lingered over one picture of herself holding a stuffed unicorn and said she regretted not knowing what had happened to "Danny," who had been given to her by those foster parents and had disappeared after the move to Roberta's. When we came to a picture of Abby, Lily enthusiastically said, "Isn't she pretty?" without a trace of jealousy or the complicated feelings that must arise between siblings when one of them is blatantly favored by a parent while the other is a scapegoat.

When we had finished looking at all the pictures, Lily asked me if I'd like to see another album that she thought might have been put together by her birth father. She apologized for the fact that it had only seven pictures. They were pictures of a good-looking blond man, probably in his late twenties, who looked like Lily, and there were also pictures of an uncle and grandfather. Looking at them prompted Lily to ask me if I thought it was okay for her to wonder what had happened to her birth family. She was especially interested in finding out what had become of a baby brother who was born after the other children were removed from the home. I told her it was absolutely normal to want to know about the people in her birth family and her history with them. It pains me to know that Lily has been denied even the most basic information about these people, even whether they are still alive, in this era of supposedly enlightened child welfare work. Even early in my career, social workers were taught about the importance of creating "life books" so that children would have information about their family history. Lily came into care only eleven years ago. How is it that things were allowed to go so terribly wrong for her?

My role in Lily's adoption was actually quite limited. Other than to ascertain that Jan and Mark met all the state requirements for adoptive parents and that Lily was happy and wanted to be adopted by them, I had no authority in this matter. I felt fairly confident that, after all their struggles to get to this point, Jan and Mark and Lily would be allowed to become a family. Jan and Mark had reached a level of determination that wouldn't be easily denied. They had an excellent attorney to guide them through the process, and it seemed inconceivable that the courts would force Lily to return to Roberta's home against her will. It might not happen quickly or easily or inexpensively, if Roberta decided to object, but I believed that Lily would ultimately become Jan and Mark's daughter. That won't be the end of the story, though, because she will still face the enormous challenge of coming to terms with her past. Amazingly, it appears that Lily has somehow, despite everything, found just the right parents to help her take it on.

Conclusion

<hr>

L OOKING BACK, IT IS fascinating to see how rapid the pace of change has been over the course of my career.

Some of this change, such as widespread acceptance of gay parenthood, is simply a reflection of change in the mainstream culture. Until almost the twenty-first century, most gay or lesbian prospective adoptive parents had to omit/conceal/misrepresent information about their sexual orientation. Although these parents sometimes were able to adopt children, there was no societal acknowledgment that they were, or should be, allowed to become parents.

This is the way things were in 1993, when I met Joe and Alex. Fourteen years later, in 2007, Cameron and Mitchell—the gay couple on the sitcom *Modern Family*—and Lily, their daughter from Vietnam, became one of the most beloved of all television families, and they have been holding that position ever since. Of course, there is still outrage from some conservative factions, which are absolutely correct in their fears about the effect this show has had on normalizing gay parenthood. The Supreme Court decision in favor of same-sex marriage, groundbreaking as it was, was really just an acknowledgment of the fact that attitudes changed dramatically over a short period of time.

Personally, I also give a lot of credit to *Queer Eye for the Straight Guy* for introducing (way back in 2003) a generation of MTV viewers, who are now voters, to the idea that gay guys aren't scary. According to the show, quite a few of them just want to fix up your house and wardrobe and teach you how to cook a good meal; all of this is aimed at helping you impress your girlfriend so she'll want to come over more often. I don't know if the show was designed specifically with the idea of bringing about cultural change, but I think it helped mainstream Americans take some of the first significant steps in that direction.

Other changes in adoption have been brought on by advances in reproductive technology, the most notable being embryo transfer and gestational surrogacy, which have created a dense thicket of new legal issues needing attention. There are various forms of transfer and surrogacy: the embryo can be created with sperm and egg from the intended parents, or from the intended father and an egg donor, or from the intended mother and a sperm donor, or from both donated egg and sperm, then implanted in either the intended mother (the "adoptive" mother) or a surrogate mother who will grow and deliver the baby.

In "traditional" surrogacy, in which the surrogate mother also provides the egg, the surrogate is the biological mother of the child. Some years back, I did a home study for a woman who, after she and her husband provided the egg and sperm for their surrogate adoption, was being required to adopt her own biological child because the law defined a mother as the person who gave birth to the baby no matter what the baby's biological origins. The woman who was giving birth (the surrogate mother) was a dear friend (incredibly dear) of the child's genetic parents. That woman had the full support and involvement of her husband, and they both were motivated purely by the desire to help their friends have the child they longed for.

Everything about the arrangement was amazing and loving . . . except in the eyes of the law, which did not recognize the child's biological mother as its legal mother. Her husband, who was also the biological parent, could legally be named as the father on the birth certificate, but the mother could not. So, on top of all the other expenses this couple had paid for during years of infertility treatment (not covered by insurance) and the egg retrieval and implantation procedures for this pregnancy (not covered by insurance), they now had to come up with many thousands of dollars in legal and adoption fees. They also had to deal with the significant emotional insult of the legal distancing of this mother from her own baby.

This maddening legal problem existed simply because the law was written prior to the ability to implant an embryo, and updating the law seemed to be both ethically confusing for some lawmakers and low on their list of priorities. So they held on to an interpretation of the law, which hadn't foreseen the possibility of a woman giving birth to a child who wasn't biologically hers.

Although it has now been more than thirty years since gestational surrogacy became a realistic option for people, reproductive law still doesn't adequately understand or address the subject with anything close to clarity and conformity. There are no federal laws governing either gestational or traditional surrogacy arrangements in the United States, with some states viewing the practice favorably, while others ban it entirely. There are complicated, sometimes even conflicting, policies between and even within states, and sometimes interpretation of the law is left up to the discretion of individual judges. Clearly, this is not a system that inspires confidence, nor is it fair and equitable.

It's safe to assume that there will be other advances in reproductive technology in the not-too-distant future, and there are legitimate concerns about just how far science will be allowed to go. But back in 1978, there was a tremendous uproar about the first "test tube baby," with dire predictions about her fate and the inevitable devaluing of human life that would result from this new technology. Instead, in the intervening years, we have had several generations of much-wanted and loved "test tube" children and no apparent dire consequences.

There is still some theological posturing about the evils of assisted reproduction, but even people who identify as strongly conservative in regard to this issue find that they are able to revise their thinking when it becomes personal. Most people who need high-tech help to bring children into their lives do not forgo that opportunity, or deny it to their loved ones, even when they previously held beliefs that opposed taking this sort of action to achieve a pregnancy or carry a baby to term.

Profound shifts in the geopolitical balance of wealth and power have brought about equally profound changes in international adoption. These days, my familiarity with international adoption is more personal than professional, and I can't help but view these changes from my perspective as the parent of a child adopted from another country. But I am not blindly or willfully self-serving in this, and I accept and empathize with a perspective that questions the ethics of international adoption. It is important to carefully monitor these adoptions and to increase awareness and concern about the vast inequalities between placing and receiving countries.

There was great hope that the changes in policy put in place after The Hague Adoption Convention of 1993 would lead to better regulation of unethical international adoption practices. Tragically, along with improved regulation, the Hague convention appears to be responsible for unconscionable delays in processing adoptions. Children, even those who already have an identified adoptive family waiting for them, have languished in crowded children's homes for years while someone somewhere works through the mountains of paperwork required to process their adoptions. The number of international adoptions from all of the placing countries has plummeted by 75 percent in the past decade, while the cost has skyrocketed. Although it was assumed that there would be a period of adjustment for a few years after the Hague regulations went onto effect, that adjustment period is now close to a decade long, and children who were infants when they first came into care have become ten-year-olds who have virtually no chance of finding an adoptive family. And they are ten-year-olds who have suffered the effects of having been raised in institutions and will face enormous hardship when they are turned out on their own in a few more years to make room for all the new babies. It is astounding and heartbreaking that this situation wasn't foreseen and even now isn't being addressed with the urgency it deserves.

I understand that there are legitimate reasons to oppose international adoption. I also understand and empathize with the unhappiness of some Korean adoptees about the loss of their families and culture, and I think the attention these people have drawn from the Korean government should be viewed in a positive light. It brings questions about Korea's treatment of single mothers and their children into the open and might even help change long-held attitudes about them within the country. Ideally, this would result in a societal change allowing single women to feel confident that they can now raise their children without the hardships and stigma they faced in the past. It may also bring about increased acceptance of adoption within Korea, leading to policies that more effectively encourage Korean families to adopt. On the other hand, it is also possible that the negative attention focused on Korean adoption will encourage individuals who feel happy about their own adoptions, and believe that international adoption is a reasonable response to the plight of real children, to call attention to their very different stories and perspective. People on both sides of this issue deserve to be heard and respected.

Another significant (and quite unexpected) change I have witnessed has been in the degree of openness between adoptive families and birth parents in domestic adoptions. Openness was brought about by the recognition that secrecy was harmful to all members of the adoption triad: birth parents, adoptive parents, and adoptees. Ongoing contact was encouraged by adoption professionals who felt that it promoted healthy relationships between all of these people and promoted healthy attitudes toward adoption.

Once the adoption was accomplished and the professionals were out of the way, birth and adoptive parents were free to carry on with whatever sort of contact they wanted—which, for many of the people we worked with, turned out to be surprisingly infrequent. This wasn't due to broken promises or to problems in the relationship; it seemed, for most people, to reflect the fact that these people were simply busy with their day-to-day lives. Most birth and adoptive families continued to be extremely interested in one another, and they definitely appreciated the reassurance that openness provided, but they didn't actually end up choosing to spend a lot of time together. Even more surprising, the birth parents were almost always the ones who made the decision not to pursue more contact.

The majority of the birth parents we worked with at Adoption Connections, which encouraged open adoptions, decided not to have a significant degree of in-person contact after the first few years of the child's life. While this was not what we thought would happen, the lack of visits did not indicate that something had gone wrong or that someone was unhappy. Instead, it appeared to just be the way people wanted it to be, with a few exceptions. I periodically get calls from one birth grandmother, for example, who wishes the relinquished grandchild, who is now a teenager, would give her a call. She had heard somewhere that when a child reaches age fourteen, she can make the decision on her own to contact the birth family, and the grandmother expected the girl to be getting in touch. But the girl is not interested in contact right now and wants to wait until she is older before exploring relationships with her birth family.

This degree of remove may not be possible to maintain, however. As in so many other aspects of life, privacy and control have often been rendered obsolete by the Internet. In this particular case, the girl's birth mother has already found her daughter on Facebook and could choose to contact her at any point. But the birth mother is cautious and is focused on her own marriage and two young children, so she is waiting, at least for now. She is also being respectful of her daughter's feelings and wishes, and that bodes extremely well for their future relationship.

We have been fortunate, for the most part, at Adoption Connections, but not all situations in which one party unexpectedly makes contact are handled amicably. If there hasn't been some type of ongoing communication between the birth and adoptive families prior to the child's teenage years, the stage is set for some complicated and possibly upsetting interactions. People who adopt a child these days have to assume that their family's online presence will make them visible not only to the child's birth parents but also to the extended birth family. They should also realize that some member of that extended family, not necessarily a birth parent, may take it upon themselves to contact the child by early adolescence. It's probably not realistic for adoptive parents to feel that they can continue to exert sufficient control over their child's use of computers to avoid this sort of contact, which can be extremely upsetting if it is unexpected or unwanted.

Although I am a proponent of openness and honesty with children, beginning at a very early age, I am not a proponent of anyone contacting children without the permission of their parents. I expect that we will soon be hearing more stories about unfortunate encounters that take place in this way, and as a result, there will be a backlash against openness in adoption.

Adoptive parents will understandably view instances in which they and/or their children have been upset or harmed by this type of contact as a reason to fear the concept of openness in general. It is distressing to think that the gains that have been made in the last twenty-five years regarding attitudes toward birth parents and openness could be jeopardized because we find ourselves unable to regulate the actions of those few people who, for one reason or another, do not act with the child's best interest in mind.

There will continue to be some adoptions, such as those where parental rights have been terminated rather than voluntarily relinquished, in which openness is not advisable or even safe, usually due to the birth parents' criminal involvement, substance abuse, or mental-health issues. In these situations, adoptive parents likely will have to restrict contact with the birth family. There are other situations in which the problems are less extreme, but contact is emotionally difficult for the child. This might happen, for example, with birth parents who tell the child that the adoption had been done against their wishes, or who expect the child to feel bonded with and loyal to the birth family in a way that doesn't come naturally to him or her. It is especially difficult for a child when this sort of contact/expectation from the birth family is made during adolescence, as it often is, when they are already trying to assert independence from parental control.

For the past three years, I have gotten calls every six months or so from a birth father I worked with seventeen years ago, when he was just finishing high school. He is eagerly waiting to tell his daughter that he was always opposed to the adoption but was forced to comply by the birth mother. He thinks this will make the girl feel that he really loves her and will also absolve him of the guilt he seems to harbor about the adoption. I know, of course, that birth fathers can't be forced to agree to adoptions. I also know that, in this particular case, the paternal grandmother was the one who was opposed to the adoption and would happily have raised her son's child if he had allowed her to do so. The birth mother could have done nothing to compel him to go along with her wishes to have the baby be adopted. I remember being surprised at the time by the maturity of this young couple's decision not to let the baby be raised by either grandmother, one of whom had mental-health issues and the other who was in poor physical health and actually died a few years after the baby was born.

For the past seventeen years, the adoptive parents have been sending letters and pictures to both birth parents, and everyone expects that the girl herself will initiate in-person contact when she decides the time is right. I can only hope the birth father will have given up his revisionist history by then. Each time he calls, we rehash his feelings about the adoption, and he, once again, comes to the conclusion that he did what he felt was best at the time. I assure him that that is the message his daughter will want to hear. It is also the truth. But, sadly, he seems to forget everything between conversations, and when he calls again he is right back to square one, insisting that the adoption was done against his will. I don't know what else to do for him, and I worry that when he does finally meet his daughter, his neediness will cause her to feel concern and doubt rather than the connection and understanding that he is seeking.

I expect to hear a lot more in the coming years from both birth and adoptive parents who worked with Adoption Connections. I also expect to be hearing from the babies who are now young adults—a wonderfully exciting prospect. This generation of adoptees is the first of Adoption Connections' "children" and they have almost all grown up with some degree of openness in their relationships with their birth parents. They won't need to undergo lengthy searches to locate their birth families, nor will they face the unknown as to how they will be received. They may not have had much contact with their birth families over the years, but they always have had access to whatever information their birth parents provided; they've known that they could choose to pursue in-person contact whenever they felt ready. I am eager to see how they handle their relationships with their birth families as adults, and it is going to be a pleasure and a privilege to learn what they have to teach us all about this next stage of open adoption.

This rapid change and the lessons I am constantly learning have made for a career that is in equal parts fascinating and rewarding. Most of the pleasure I take in my work comes from the individuals I meet and from their willingness to allow me to participate in such an important part of their lives. I am humbled by the birth mothers who trust me to be fair and helpful at a time when they are struggling, and life must seem especially cruel. I am amazed by the families who stay strong and loving while coping with infertility and an arduous adoption process, then share their happiness with me when their child finally arrives.

Recently, I was honored to be present at Lily's adoption finalization and was deeply touched at being included by her and her new parents in the group they wanted at this event. There have been countless such moments of connection with individuals that I will always remember and treasure. I am privileged to be able to feel that my work is important and meaningful, sometimes very much so, and I am honored to be in a position to help with such a profound event as an adoption. Even when things go wrong, I can at least listen and try to provide some understanding and comfort.

The psychological rewards of my career have been abundant, and the large collection of photographs I have amassed over the years serves as a powerful reminder. It includes forty-year-old pictures of the children I knew in foster care, pictures of children from all around the world with their new American families, and lots of pictures of newborns with both birth and adoptive parents. I cling to the tradition of sending holiday cards because every December I get updates from families I worked with years ago and add these new pictures to my collection. Seeing the children grow and thrive is a source of great happiness. I feel that my job has allowed me to be the fly on the wall that that teenaged birth mother I knew so long ago said she wished she could be in order to share in the joy that her baby brought to his adoptive parents. I have been able to share in so much joy, and I am so grateful.

Acknowledgments

THERE ARE MANY PEOPLE who have been instrumental in helping me throughout my career. I am grateful to my fellow child welfare workers, most specifically Connie Mendenhall, Louann Edwards, Joyce Weigel Sweeney, Mike Dorenkamp, James Johnson, Rocky Gonet, and Mel Kaufman, for sharing that life and those stories with me. I also want to thank the World Association of Children and Parents for ten years of experience in working with their dedicated staff and the wonderful families they created through adoption. I owe a special dept of gratitude to Helen Magee and the Options for Pregnancy program for introducing me to the concept of truly ethical birth-parent counseling and open adoption. I want to thank Nita Burks and Dee Talarico for having the courage to start their own adoption agency and then to turn it over to me and Patti Beasley when the time seemed right. I also want to thank attorneys Mark Demaray, Albert Lirhus, Rita Bender, Raegan Rasnic, and Dave Anderson for decades of wise and compassionate legal expertise. I especially want to thank my fellow adoption specialists Ann Lawrence, Dru Martin Groves, and Patti Beasley for their counsel, support, and friendship. And, of course, I want to thank Patti for all the years of partnership at Adoption Connections.

There are others who were helpful to me specifically in the creation of this book. First among them is Nancy Beardsley, whose early gift of enthusiasm and appreciation came at just the right time. Karen Toler, Ann Lawrence, Nancy Johnson, Kathy Seeley, Shari Levine, Victoria Scott, Carolyn Scott, and Mary Stowell all provided encouragement at crucial points along the way.

Writers Kathryn Joyce, Rebecca Wells, Claire Dederer, and David Guterson generously gave their support and friendship. David was especially valuable and appreciated as a fellow adoptive parent who shares many of my sensibilities about the complicated ethics of adoption.

I want to thank Suzanne Staszak-Silva and Elaine McGarraugh, my editors at Rowman and Littlefield, for seeing value in this book and supporting a first-time writer. And I want to thank Jamie and Erin Quick at Stoke Strategy for their considerable skills and enthusiasm.

Most importantly, I want to thank Fred, Erin, Caitlin, and Jocelyn for every single thing. There would be no book without each of them and their abundant love, encouragement, and willingness to listen to my stories.

Index